Occasional Paper 95

The Carlyle Collection of Stone Age Artefacts from Central India

Jill Cook and Hazel E. Martingell

Department of Prehistoric and Romano-British Antiquities
1994

BRITISH MUSEUM OCCASIONAL PAPERS

Publishers: The British Museum
                         Great Russell Street
                         London WC1B 3DG

Production Editor: Anne Marriott

Distributors: British Museum Press
                         46 Bloomsbury Street
                         London WC1B 3QQ

Front cover image: drawn by Hazel E. Martingell

Occasional Paper No. 95, 1994:
The Carlyle Collection of Stone Age Artefacts
from Central India

Jill Cook and Hazel E. Martingell

© The Trustees of the British Museum 1994

ISBN 0 86159 095 3
ISSN 0142 4815

Orders should be sent to British Museum Press.
Cheques and postal orders should be made payable to
British Museum Publications Ltd and sent to
46 Bloomsbury Street, London WC1B 3QQ.
Access, American Express, Barclaycard and Visa cards are accepted.

CONTENTS

List of figures		iv
Preface		v

PART ONE: BACKGROUND

I	Archibald Campbell Carlyle	2
II	Frameworks: the Stone Age Prehistory of Central India	16

PART TWO: GLOSSARY AND CATALOGUE

III	Glossary	30
IV	Catalogue	45

Appendix 1	Carlyle material in other Museums in Britain & Ireland	99
Appendix 2	Stone Age collections from India, Pakistan & Sri Lanka in the British Museum	101
Bibliography		114
Index to Glossary		122
Index to Catalogue		123
FIGURES		124

LIST OF FIGURES

Figure 1 The Indian sub-continent showing areas enlarged in figures 2-6
2 Central India in the late nineteenth century
3 Modern states of Central India
4 Physical geography of Central India
5 Districts and main towns visited by Carlyle
6 Location of Carlyle's sites
7 Artefacts collected by Carlyle and sold by Charles Seidler to Sir Wilfred Peek before acquisition by the British Museum for the Christy Collection
8 Flaked artefacts
9 Complex cores
10 Nomenclature used to describe features of struck flakes and blades
11 Flake and blade tool types
12 Retouch types
13 Microlith forms
14 Polished stone implements
15 Hammerstones and utilised pieces
16 Artefacts from Amila Nala, Barkor, Bhagatpura, Bharkura and Mahrela Chacki
17 Artefacts from Baghai Khor
18 Artefacts from Baghmara Pahar
19 Tools from Banda
20 Saw and palettes from Bharkacha
21 Utilised sandstone slab from Bharkacha
22 Microliths from Bundelkhand
23 Microliths from Bundelkhand
24 Microliths from Bundelkhand
25 Prepared and retouched flakes from Gaur River gravels
26 Artefacts from Gaur and Ken River valleys
27 Bifaces from Marfa
28 Picks from Marfa
29 Prepared flake and scraper from Marfa
30 Prepared flakes from Marfa
31 Flakes from Marfa
32 Palette from Morhana Pahar
33 Palettes from Morhana Pahar
34 Biface and prepared flake from the Narmada Valley
35 Tools from Manohar Tali Pahar, Moretha Pahar, Nao Gaon, Naon Ka Pahar and Naro

PREFACE

Archibald Campbell L. Carlyle had every intention of writing a report on the 'great numbers of beautiful little implements' which he had found on prehistoric sites in and around the Central Provinces of India while working as First Assistant to the Archaeological Survey. His good intentions came to nothing but the implements, many made of semi-precious stones, as well as of chert and basalt, have been curated by the British Museum since they were acquired in the late nineteenth and early twentieth centuries. This volume brings the material to public attention for the first time. Its intention is not only to provide a catalogue of the objects but also to establish their intrinsic interest and archaeological value by providing some background on Carlyle's role in the historical development of research into the Stone Age of India and the significance of his finds in the context of modern archaeology.

Several people have helped the authors in the preparation of this volume. In particular, we wish to thank Nick Ashton, Alison Roberts, Michael Lindop, Tracy Newman and Karen Perkins, curators in the Quaternary Section of the Department of Prehistoric and Romano-British Antiquities at the British Museum. Thanks are also due to Robert Knox for providing access to objects housed in the BM Department of Oriental Antiquities and to Dr Rita Gardener of Kings College London for her advice on the identification of raw materials. We are also grateful to Raghnall O Floinn in the Department of Irish Antiquities at the National Museum of Ireland for providing copies of documents relating to the Carlyle material curated there. Dr Elizabeth Goring of the Department of History and Applied Art of the National Museums of Scotland, Dr Robin Boast of Cambridge University Museum of Archaeology and Anthropology and Ray Inskeep of the Pitt Rivers Museum, Oxford also provided information about Carlyle artefacts in their care. We also owe particular thanks to Dr John Allan of the Royal Albert Memorial Museum, Exeter who arranged for unaccessioned and previously unidentified Carlyle material to be donated to the British Museum. Christine Baird, Dr Andrew Sherratt, Peter Saunders and John Parsons of the Liverpool, Ashmolean, Salisbury and South Wiltshire and Sheffield Museums respectively assisted by checking their records for Carlyle material. Help also came from the staff of the British Library Oriental and India Office Collections, the Royal Geographical Society and the National Archive of India in Delhi. For their encouragement and support, we owe a great deal to Dr Ian Longworth, Keeper of the Department of Prehistoric and Romano-British Antiquities at the British Museum, Dr Roger Jacobi of the Department of Archaeology, University of Nottingham, Dr Ian Glover of University College London, Institute of Archaeology and Anne Marriott, Editor of Occasional Papers. Finally, we are most grateful to Tim Clark for his infinite patience and skill in typing and formatting the manuscript and to Graphics Officers Karen Hughes, Meredydd Moores and Phil Dean for preparing the maps and assisting with the final presentation of the illustrations.

PART ONE

BACKGROUND

I. ARCHIBALD CAMPBELL CARLYLE

In the context of Stone Age archaeology it can fairly be said that a collection of stone artefacts is only as good as its collector. Archibald Campbell Carlyle (or *Carlleyle* as his name was spelt in India) devoted most of his adult life to the antiquities of India and a thoughtful look at any of the serried ranks of microliths or arrowheads in his collection reveals immediately that he had the wit to recover and record artefacts which were generally ignored by contemporary antiquarians whose interests focussed on the great wealth of the subcontinent's historical antiquities. In this respect, Carlyle was exceptional and his collection equally so. But as his biography reveals, his personality and personal circumstances, as well as the inherent difficulties in the branch of archaeology he pursued, prevented him from taking a place among the eminent scholars of his day.

Little is known about Carlyle's early life or education. He was born on 25 April 1831, had at least one brother, a Hildred E. Carlyle who lived in London (Sieveking, 1960) and believed himself to be a 'representative of the extinct Earldom of Cairnworth' (National Archive of India (NA of I), Delhi, Home Dept. 'B': letter, 1884). Writing in 1884, Alexander Cunningham, Director General of the Archaeological Survey of India, described him as a naturalist and geologist who originally went out to India as a tutor to the sons of the Raja of Vizianagram for a salary of one thousand rupees a month (NA of I, Delhi, Home Dept. 'B': letter, 1884). From these few facts, it might be surmised that Carlyle had a genteel background which gave him an education but no fortune or connections in high society. Perhaps to avoid the virtual servitude of being a tutor to the moneyed classes in England or the spartan existence of a Victorian schoolmaster, Carlyle sought his fortune in India. He did not do this by joining the army, in which his background might have precluded him from rank, or by entering competition for the Civil Service. Instead, he went to India as a gentleman, a position he could not sustain without wealth, ingenuity or influence in the class system of Victorian England but which was perhaps easier at least to imagine in the society of the Raj. That he needed at least to imagine his status to cover what he almost certainly regarded as the demeaning circumstances of his origins is suggested by the tone of pride and independence pervasive in all documents about or by him, as well as his own recalling of aristocratic forbears and the affectation of spelling his name 'Carlleyle', instead of the more common form 'Carlyle', while he was in India. It might even be conjectured that, denied the privileges of rank and the opportunities of wealth or academic qualification, Carlyle realised that he could not easily contribute to the study of India's art, architecture, history and literature which were so fashionable and debated in the more socially elite scholarly circles of the Raj. Instead, he turned his talents to prehistory and, as human evolution and the length of human antiquity became the burning issues of the life sciences in Europe during the 1850s and 1860s, he began to seek evidence of the Stone Age in India.

Early Days in India

Carlyle's job as a tutor may not have lasted long as he was subsequently employed in the Indian Museum in Calcutta (NA of I, Delhi, Home Dept. 'B': letter, 1884) and then, following his dismissal, as Curator of the Riddell Museum in Agra (NA of I, Delhi, Home Dept. 'B': letter, 1871). According to his own notebooks (Smith, V.A., 1906), he had already begun collecting stone tools around Sohagi Ghat on the northern scarp of the Vindhya Hills by 1867. It was at this time that he also discovered rock-paintings in a group of rockshelters subsequently identified from his descriptions as those at Morhana Pahar, isolated in difficult terrain high above the Ganga valley (Allchin, B., 1958). In his notes, Carlyle records that the paintings illustrate:

> ...in a very stiff and archaic manner scenes in the life of the ancient stone chippers, others represent animals or hunts of animals by men with bows and arrows, spears and hatchets...
> Carlyle notes quoted by V.A. Smith, 1906, p.187.

As he found no metal objects, polished stone implements or ring-stones and only occasional fragments of 'very rude and sometimes much worn' pottery (ibid.), Carlyle deduced that although the paintings were 'apparently of various ages' (PRBA, QS archives) some were the work of the makers of the thousands of microliths he had recovered in association with

> ...pieces of a heavy red mineral colouring matter called *Gerû* ... rubbed down on one or more facets, as if for making paint, this *Gerû* being evidently a partially decomposed haematite.
> ibid.

Although the age of these paintings is still a matter for research, Carlyle's recognition that some of them must be prehistoric is notable because it had no precedent in Europe, where the possibility of paintings surviving from the Stone Age was not discussed until after the discovery of Altemira in 1895. However, Carlyle did not publish his thoughts on the paintings or communicate the whereabouts of the sites until 1883. This delay may have been caused by the fact that he 'desired to work the sites himself' (Allchin, B., 1958; Cockburn, 1899) and was prevented from doing so by his appointment as an assistant to the formidable Major-General Alexander Cunningham, Director-General of the Archaeological Survey of India.

Carlyle's appointment to the Survey was made on Cunningham's recommendation in 1871 and suggests that the Major-General, himself an able and energetic antiquarian and surveyor, was impressed by Carlyle's work. A less generous view of the appointment was subsequently published by Cunningham's rival, James Fergusson, who claimed that Carlyle had been appointed because he was incompetent and would not outshine the Major-General or forestall any credit that the latter thought might accrue to him for his work in Indian archaeology (Fergusson, 1884, p.77). This, together with other outpourings of rancour against Cunningham and his assistants, appears in a volume written by Fergusson to counter criticism by Cunningham and the Indian Sanskrit scholar, Babu Rajendrala Mitra, of his claim that stone buildings had appeared in India only as a result of European influence in the time of Alexander the Great. The odious tone of the book suggests that Fergusson was hardly capable of forming an objective view of Carlyle's abilities and, as no other source suggests that he was, by the standards of the time, incompetent, Fergusson's assessment should be distrusted. With the opportunity to travel, explore, excavate and record under the auspices of the Survey, Carlyle was in fact in his element. Despite the risks and difficulties of such work, as well as the inconveniences it must have brought to his wife and two daughters, he toured and reported tirelessly until his early retirement in 1885. Throughout this time his shortcomings and successes have to be viewed within the context of the waxings and wanings of the Survey.

The Archaeological Survey of India

The Archaeological Survey of India had its roots in the enthusiasms of eighteenth-century colonists who encountered cultural traditions to which they responded with awe, fascination and, sometimes, repugnance. Writing from England in 1774, Dr Samuel Johnson and the linguist and scholar, Sir William Jones, urged Warren Hastings in India to:

> survey the remains of its Edifices, and trace the vestiges of its ruined cities...
> quoted in Roy, 1961, p.9.

Ten years later, when only Bihar, Bengal and Orissa had been brought under British control, Sir William Jones founded The Asiatick (*sic*) Society in Calcutta where he had been appointed Judge of the Supreme Court. The aim of the Society was to enquire into 'the Antiquities, Arts, Sciences and Literature of Asia' (Roy, 1961, p.10). It was to provide a forum in which members could exchange information and ideas, as well as an annual journal in which they could publish their research on a wide range of topics including art, architecture, epigraphy, coins and natural history. Over the years that followed, antiquarians and natural scientists investigated and recorded what was for them a new world and by 1824 John B. Seely, writing of his travels through the Mahratta Confederacy of Western India, advocated that:

> ... some little attention be bestowed on these truly wonderful monuments of antiquity. A powerful, scientific, and generous nation like the English, ought not to allow any injury to happen to these mighty works, which can, by a very little trouble, and by incurring no expense, be prevented .... Affecting to venerate antiquities, and the monuments of a passed age and mighty people, it is our duty to endeavour to maintain, as far as we can, their original beauty and design; for while we esteem and admire these venerable works, it becomes us imperatively to preserve them.
> ... I humbly implore the chief civil and military authorities, who may be stationed not far distant, to look to it. How much science and posterity will be indebted to them is needless to urge.
> Seely, 1824, pp.181-2.

Seely's plea was not in vain. As antiquarian interests continued to develop, it became increasingly apparent that without a centralised system for investigation and recording, much information about Indian antiquities would be irretrievably lost. The call for such a system was led by Major-General Alexander Cunningham, CSAI, CIE, who, in 1848, began negotiating with the authorities for a department with responsibility to survey and record all historically interesting buildings and monuments. Progress towards setting up such a department was slow but Cunningham's persistent efforts had good effect.

In November 1861, he presented a memorandum to Lord Canning, Governor-General and first Viceroy of India, in which he stated that:

> ... it would redound ... to the honour of the British Government to institute a careful and systematic investigation of all the existing monuments of ancient India.
> quoted in Roy, 1961, p.36.

Canning agreed and noted that:

> ... everything that has hitherto been done ... has been done by private persons, imperfectly and without system ...

adding:

> ... there are European Governments which, if they had held our rule in India, would not have allowed this to be said.
> ibid.

With national pride in league with gentlemanly scholarship, Cunningham was able to retire from the army and start the Archaeological Survey of India with 450 rupees a month and a field allowance of 250 rupees (Roy, 1953).

For the next four years Cunningham seems to have carried out most of the recording himself with the support of surveyors and draughtsmen from the army but government enthusiasm gradually waned and, in 1866, the Survey was abruptly ended when Cunningham left for England. However, government still recognised a duty in this field and in 1867 allotted 52,000 rupees to local authorities for the listing, photography and casting of monuments. The results varied in quality, effectiveness and value for money. Once the inadequacies of this relatively expensive scheme had been pointed out to the newly appointed Governor-General, Lord Mayo, he welcomed the idea of removing responsibility from government and, in 1871, reinstated the Archaeological Survey with Cunningham as its Director-General. With an annual budget of £5000 per year, Cunningham was to employ two English assistants and indigenous people who were to be trained in photography, surveying, excavation and epigraphy. Cunningham immediately appointed Carlyle and J. D. Begler as his assistants. Their job was to explore and survey the antiquities of particular districts or cities systematically. An extract from their brief, published in 1873, shows that their work was not to be restricted to the survey of buildings and monuments but was, where possible, to include excavation and the description of artefacts:

> ... The fretted ceilings of Hindu temples are often of singular beauty, which is not surpassed by the finest specimens of Gothic fretwork. All the finer examples of these ceilings should be noted, stating their size and the general nature of the design. In many of the older villages will be found fragments of sculpture, together with curiously shaped or coloured stones, collected together under some large tree, generally either a banyan or a pippal. In the same place also, as I have been informed, are sometimes found stone celts and splintered arrowheads of stone. On the sculptures I have frequently found traces of inscriptions; but more usually these fragmentary remains, heaped together under the village trees, are much worn by the daily libations of water and anointments of red lead to which they are subjected. They serve, however, to show what was the religion of the former occupants of the village when the sculptures were executed. Connected with the stone celts are the large earthen barrows, stone circles and stone houses or dolmens, which are found in many of the hilly parts of India. The positions and dimensions of all these should be noted for further research and future excavation. Smaller monuments may perhaps be opened at once, as the work will not occupy more than a few days; but all the larger barrows must be left for more leisurely exploration. Monoliths or menhirs are more rarely found; but these, as well as dolmens and circles, need not be looked for in any place except where stone is plentiful, and in positions where their removal would give more trouble than the procuring of similar stones from the quarry. For this reason, such Buddhist topes as were erected on hills, have been generally spared by the spoiler, while those built in the plain afforded the most tempting quarries of dressed stones, or burnt bricks ready of removal.
> Cunningham, 1873, p.viii.

Following these guidelines, Carlyle toured, surveyed and reported on an astonishing number of buildings and ruins in Agra, Rajputana, the Central Doab, Gorakphur and Ghazipur districts (Fig. 2) until 1885. During this time, he contributed to five of the *Archaeological Survey of India Reports*. Reading between the lines of these reports, it is possible to detect some frustration at the lack of interest he encountered amongst other members of the Survey for the prehistoric or aboriginal sites and stone artefacts to which he was devoting an increasing amount of attention.

Stone Tools

Carlyle was not the first person to collect stone artefacts in India. This laurel has been credited to Colonel Philip Meadows Taylor, a gifted linguist and administrator, whose excavations of cairns on the Deccan Plateau published in 1862 with plans of the cairn fields, section drawings through the mounds and illustrations of the antiquities found in them were probably an important stimulus to Carlyle's prehistoric interests. In 1842, shortly after his appointment to administer the principality of Shorapur during the minority of its Raja, Taylor reported finding a ground or polished stone axe at Lingsugar (Sankalia, 1963) and noted its similarity to implements found in Europe. In the same year, a Dr Primrose noted a bagful of stone knives and arrowheads which he found whilst clearing his garden in the Raichur District (Allchin and Allchin, 1968) and, over the next twenty years, similar finds, usually from the surface or disturbed contexts, were reported regularly from various parts of the country (Ball, 1867). However, as in Europe at this time, these reports were generally anecdotal in character and treated the objects as curiosities of only intrinsic interest. They offered little scope for research into the length of human antiquity or for progress in developing a typological or chronological framework for Stone Age prehistory because they satisfied antiquarian interests without raising any doubts about the accepted view of a short prehistoric chronology. This challenge was to come from Europe where the demand for proof of human antiquity and evolution had stimulated a new phase of archaeological research.

In India, the first paper to attempt to relate stone implements to a geological deposit and to interpret their age on the basis of their stratigraphic context was published in 1863 by Robert Bruce Foote. Foote's paper describes the discovery of handaxes in laterite formations in southeast India. It was clearly influenced by the flurry of papers published in 1860 by John Evans, Hugh Falconor, John Flower, Charles Lyell and Joseph Prestwich, *inter alia*, which put forward the view - based on the evidence of fossil bones and artefacts recovered from various caves and, more particularly, the Somme Valley - that people had co-existed with extinct mammals at a time when the earth was not yet modern in form. Even Foote's title, *On the occurrence of stone implements in laterite formations in various parts of the Madras and North Arcot districts*, echoes that of Evans' (1860) paper which vindicated the significance of Boucher de Perthes' discoveries in the Somme Valley and which changed the question of whether human life had an antiquity greater than 4004 BC as calculated by Bishop Ussher for the Biblical Creation, to how long that antiquity might be. By 1866, Edouard Lartet and Henry Christy's 1865 monograph on the excavations in caves and rockshelters of southwest France, *Reliquiae Aquitanicae*, was available in India (Blanford, 1867) and, as with the papers on the Somme discoveries, its lessons on the relevance of context and stratigraphy in demonstrating the relative age and variation of artefacts through time were noted. But in the midst of so much historical treasure, Carlyle was among the few who tried to advance the investigation of the Stone Age in India.

Although he found little support for his efforts from Cunningham, whose interests were entrenched in architecture, epigraphy and numismatics, Carlyle continued recording and describing the stone artefacts he discovered when he joined the Survey. His purpose was the same as that of his English counterparts such as John Evans, Canon Greenwell, Worthington Smith and Boyd Dawkins but he was a world apart. He was working alone and although he corresponded with Reverend Gatty in England, Charles Seidler, curator of Nantes Museum, and Vincent A. Smith, a keen amateur archaeologist in the Indian Civil Service (Smith, V.A., 1906), he was not part of a scholarly community. He was elected to membership of the Asiatic Society of Bengal in 1880 but his absence on survey tours would have prevented him attending meetings and there is no evidence for any contact with other investigators such as Hackett, who was collecting stone artefacts in the Narmada Valley, or Robert Bruce Foote, who maintained his interest in the Indian Stone Age until his death in 1912. How much this was due to circumstance and how much to his own choice and personality is difficult to determine but it is clear that he did not welcome Cockburn's interest in his discoveries of cave-paintings (Smith, V.A., 1906). However, isolation was not Carlyle's only problem in his work. Stratified sites from which he could develop a chronological and typological framework for his material eluded him and, as an employee of the Survey, he lacked the freedom and time to pursue his own interests to the exclusion of his duties. Perhaps as a result of these circumstances, he produced no publication devoted purely to stone tools. However, in the reports of his tours for the Survey and his unpublished notes, Carlyle shows that he was not just a magpie collector of curious coloured stones but an archaeologist concerned with their form, technology, age and significance.

First Tours for the Archaeological Survey, 1871-1874

Carlyle spent most of the two years from 1871 to 1873 in the field, first in Agra and then in eastern Rajputana/Rajastan. These tours were subsequently published in volumes 4 and 6 of the *Archaeological Survey of India Reports* for 1877 and 1878 respectively. They reveal that conditions were not easy. Carlyle travelled on horseback with men on foot and baggage camels with his camping and surveying equipment. Sometimes he would make an excursion into the hills on foot to allow his horse to recover from being sick and fagged out. On one day in the jungle he had a dog taken by a tiger, on another, at the town of Sanchari, he records a meal which included oranges and remarks how delicious they were to the taste of the tired archaeologist-explorer who had been living on a meagre fare of dry chapatis. At night he slept in a tent probably equipped with a camp bed and table while his men slept rough, although after one expedition he wrote:

> I've often come home late at night from surveying and had besides to remain, once all night, in the porch of a deserted temple on account of the rain.
> Carlleyle, 1878, p.192.

Despite these deprivations, which made his task much harder than that of his contemporaries working in Europe, Carlyle applied himself assiduously. In the main, his reports describe temples, forts and Buddhist *stupas* or tombs but there are also a number of references to prehistoric or aboriginal sites which evidently excited his enthusiasm. At Khera, he recorded stone cairns and nearby megaliths on the hills above the village, at Rup-bas (Rup-vas) more standing stone circles and dolmens and at Puranigam an ancient village where the drystone architecture reminded him of Skara Brae in Orkney. Thirty ancient cairns at Satmas warranted careful attention. Their types were classified as flat topped, conical and subterranean and he prepared detailed illustrations, plans and sections of them. South of modern Machadi he excavated into the interior of a megalithic tomb to find only bone ash, a stone ball and some flakes which he noted with a sketch of the structure. So the inventory runs on. In some places he would have excavations made by his men, at others he would spend some days measuring and drawing plans or architectural details. At Deosa, he found an important concentration of stone circles, standing stones and dolmens. Within one of these structures he found stone artefacts:

> ... of the last named I may mention a flat piece of hard black stone, shaped exactly like the fragment of a sword blade, it having a sharp edge on one side, while the opposite one was thicker and blunt. This fragment was about three inches in length, but I think rather less than two inches in breadth, with a thickness at the thickest edge of about a quarter of an inch. I believe it to be a fragment of a stone knife or dagger. I also found a stone ball and a bulb shaped, or conical shaped, quartz implement, very thick at one end and sharp pointed at the other - perhaps a rude borer.
> ibid. p.107.

Rude stone implements attracted his attention in the gravel pits at Shiv-dungr where he noted the geology as:

> ... beds of quartz marked here and there with efflorescence of gold and beds of decomposed red haematite and hard micaceous red iron-clay.
> ibid. p.132.

At Bachera (Vyaghera) he was quick to note an iron axe hafted as a prehistoric stone axe might have been and made a careful description of how it was bound. But Carlyle's genius really lies in his appreciation of the relationship between prehistoric sites and the landscape, which was extraordinary for his time. For example, writing of Rajputana he first describes the surface geology and then identifies the location of the oldest sites:

> ...But there are also certain other parts of Rajputana which possess very peculiar characteristics, differing in many respects from any of the former. In such parts of the country, the soil is composed of alluvium or of gravel. Where it is composed of alluvium, the surface is covered with a growth of thick rank grass. Now, it is on the surface of these two last mentioned formations, the gravelly and the alluvial, that we find the remains of the earliest human settlements; while on the salt plains, and in the sandy desert parts we find no remains of the occupation of man older than the middle ages of Man's history, but where in general the majority of the human settlements are even of comparatively recent date.
>
> As illustration of proof of these statements, I may mention that on the saline plains to the north of Jaypur or between Jaypur and Sanbhar to the south, and Madhupur Uncha Pahar and Sikar to the north, I could neither find nor hear of the remains of the human settlements which were older than what we may, for convenience sake, call the middle ages of Indian history.
> ibid. p.147-9.

As he did not develop his ideas or observations, his contribution to a human geography of the past was overlooked and it is only possible with hindsight to appreciate his grasp of the human landscape.

Survey Tours 1874-1880

India Office Records for 1872 record:

> the disappearance of Mr Carlyle and his colleagues...

but there is no clarification of this tantalising entry and by the spring of 1873, he was back to write up his report and prepare his illustrations before his next survey tour which began in 1874. This tour took him into the Vindhya Hills and thence north of the Ganga into the plains (Figs. 2,4,5). It began in the Central Doab and Gorakphur (Carlleyle, 1879) where he remained until 1877 (Carlleyle, 1883) when he moved on to Saran and Ghazipur and stayed until 1880 (AS of I Reports, 22, 1885). What became of his wife and daughters during this time is unknown but it is clear from the reports that Carlyle was becoming increasingly dogged, if not obsessed, about his work. Although he evidently felt his researches into prehistory to be constrained by his work for the Survey, he performed his duties assiduously. His concern for antiquities is revealed in an unusual entry in his report for 1875-6 (published in 1883):

> I will not any longer be directed to injury, disfigurement or destruction of ancient historical buildings, but to their preservation, and where practicable to their repair.
> Carlleyle, 1883, p.76.

The cause for his concern is not specified. It is evident from Cunningham's *Memorandum of Instructions* published in 1873 (Cunningham, 1873) that the preservation of India's architectural heritage was one of the aims of the Survey and there is no evidence to suggest that members of the Survey were ever required to disfigure or destroy buildings or to remove objects. It may be that Carlyle was referring to damage which may have occurred during or after excavations made to expose structures prior to survey. Once exposed, they would be subject to weathering and open to the ravages of souvenir hunters and antiquarian collectors, as well as the bigots who saw evil in the erotic statuary and carvings of some Hindu temples. Such people had been a menace to India's ancient monuments since the early part of the century (Seely, 1824, pp.21, 181-182) and it is a credit to Carlyle that he did not want to join their ranks or by any of his actions assist their deeds, which were eventually legislated against in the Treasure Trove Act introduced by Viceroy Lord Lytton in 1878 (Roy, 1961).

Alternatively, and perhaps more remarkably, Carlyle may have been objecting to restorations such as those carried out by Beglar under Cunningham's orders at Buddha Gaya. Writing in 1884, Cunningham's rival, James Fergusson, complains that the question of the age of Buddha Gaya which for some time past had ruffled the surface of the puddle of Indian archaeology (Fergusson, 1884, p.76) would never be resolved because of Beglar's restoration work. Refering to Beglar as even less accomplished in the field of architecture than Cunningham and describing his reports as like the productions of a half-educated schoolboy (ibid. p.77), Fergusson states that having discovered some features dating to *c*.250 BC:

> ...it was natural that General should wish to clear away all the rubbish which encumbered the terrace of the temple. In doing so he made some very interesting discoveries, but there was no occasion why he should immediately undertake a restoration, which nearly amounts to a rebuilding of the whole, and has practically obliterated almost all the ancient features.
> ibid. p.77.

The implication of Fergusson's writing is that Cunningham was obliterating evidence which might contradict his opinions on the origins of Indian architecture. If Carlyle's comment of 1876 relates to a similar incident, his concern for the monuments and his audacity in speaking out to the Major-General reveal his determination and independent thinking. In this case, the fact that his remarks appeared in print and he remained in his post may vindicate Fergusson's claim that Cunningham did not always bother to edit reports for publication (ibid. p.82).

Excavation at Joharganj

By 1879, Carlyle's commitment to prehistory and his wish for a deeply stratified site caused him to excavate a mound beneath a temple at Joharganj west of Saidpur on the Ganga Plain in Gazipur district. His original intention had been to survey only the temple but the geology excited him to exceed his remit. The extra time taken to do this work resulted in additional wages having to be paid to the men and as extensive excavation was not one of the activities authorised by the Survey, Carlyle had to pay the costs from his own pocket. As reminders to the Survey of his out-of-pocket expenses show (NA of I, Delhi, Home Dept. Proceedings, August 1885, p.2519), this was not an isolated occurrence.

In his description of the excavation, Carlyle notes the changes in the deposits through the depth of the mound:

> ...When I had got down to the bottom of the debris of the ruins of the old temple, I carried the excavation still further down below it in order to see if I could find anything still older beneath it. At length I reached firm clay interspersed with layers of sand and KANKARY (*sic*) gravel, and in that I found a few specimens of what are (whether rightly or wrongly) generally called pre-historic remains. (Although, as to whether they are really entirely pre-historic or not, after all, may be at least a doubtful question. At any rate these were lying in very unhistoric looking clay etc. and at great depth, apparently about on a level with the river).
> Carlleyle, 1885, p.100.

He then goes on to give careful descriptions of the artefacts he found, apparently realising that their types might be a useful indicator of the relative age of the deposit:

> These few remains consisted, in the first place, of a curious looking little celt, made of very dark coloured stone, and polished, especially towards the edge, and of which the width across the blade measures a little less than 1½ inches and the breadth backwards about 1⅛ inches, the width across the narrow butt-end at the back being three-quarters of an inch. But evidently the back of the implement must once have ended in a long conical point (for insertion into a handle); and the point having probably got broken off in the course of use, it had been rubbed down pretty smooth into a blunt sort of butt. The cutting edge spreads out wide, like that of a small broad axe.
> ibid.

He compares this implement with a small, trapezoidal polished stone axe from Guernsey illustrated in Evans (1872, fig. 71) and adds:

> These kinds of implements, if pushed with the blade forward, would do as fleshing instruments for cleaning the inside of raw hides.
> ibid.

After describing a small, stone rubber, Carlyle reports finding two pieces of red haematitic clay ironstone (ochre) called *Gerû* for making paint and colour, noting how he found this in other sites:

> I found similar pieces of rubbed-down *Gerû*, or red haematite, along with stone implements, in excavations which I made in some caves, in the north Rewa hills, on the south of the Mirzapur District.
> ibid.

Finally, he records the occurrence of cores and a bladelet, possibly an armature, in the lowest level of the site and concludes:

> ... It is worthy of remark that not a single item of metal, nor any pottery either was found with the stone implements in the lowest stratum which I reached at the bottom of my deep pit of excavation. The greatest depth reached in my excavation was about thirty three feet below the top of the mount, or about from 18 - 20 feet below the mean level of the surrounding ground.
> ibid.

It is a tribute to Carlyle's description that over a century later, it can be suggested that the temple mound was constructed on a riverside pre-pottery Neolithic site and noteworthy that lacking any evidence by which he can assess the relative age or typological affinities of the material, he avoids interpreting the significance of his finds. Consequently, his work remains that of an avid collector and reporter, accumulating essential facts but unable to use them to interpret sites or develop hypotheses exploring their potential relevance to prehistory.

Retirement and Later Life

After completing his work at Joharganj, Carlyle seems to have been living in Mirzapur, a small town on the Ganga between Allahabad and Varanasi (Benares), about thirty miles north of the northern scarp of the Vindhya Hills. Here in 1880 he joined the Asiatic Society of Bengal and settled to write up his report of the Gorakhpur, Saran and Ghazipur seasons. As the publication of this work was delayed until 1885, Carlyle was able to add a summary of his field investigations after 1880 (Carlleyle, 1885). This summary makes no mention of the Survey and refers to expeditions in the Vindhya Hills collecting prehistoric stone tools, recording and excavating rockshelters and noting rock art. He worked in four distinct regions (Figs. 4-6). At first he concentrated on Baghelkhand in the southern part of Mirzapur District and then moved further west into north Rewa District. From there, he moved south to the Kaimur Hills that formed the border between Rewa and Sidhi District before collecting on the low ground in the Banda and Satna Districts of Bundelkhand. Writing of the stone artefacts he states:

> ...I have found worked flakes and stone implements in the fields in the immediate neighbourhood of the town of Banda; besides celts, or stone hatchets, and stone hammers and other stone implements, through the whole of Bundelkhand, and Patar Kachar, and through the Sohawal state, stone implements also in the Nagod state, and thence down to the south of Maihar; and also, above all, among the hills of the Rewa plateau and in the southern part of the Mirzapur District, and lastly, I have found some worked flakes, of agate and chert, in the fields in the immediate neighbourhood of the town of Mirzapur

and goes on to conclude:

> The question now, therefore, is not where are stone implements to be found, but rather where are they not to be found. For, as my own experience goes, they appear to be findable almost everywhere in India, at least!
> Might it not perhaps turn out to be the same in other parts of Asia, as well as in Europe and America; or possibly in all parts of the world. Indeed if people only had eyes to see such things! Stone implements have hitherto been looked upon as rare wonders, but they cannot and should not be so any longer.
> Carlleyle, 1885, p.117.

Unfortunately, this was to be his last published comment on the subject as a paper entitled *Notes on lately discovered sepulchral mounds, cairns, caves, cave paintings and stone implements*, announced as forthcoming in the 1882-3 volume of the *Proceedings of the Asiatic Society of Bengal*, never appeared although the notes for it survive in the Carlyle archives at the British Museum (PRBA, QS archive). The loss of this paper may have been due to Carlyle's increasing problems with officialdom. In 1882, a complaint was brought against Carlyle by the political agent of Nagod state and an official letter, preserved in the National Archive of India, describes him as:

>...a violent lunatic, dangerous to approach and causing great disturbance among the inhabitants of Nagod State

adding that he had:

>...returned to a comparatively sane condition of mind ... but insane or not Mr Carlyle is a person unfit to be sent on independent duty into native States where his wildness and apparent madness cause much alarm and embarrassment.
>NA of I, Delhi, Home Dept.'B':letter, 12 April, 1882

It is clear that Carlyle's insanity was simply a way of saying that in the practical way in which he went about his survey work, he had not conformed to what was expected of a British government employee and minor official. In 1882, a European with one servant, living rough, without bed and bedding and without a change of clothes or proper food for six weeks had to be mad. On this occasion, Carlyle had left Banda at the beginning of the cold season, in late February, on a surveying tour with servants and twelve camels loaded with equipment. By March, he was in the jungles of Nagod District, living in a hut built by himself and his servant inside the fort of Shankargarh. Somehow he had become separated from his other servants and camels and they were alone for a month. The Raja of Nagod, suspecting he had an escaped criminal in the fort, sent an official to question him. Carlyle, furious, refused to give his name and threatened the official with a gun. The official retreated and Carlyle moved on. He was next seen in a nala near Kharwai in Rewa District where he spent two days surveying before moving back into the jungle in Maihar District where he again set up camp in a fort. It was while he was here that his men appear to have left him, without explanation, for on 2 April, he wrote the following letter which was delivered by hand to the deserters:

>To
>>The Servants and Camel Men, said to have gone to Satna (?)
>>To the Khansaman, Khidmatgar and Chaprasi Ram Gopal, and to the head Camel Man
>>You scoundrels! What have you done with my baggage? If you do not bring my baggage to me immediately on receipt of this order which I send by my Dhobi, I will have you all put in jail! - I command you to bring my baggage to me immediately at your peril!
>>For a whole month and more, you have kept away from me, and you have kept my baggage away from me; and I have not been able to get even a change of clothes for a whole month, and my clothes are all torn and dirty, untill (sic) I am ashamed to show myself! - And I refuse to see or to mulakat any one, untill I get a change of clothes, and everything that is proper for my dignity as your master!
>>For a whole month and more you left me to wander in the jangal (sic) - alone by myself, without any bed or bedding, without any table chair, and without any proper food!
>>I have suffered much and my business has been entirely ruined.
>>You have thus injured me, by your wickedness and rascality; and now you must be punished! - So as you have neglected me for a whole month; and as you have been absent from me for a whole month and as you have not done any service whatever for me for a whole month, therefore you have forfeited a full month's pay, and I hereby fine you a month's pay, - which therefore I refuse to pay you! And if you wilfully have gone into debt anywhere, while absenting yourself from me, against and in defiance of my orders, I refuse to pay your debts! Your debts are nothing to me. My Dhobi, with this order, is commanded to bring my whole baggage three or four times, and if it does not come now, I shall put you all in jail!
>>Your Master
>April 2nd 1882 Mr C Gillespii
>>NA of I, Delhi, Home Dept. 'B': letter, 2 April, 1882

This letter adds a personal note to the otherwise official account of Carlyle's problems. It reveals a charming if patronising mixture of emphasis and humour, much in the manner of letters written to children at this time. Even the signing of the note as from a Mr C. Gillespii would not be unusual as the use of nicknames was quite common. Unfortunately, such informality was anathema to the more conventional officials. On 7 April, Carlyle, his servants, camels and a government officer all met up at Satna in Baghelkhand where Carlyle accused the men of running away from him while they in their turn said Carlyle had wandered off from them. There was no evidence one way or the other but Carlyle's excitable behaviour had upset the officials. As a result, he was subsequently restricted to British territories and was not to be permitted to work in Bundelkhand and Baghelkhand. Furthermore, the state of his mental health was to be reviewed by a medical surgeon. This was the beginning of the end of Carlyle's work in India. Pilloried for his unorthodox activities by official cant and Victorian social mores, Carlyle was held in limbo for the next three years. Back in Allahabad in June 1882, he was visited by the Civil Surgeon of Allahabad on behalf of the District Collector. The surgeon found him nervous and flighty but could not identify anything amounting to insanity. Understandably but certainly injudiciously, this interview led Carlyle to write an irate letter to the Collector complaining about such an unjust, impertinent and degrading kind of enquiry. As a consequence, he received another visit, this time from the junior Civil Surgeon who had known Carlyle at the Riddell Museum in Agra and who found him:

> ...to be exactly what he was then - intelligent and gentlemanly in manner - a very hard worker if allowed his own ways, but most difficult to manage otherwise, proud, excitable and violent in his threatening when he fancied himself injured but never actually resorting to force as was known to me. Apparently he is just as fit for employment now as he was eight years ago at Agra - requiring however the most positive orders regarding what he may or may not do. I regard him as a very peculiar man not ordinarily insane, but liable to outbursts of eccentric action and evil temper - which may be regarded as insanity for the moment.
> NA of I, Delhi, Home Dept. 'B': letter, 14 July 1882.

This appraisal did little to alleviate Carlyle's situation because it emphasised an ungovernable temperament which made officialdom recoil. Major-General Cunningham's opinion was sought before any decision was made about his future employment. It took Cunningham two years to reply and his statement of October 1884 (NA of I, Delhi, Home Dept. 'B': letter, 13 October 1884) that Carlyle was eccentric but not insane and still a very able man came too late: Carlyle was almost destitute. In April 1885, he wrote to the Survey enquiring about his retirement which had been due in March and also informed the government agent that he was subsisting in impoverished conditions (NA of I, Delhi, Home Dept. 'B': letter, 15 April 1885). He had been carrying out excavations at Sansaripur for nine months, living in a tent at starvation level while his wife and daughters were also starving at Dehra Dun. Cunningham sent him one thousand rupees and, much to the relief of the government agent, he returned to Allahabad.

By this time Cunningham himself had decided to retire and had advised the Government that the Director-General's post should be abolished and the Survey disbanded so that the listing of monuments could be more cheaply achieved by three independent units working in the areas of the Punjab, Sind and Rajputana, Uttar Pradesh and the Central Provinces and Bengal (Roy, 1961). Each area was to be managed by a separate surveyor who would be accountable to the local governments and political agencies. Beglar was put in charge of Bengal but in May 1885, Carlyle was retired aged 54, five months before the 71-year-old Cunningham himself left India.

After leaving India in 1885, Carlyle lived another twelve years - probably with his daughter in London for it was at her home in Grattan Street, Hammersmith that he died in 1897. Possibly disillusioned, certainly in ill health and with continuing financial problems, Carlyle published nothing more after returning to Britain but he did complete a list of his collection, which became the focus of his interest in his last years and the most enduring aspect of his work on the Stone Age of India.

The Carlyle Material in the British Museum

On his return to London, Carlyle began to dispose of his collection by giving or selling groups of implements to various museums in Britain, as well as in Europe and America. This may not have been entirely to his liking but a letter from Charles Seidler to the eminent Victorian antiquarian Canon Greenwell, which refers to Carlyle as a poor man in need of the payment of a guinea (PRBA, QS archive; Sieveking, 1960), suggests that it may have been an economic necessity. However, the collection hardly represented a fortune. In a letter dated 7 October 1892 written by Seidler to Major R. F. MacEnery, Curator of the Royal Irish Academy Collection which had been incorporated into the National Museum of Ireland in Dublin, the purchase price for fifty pieces is quoted as just one pound (File G, S & A Museum Registry. No 590. 11 October 1892).

Seidler was a dealer who, after retiring as curator of Nantes Museum, came to live in Hammersmith near to Carlyle and was responsible for the piecemeal sale of his material. Referring to his success in this respect, Seidler noted in a letter offering material to the National Museum of Ireland in Dublin that he had:

> ...succeeded in inducing the following Gentlemen and Museums (amongst others) to take a small series viz Sir John Evans, Canon Greenwell, the Soc. of Antiquaries of Scotland, the Scottish Museum of Art and Science, as well as the Cambridge, Salisbury, Exeter, Liverpool and Sheffield Museums. Mr Franks of the British Museum also took a large quantity from Mr Carlyle.
>   ibid.

As this letter indicates, the British Museum did not acquire any of its collection direct from Seidler. It was acquired in stages. In 1887, Augustus Wollaston Franks, a Keeper at the British Museum whose own scholarly interests had led him to recognise the importance of collecting Stone Age antiquities from all parts of the world, purchased a selection of Indian microliths for the Christy Collection. He obtained them from an exhibition sale at the Royal Albert Hall of Arts and Science in 1887 (Sieveking, 1960). Subsequently, in 1919, the Sturge Bequest brought to the Museum not only the material which Sturge himself had purchased from Seidler but also the artefacts which had been acquired first by other collectors including Canon Greenwell, G.F. Lawrence, J. Allan Brown and H. W. Seton-Kerr and then by Sturge. In 1926, the Department of Ethnography purchased a small but informative group of microliths sold by Seidler to Sir Wilfred Peek of Rousdon, Devon for the Christy Collection. These artefacts were transferred to the Department of Prehistoric and Romano-British Antiquities, formerly British and Medieval Antiquities, in 1939. Another acquisition of Carlyle finds was made in 1982, as part of the Wellcome Collection and the latest, in 1993, came from the Royal Albert Memorial Museum in Exeter. Inevitably, this dispersal and recollection has resulted in the loss of some information but Carlyle's material has at least retained its integrity and although its post-acquisition sorting and curation by site has made it difficult to be certain of the source of acquisition of a large number of artefacts, cataloguing has helped to restore it to a useful archaeological resource. Carlyle material held by other museums in England, Scotland and Ireland is noted in Appendix 1.

Using Carlyle's lists and his notes on the collection published by Black (1892) and V.A. Smith (1906), it has been possible to reclassify the material using modern terminology. This has provided insight into the range of Palaeolithic and Neolithic sites which Carlyle investigated and the chronological framework which had eluded him. Like all nineteenth-century collections, the archaeological value of Carlyle's material is variable. Although many of the implements are marked with site names, there is often a problem in attributing material to a specific provenance because in these districts many villages have the same name (Allchin, B., 1958). Usually, it is only possible to be certain of a provenance if there is a cluster of site names in the proximity of a named river with an adjacent temple or fort located and recorded in the Survey. It must also be pointed out that in some areas much of Carlyle's collecting was achieved by fieldwalking rather than excavation and artefacts may have been gathered from a wide area around the named location. Although many of these objects are of intrinsic interest and indicate the distribution of Stone Age material in the areas concerned, it is the material from sites such as the rockshelter of Morhana Pahar (Catalogue entry 38) on the northern scarp of the Vindhya Hills (Fig. 6), where Carlyle excavated microliths and recorded rock art, which are of the greatest archaeological significance now. However, it is also evident from what remains of the nineteenth-century organisation of parts of the collection that Carlyle was developing a typology for Indian stone artefacts. Although this typology utilises modern functional terms such as knife, razor and saw, the groupings, particularly of the microliths, correspond quite closely to those achieved by modern definitions based on technological description. He certainly distinguished between geometric and non-geometric microliths, recognising crescentric (lunate), triangular and trapezoidal forms among the former and various forms of backed and/or truncated bladelets among the latter but, in the absence of publication, his observations had no influence on the development of Stone Age archaeology in India.

Isolated from European scholarship although familiar with its trend, Carlyle pursued his research with seemingly endless endurance against difficult conditions, personal hardship and officialdom. In his own day, his frequent irritation and lack of composure with authority, as well as his determination to go his own way caused him to be regarded at best as an unmanageable eccentric rather than as a scholar with a worthwhile purpose. A century later, it is possible to appreciate that what he was trying to do was to establish the very nature and time-depth of the Stone Age in India. In this work, he often showed remarkable insight - as in his appreciation of the human geography of the past and his recognition of the antiquity of rock art. In the legacy of his collection he also provided material which is still relevant to modern archaeological research. The preparation of a new catalogue has provided an opportunity to review the classification and nomenclature used in the description of Indian stone artefacts (Chapter III) and discuss the Stone Age archaeology of the Central Provinces (Chapter II), albeit at a distance. Moreover, it has made clear the extent of Carlyle's achievement in establishing the existence and variety of Stone Age sites in the areas of India in which he worked.

II. FRAMEWORKS: THE STONE AGE PREHISTORY OF CENTRAL INDIA

The majority of stone artefacts in Carlyle's collection were found during his tours in Central Provinces of Uttar Pradesh and Madhya Pradesh between 1874 and 1884. Although primarily aimed at recording standing monuments, these tours took Carlyle to the southern edge of the Yamuna-Ganga Plain and into the Vindhya Hills where the geology and geomorphology favoured the preservation and exposure of different types of prehistoric Stone Age sites. Over the past fifty years, these areas have again been the focus of attention for archaeological investigations and, as a result, it is possible to review Carlyle's discoveries in the context of more recent research. This will be dealt with in two sections, the first covering the physical context of the sites and the second their archaeological position.

1. The Distribution and Geographical Contexts of Carlyle's Sites

The distribution of known Stone Age sites in Central India has changed little since the period of Carlyle's work. In some respects this simply reflects a similar manner of searching and recording. Carlyle would set out from a major centre such as Allahabad, Mirzapur or Rewa and travel along the better roads, stopping to collect if an opportunity arose - as for example at Bhainsaur, which the *Gazetteer of Mirzapur* (Drake-Brockman, 1911) describes as a government encampment and inspection bungalow on the Great Deccan Road southwest of Mirzapur, just beyond the Katra Pass which leads up into the hills (Figs. 4, 6). This location and its facilities provided a base from which Carlyle could leave the main road to search for rockshelters or sites around rocky outcrops or exposed in river valleys (see Catalogue entries 2, 5, 8, 10, 11, 17, 20, 33, 38). Much the same approach to survey has been adopted in recent times and, as a result, the northern part of the Jamuna-Ganga Plain and the Himalayan foothills have remained largely unexplored in terms of prehistory, whereas the number of known sites has increased in the areas explored by Carlyle on the southern edge of the plain and in the Vindhyas (Pant, 1982; Sharma, 1973a, 1973b).

The areas of eastern Madhya Pradesh and southeastern Uttar Pradesh explored by Carlyle (Fig. 6) include the southern part of the Yamuna-Ganga Plain, the Bundelkhand uplands which lie between the Yamuna and the curved northern scarp of the Vindyhan Hills to the south and the Aravalli Hills to the west, the Vindhyas, including the Kaimur range in the east, and the upper reaches of the Narmada Valley to the south. Within these physiographically and geologically distinct regions, stone artefacts occur in a variety of contexts and localities, most of which are reflected in Carlyle's material.

THE YAMUNA-GANGA PLAIN

The Quaternary alluviums of the Yamuna-Ganga Plain (Fig. 4) are thought to fill a deep depression between the Himalayas to the north and the plateaux to the south and constitute the most recent physiographic region of this part of India (Misra, 1977). The most recent Holocene alluviums or *khādar* occur on the low-lying flood plain adjacent to the meandering, modern courses of the rivers. The Plain is formed by older Pleistocene river deposits with the *bangar* or oldest alluvium forming the higher ground (ibid.). In this region, stone artefacts have been found on the surface or derived in river deposits subsequently exposed by the downcutting of more recent tributary and ephemeral streams or the excavation of modern pits and channels. In both circumstances, artefacts may occur over extensive areas, as in the case of Bayiari, 18 km east of Kausaubi, where Palaeolithic bifaces, cleavers, flake tools and debitage as well as microliths have been recorded from terrace deposits and as surface finds over an area of 8 square kilometres (Ghosh, 1956; Misra, 1977). Carlyle's finds around Banda (see

Catalogue entry 7) may have come from a similarly extensive area and he also recovered derived artefacts from alluvial deposits of the river Ken, a tributary of the Yamuna (see Catalogue entry 27).

THE BUNDELKHAND UPLANDS

The Bundelkhand uplands (Fig. 4) are formed on volcanic rock extruded as massive lava flows. The uplands slope from northwest to northeast in a series of three plateaux at an average elevation of 300, 150 and 100 metres but mesas and buttes rise above these general levels (Anon., 1968). The long, narrow ridges of quartz reefs and trap dykes as well as numerous lakes and waterfalls make for a rugged topography in which Stone Age surface sites often occur near sources of stone suitable for toolmaking. However, the condition of cortex remnants on artefacts collected by Carlyle suggest that the pebbles of chalcedonic silica utilised as raw materials derive mainly from river beds or, occasionally, screes rather than directly from the cavities in the lavas in which they form. This contrasts with the exploitation of igneous and metamorphic rocks which at sites such as Marfa (see Catalogue entry 36) seem to have been exploited at source.
  The Vindyha scarplands (Fig. 4) rise abruptly in the south of Bundelkhand and are composed of horizontally bedded sedimentary rocks consisting of the predominantly calcareous strata of the Lower Vindyhan geological formation, unconformably overlain by the sandstones of the Upper Vindyhan which are intruded in places by lava dykes and sills. The sandstones form the surfaces of three plateaux: the Bhandar, Rewa and Kaimur. These descend in steps from west to east and are much reduced and dissected by erosion (Anon., 1968). Naturally weathered-out hollows and overhangs occur in the sandstones exposed along the escarpment, especially those occurring along the flat tops of small hill ranges (Pant, 1982). Some of these *tafoni* may have formed as a result of extreme diurnal and seasonal temperature and humidity changes during the Late Pleistocene (Jacobson, 1980). Many were certainly favoured for habitation from this time onwards (Pant, 1982). It is possible that Carlyle realised the potential of such sites for he collected or excavated in at least five (see Catalogue entries 5, 8, 11, 20, 38), perhaps the most notable being Morhana Pahar (see Catalogue entry 38) where he also recorded rock-paintings (Allchin, B., 1958; Carlleyle, 1883; Cockburn, 1883, 1884). However, it is only in the last thirty years that systematic excavations at a few sites have shown their importance for evaluating at least the relative age of artefacts, as well as distinguishing variation in the technology and composition of lithic assemblages through time. More commonly reported are the many open sites in the Vindhyas at which stratigraphy may be lacking and the finds confined to the surface. Such sites tend to be associated with identifiable features in the terrain such as low hills (Jacobson, 1980). As is evident from the catalogue, the most common raw materials on both types of site are chalcedony and chert. These silicas formed in cavities in the Deccan Trap which covers some of the sandstone hills. However, judging by the staining, abrasion and chattermarking of many of the natural surface remnants on artefacts in the Carlyle Collection, most pebbles of these materials were obtained from stream beds.

THE NARMADA VALLEY

The Narmada river rises on the Amarkantak plateau (22°40'N, 81°45'E) and flows west through a tectonically formed rift in rocks running parallel to the Vindhya Hills (Ghosh, 1989) to the Gulf of Cambay (Figs. 2, 4). The trough it occupies favoured the massive accumulation of alluvial sediments which in places reach a depth of 150 m (ibid.) and incorporate mammalian fossils and artefacts dating from the Middle Pleistocene onwards. The first faunal remains were reported by Theobald in 1860 (Theobald, 1860) and Carlyle was probably aware of this and other early work (Blanford, 1869; Medlicot, 1873; Oldham, 1868) as he also took care to note the occurrence of animal bone whilst collecting in the area south of Jabalpur (see Catalogue entry 19) and referred to the gravels of the tributary Gaur river as being the same age as those of the Narmada. However, as is evident from the artefacts he recovered (see Catalogue entries 19, 21, 43), much of the archaeological material from these deposits is derived and mixed. This has proved a particular problem for workers who have attempted to associate distinct industries with the geological and climatic succession suggested by de Terra and Paterson (1939) following a two-week field survey between Hoshangabad and Narsinghpur in 1935. In brief, this survey recognised a Lower and an Upper Group of Pleistocene gravels and silts resting on laterite overlying quartzitic bed rocks. Artefacts were noted in the Lower and Upper Groups, as well as in the late Pleistocene gravel and Holocene soil which were reported as capping the 'sequence'. Inevitably, this scheme and the simplistic correlations based on it have proved untenable (Dennell in Rendell et al., 1989; Ghosh, 1989; Khatri, 1961; Sankalia, 1963) and its use as a framework or model for Central India has been problematic (see below). However, in addition to its alluvial sediments the Central Narmada Valley is also important for rockshelters such as Adamgarh (Ghosh, 1989) and those at Bhimbetka (Misra, 1978, 1982; Thapar, 1975) which contain stratified deposits incorporating *in situ* material remains from the Lower Palaeolithic to the Chalcolithic. Carlyle makes no mention of having visited these sites but in more recent times they have provided important information towards understanding the Pleistocene archaeology of Central India, as may be seen from the chronological review which follows.

2. The Archaeological Context of Carlyle's Finds

Although he was undoubtedly aware of the basic division of prehistory into Stone Age, Bronze Age and Iron Age which had been in use in Europe since the 1830s (Daniel, 1967), Carlyle did not explicitly apply this classification in his work and made no use at all of the subdivisions of the Stone Age which were beginning to come into use in the 1870s and which must have been known to him at least from Evans (1872) *Ancient Stone Implements*, to which he occasionally referred in his work. His reticence in classifying material may have resulted from the fact that a large portion of his discoveries were 'pygmy flints', bladelets and microliths which had received little attention in Europe at that time and which were not incorporated into general classifications until the 1890s (Daniel, 1967). However, although recourse to European ideas hindered Carlyle, as well as his contemporaries and to some extent his successors, from developing a relative chronology and typological framework for the material he found, this was not the only problem. There was also a paucity of stratified sites in which different stages of the Stone Age in general and the Palaeolithic in particular could be distinguished. Animal remains which in Europe had helped to distinguish chronological periods were rare with or without association with artefacts and, in remote regions, the continued use of stone tools into recent times could confuse the distinction of archaeological periods simply on the grounds of typology and technology. Indeed, these problems, as well as the contrasts in the preservation and character of the archaeological record in different regions and a lack of data about how Pleistocene climatic changes affected the subcontinent, have continued to inhibit the modelling of frameworks (Allchin and Allchin, 1982; Rendell et al., 1989; Wickramapathirana, 1984).

After Carlyle, Foote (1916) used a simple four-age scheme which did not identify the Mesolithic or subdivide the Palaeolithic in his notes on his collection from Southern India for Madras Museum. In 1930, after a brief visit to India, Cammiade and Burkitt proposed that Older Stone Age material could be classified into four series numbered 1 to 4. This scheme, based on a short period of fieldwork in Madras, suggested that the earliest, or series 1, industries were characterised by quartzite handaxes, whereas flake tools predominated in series 2 assemblages, giving way to blade tools in series 3 and microliths in series 4 (Cammiade and Burkitt, 1930). As these series corresponded loosely with the Lower, Middle and Upper Palaeolithic and Mesolithic respectively, the tendency to apply the European terms soon developed. Certainly, the series terminology had less impact than the nomenclature for the earlier Palaeolithic derived from the results of de Terra and Paterson's fieldwork in the Soan and Narmada Valleys in 1935 (de Terra and Paterson, 1939). In the Soan Valley, where he found no bifaces in the Palaeolithic assemblages, Paterson (ibid.), mindful of his work on the British Clactonian (see Dennell in Rendell et al., 1989), divided and named his material Early and Late Soan, the former characterised by pebble tools followed in the latter by industries in which flake tools predominated. As this subdivision was tied into the geological chronology and interpretation of Pleistocene climatic fluctuations described in the same work by de Terra, the scheme invited typological comparisons and correlations in much the same way as the Swanscombe 'sequence' did in Britain. However, in peninsular India, the scheme could not be applied directly because biface assemblages referred to as Acheulian, Chellean-Acheulian or Madrasian (Krishnaswami, 1947; Menghin, 1931, p.119; Paterson, 1940) predominated, with the consequence that many years were 'spent in a futile search for the meeting ground of the Sohanian and Madrasian culture' (Khatri, 1961, p.521) in the hope of correlating and extending the framework.

To break out of such circular arguments, Sankalia (1956) attempted to reintroduce the series nomenclature, this time applying Roman numerals I-III to distinguish biface-cleaver-core assemblages (I) from flake tool (II) and microlith (III) assemblages. Subsequently Sankalia and Banerjee (1958) used the term Nevasian for series II or Middle Palaeolithic assemblages. This name derives from the site of Nevas on the Pravara River in Maharashtra where Series II flake tools were found stratified in gravels above bifaces and cleavers (Sankalia, 1956; Sankalia and Banerjee, 1958) but it has not been widely applied and seems to have fallen out of use in recent literature.

In parallel with Sankalia, influenced by developments in the Stone Age archaeology of Africa and controversy about the existence and nature of an Upper Palaeolithic, Bridget Allchin (1963) proposed a threefold Early, Middle and Late Stone Age scheme which corresponded with Series I-III. However, more recent research and debate have restored the Upper Palaeolithic and drawn most Indian archaeologists back to the four-age (Lower, Middle, Upper Palaeolithic and Mesolithic) scheme, in which regional variations are beginning to be recognised (Allchin and Allchin, 1982; Sharmer, 1982; Wickramapathirana, 1984). An alternative suggested by Ghosh (1970, 1973, 1982; Ray, 1982) retains the basic distinction between stone and metal ages but subdivides the former into Pebble-core, Flake and Flake-Blade elements. This techno-typological approach has limitations because it explicitly assumes progressive evolution or 'transmutation' (Ghosh, 1982, p.278f.) rather than adaptive variation and, as a result, could impair the recognition of actual archaeolgical patterns even more than the loose umbrella terms of the old four-part division of the Stone Age. Consequently, it is the latter scheme which has been used to reappraise and catalogue Carlyle's material but it should be noted that in this context the European connotations of the nomenclature are almost irrelevant.

THE LOWER AND MIDDLE PALAEOLITHIC

Some of the artefacts in the Carlyle collection identified as Lower-Middle Palaeolithic come from the central Narmada Valley and its tributary, the Gaur (Catalogue entries 43, 19; Fig. 6). As noted above, the Narmada has been a focus for research on the Pleistocene since the nineteenth century and the publication of de Terra and Paterson's fieldwork in 1939 seemed to suggest a succession of Palaeolithic industries in Central India as summarised in Table 1 (see over).

Subsequent research has shown this scheme to be generalised and inadequate. The deposits are not continuous along the length of the valley as assumed by de Terra, there is an unconformity between the Lower and Upper Group deposits (Table 2, over) and, on the basis of its fauna, the latter must be Upper rather than Middle Pleistocene (Khatri, 1961, 1962 and in Ghosh (ed.), 1959, 1960; McCown and Banerjee in Ghosh (ed.), 1959; Sankalia, 1962; inter alia). This imposes a number of difficulties on the interpretation of the archaeology. In places, Gravel I rests against a red clay, said to be a fluvial aggradation, which contains artefacts and heavily mineralised mammalian fossils (Khatri,

Table 1. Stratigraphy and archaeology of the Narmada Valley after de Terra and Paterson (1939)

Period	Geology	Archaeology
Holocene-Upper Pleistocene	Black cotton soil Fine gravel	Microliths
Middle Pleistocene	Pink silt = Upper Group Gravel II	Choppers, flakes and flake tools and prepared cores. Equated with Late Soan of Pakistan
Middle Pleistocene	Pink silt = Lower Group Gravel I	Bifaces and cleavers equated with the Acheulian. Pebble tools and flakes equated with the Soan of Pakistan
	Laterite	--------

Table 2. Stratigraphy and archaeology of the Narmada Valley after Khatri (1961)

Period	Geology	Archaeology
Holocene	Black cotton soil Cross-bedded yellow silts with concretions	Microliths
Uppper Pleistocene	Cemented cross-bedded sands	Bifaces, pebble tools, flakes, flake tools and prepared cores. Late Acheulian and Middle Palaeolithic
Uppper Pleistocene	Cemented sandy gravel (II)	Bifaces, cleavers, pebble tools and flakes. Early Acheulian
	↑↓ ↑↓ ↑↓ ↑↓ ↑↓ ↑↓ EROSIONAL UNCONFORMITY ↑↓ ↑↓ ↑↓ ↑↓ ↑↓ ↑↓	
Middle Pleistocene	Bouldery gravel (I) // Red clay	Bifaces, pebble tools and flakes Cholloan
	Laterite	-------

1961). The gravel itself is usually described as 'bouldery' as it incorporates clasts larger than those in a usual gravel fraction which presumably implies a high energy depositional environment. As the artefacts within this deposit must therefore be derived, collections from it cannot be regarded as discrete archaeological assemblages. More probably, they are mixed accumulations possibly derived from more than one site and, potentially, from older sediments. This also applies to Gravel II, which is separated from the Lower Group sediments by an erosional unconformity representing a time gap of unknown duration. As a result, the recognition of Soan chopper-chopping tool/flake and Acheulian or Madrasian biface traditions within the Lower Group, the Late Acheulian and Middle Palaeolithic in the Upper Group and their possible relationships is based on typology and implicit models of techno-typological evolution or 'transmutation' (Ghosh, 1982) for which there is no contextual confirmation.

Dating these deposits is also problematic. The Lower Group has been attributed to the Middle Pleistocene (730,000 - 120,000 BP) because it incorporates the fossil remains of two large mammal species, the hippopotamus *Hexaprotodon palaeindicus* and the pig *Sus namadicus*, which are known only from this period (Ghosh, 1989; Joshi, 1978; Sahni and Khan, 1988). However, as is noted by Ghosh (ibid., 311), this attribution is not well established because the fossils are derived and there is no independent evidence to confirm the age. With the exception of the two noted above, the species present in the Lower Group fauna occur throughout both the Middle and Upper Pleistocene (120,000 - 10,000 BP) and are also represented in the Upper Group. On the basis of this evidence alone, the Lower Group could be Middle or Upper Pleistocene, further compounding the archaeological problems. Similar difficulties also detract from the value of sites excavated through the alluvial deposits of Yamuna-Ganga tributaries such as the Belan, Seoti, Ken, Tons and Son (Pant, 1982; Sharma, 1973a) and of the Pravara and Godavari to the southwest in Maharashtra (Corvinus, 1968, 1969, 1970, 1981; Sankalia, 1956). However, apparently discrete artefact assemblages from stratified primary contexts at the open sites of Chirki on the Pravara, Maharashtra and at Lalitpur in Madhya Pradesh, as well as in the rockshelters of Adamgarh Hill and Bhimbetka, south of the Narmada near Hoshangabad, provide more satisfactory information about the nature of both the Lower and Middle Palaeolithic.

At Bhimbetka (77° 37'E, 22°50'N) on the northern margin of the Vindhya Hills (Fig. 4), Lower Palaeolithic assemblages have been found in the basal deposits of four rockshelters: IIIF-23, IIIF-24, IIIA-29 and IIIA-30 (Misra 1978 and in Thapar (ed.), 1975). Site IIIF-23, the largest of these shelters, contained eight levels as summarised in Table 3:

Table 3. Stratigraphy and archaeology of Bhimbetka IIIF-23 after Misra (1978)

Level	Context	Archaeology
1	Silty sand with angular clasts	Geometric microliths, grinders, querns, red and grey pottery, stone beads
2	Sandy/clayey silt	Geometric microliths, grinders, querns
3	Sandy silt	Some microliths
4	Silty clay with frequent clasts	Flakes, blades, scrapers
5	Fine silty sand	Endscrapers, Levallois flakes, blades, some bifaces
6	Silty sand with large clasts	
7	Red silt with deeply altered clasts	Cleavers, bifaces and debitage
8	Orange silty clay with deeply altered clasts	

Lower Palaeolithic artefacts occur through 2.4 m of deposit in the bottom of the inner part of the shelter over an area of 26 square metres (ibid.). No evidence of fire or organic remains were found and Misra (1978) has treated the 4705 artefacts from levels 6, 7 and 8 as a single assemblage. The artefacts are made from metamorphosed sandstone, one variety of which occurs on the spot, another having been introduced. The material is fresh although Misra (ibid.) reports that the majority of bifaces and cleavers show ancient breaks or damage. Just over two-thirds of the collection consists of debitage, suggesting that toolmaking took place within the shelter. Cleavers made on flakes and ovate and cordiform bifaces make up some 60 per cent of the tools, the cleavers exceeding the bifaces by a ratio of four to one. The flake tools include endscrapers, naturally and deliberately backed knives, notches and denticulates. A small number of prepared, Levallois flakes and cores are also present and this element, in addition to the relatively high proportion and diversity of flake tools, has led Misra (ibid.) to suggest that the industry relates to the Middle Palaeolithic and represents a 'Late Acheulian'. Certainly, in level 5 at the same site (Table 3) bifaces become rare and the frequency of flake tools and the use of Levallois technique increases in a manner which suggests a continuum. Misra (ibid.) also contrasts the Bhimbetka assemblage with those from Lalitpur (Ghosh (ed.), 1964; Misra, 1978), Chirki (Corvinus, 1968, 1969, 1970, 1981) and Adamgarh Sites 6 and 7 (Joshi, 1972). Noting that these assemblages contain choppers and chopping tools, a higher (Lalitpur) or equal proportion (Chirki) of pointed bifaces to cleavers and no evidence of Levallois technique, he suggests that the Lower Palaeolithic may be divided into two phases as summarised in Table 4.

Table 4. Sub-division of the Lower Palaeolithic after Misra (1978)

Phase 1	Phase 2
High % choppers and chopping tools	Choppers and chopping tools absent
High % bifaces	Low % of bifaces
High ratio bifaces: cleavers	More cleavers
Low % flake tools	High % flake tools
Levallois/prepared core technique absent	Levallois technique present
No blades	Some blades

This subdivision provides a useful starting point from which to begin to understand the Lower Palaeolithic of Central India although, as Misra (ibid.) notes, it is currently difficult to expand because of the problems of derived and mixed assemblages and the lack of standardised methods of analysis. There are also some difficulties with the implication that phase 1 may be older than stage 2, not least because there is no means of dating the assemblages considered. As noted by Joshi (1978), the absence of or low percentage of pebble tools might be as much due to a lack of suitable cobbles from which to make them as to age or culture. Similarly, variations in the relative percentages of bifaces, cleavers and flake tools may represent coeval adaptive variations rather than change through time.

At Chirki, the assemblage discussed above was recovered, in fresh condition, from a colluvial deposit resting directly on Deccan Trap and overlain by a fluviatile gravel incorporating flakes, cores and worked pebbles (Corvinus, 1969, 1970, 1981). In contrast to the tools from the colluvium which are made of diorite, the artefacts from the gravel are produced from chalcedony and jasper. As noted at other localities along the Pravara (Sankalia, 1956; Sankalia et al., 1960), these artefacts are smaller than those from the colluvium and were originally attributed to the Middle Palaeolithic Nevasian (Corvinus, 1970). However, Corvinus (1981) has subsequently referred to this material as non-diagnostic and suggests that this could be a light duty facies of the Acheulian. In discussing the Middle Palaeolithic material from open rockshelters (ADG-7 on Adamgarh Hill), Joshi (1978) also points out that despite a reduction in the size of artefacts, the techno-typological attributes of the material are the same as in the earlier levels. Similarly, Misra (1978) has described the separation of 'Middle Palaeolithic' flakes and flake tools from the boulder conglomerate in the cliff section at Mahadeo Piparia as 'arbitrary and unwarranted'. These examples might suggest that the separation of a Lower and Middle Palaeolithic may be inappropriate, as has also been suggested in Pakistan where Dennell (in Rendell et al., 1989) prefers to call the period prior to $c.30,000$ BP the Early Palaeolithic. However, if the diminution of artefact size and increase in the diversity of tool types noted by Ghosh (1982) and Ray (1982) can be shown to occur consistently in stratigraphically more recent levels as mooted in the sites discussed above, there may be some validity in maintaining a subdivision in Central India. However, outside Central India in Rajasthan, the recognition of such a 'Middle Palaeolithic' in a context dated by uranium series and thermoluminescence to $c.144,000$ BP at Didwana (Mishra 1992; Misra 1989; Misra et al., 1988), may indicate that there could be chronological overlap in assemblage variation rather than a continuous progression. Only the discovery of further datable, primary context sites will help to resolve this problem in Central India.

Unfortunately, Carlyle's finds have little to contribute in the context of these modern arguments although it is perhaps noteworthy that they are still representative of the type of material found from this period. It is also difficult to suggest their possible age although it does seem increasingly evident that the Lower-Middle Palaeolithic of Central India extends back into the Middle Pleistocene (Mishra 1992) and is not just a phenomenon of the Late Middle-Late Pleistocene as has been occasionally suggested (ibid.).

THE UPPER PALAEOLITHIC

An Upper Palaeolithic was not recognised in India until relatively recently (Ghosh, 1989; Sankalia, 1974; Sharmer, 1982). Although so-called 'blade and burin assemblages' had been noted in Southeast India by Cammiade and Burkitt (1930) and at Khandivli near Bombay by Todd (1939, and see Appendix 2), these occurrences tended to be grouped with microlithic assemblages in Series III or the Late Stone Age and it was generally assumed that the latter had developed from a prolonged Middle Palaeolithic. This may be the case in some areas but in Central India and to the 'southwest' in Maharashtra, an intermediate Upper Palaeolithic phase is now known from a number of both open sites and rockshelters, including some first discovered by Carlyle.

For Sankalia (1974) and Ghosh (1989), the Upper Palaeolithic is characterised by the introduction of true blade technology (Tixier, 1984; Tixier et al., 1980) alongside a continued use of flakes in assemblages such as that from Bhimbetka IIIF-24 level 4 (Table 3), including burins on thick blades, backed blades, awls, points and scrapers (see Glossary, Chapter III). An example of the indigenous development of this type of assemblage may be seen at the site of Patne in Maharashtra, where Sali (1985; Sankalia, 1974) identified five Upper Palaeolithic levels in deposits 11 to 7, stratified between the Lower-Middle Palaeolithic and Mesolithic. The oldest of these, level 11, includes burins and scrapers made on thick flakes and flake-blades like those produced in the Middle Palaeolithic layer below. Boldly retouched backed blades occur in the two subsequent levels but the pyramidal and conical cores typical of true blade production appear later in levels 8 and 7, which also contain tanged points and a decorated ostrich eggshell bead. In level 5, the occurrence of non-geometric microliths (see Glossary, Chapter III) with the Upper Palaeolithic may indicate a transition towards, or overlap with, the early Mesolithic. However, although the Patne assemblages may typify the nature of the Upper Palaeolithic of peninsular India (Sankalia, 1974; Ghosh, 1989), in Uttar Pradesh Pant (1982) characterises the same period as including a large proportion of bladelets among the blanks, a small number of microliths (usually backed bladelets and lunates), flake tools and some burins, endscrapers, points and truncated blades. Jayaswal (1989) adds that a later phase or Epi-Palaeolithic may also be recognised by an increase in microliths.

The recognition of a regionally distinct Upper and Epi-Palaeolithic in Central India is based principally on assemblages found in alluvial deposits of the Belan and Seoti valleys (Fig. 5), as well as from open, hillside 'factory' sites with shallow stratigraphy around Banda and Kalinjar (Fig. 5) and from the rockshelter of Laharaidh or Laharia-dih (Jayaswal, 1989; Pant, 1982). In the Belan and Seoti valleys, they occur in Gravel III and the overlying silt (Jayaswal, 1989, fig 12.2; Sharma, 1973a). At Daiya, on the right bank of the Seoti, the artefacts are described as *in situ* in these deposits (Pant, 1982) but in alluvial sediments this may not be meant to imply a discrete, primary context assemblage. However, even if some mixing has occurred, it seems at least possible that Gravel III and the silt are Late Pleistocene on the basis of their stratigraphy, as well as radiocarbon dates of $19,715 \pm 340$ BP for material from Gravel III on the middle terrace of the Belan at Chopani Mando (Jayaswal, 1989; Ghosh (ed.), 1967; Thapar (ed.), 1978) and $10,030 \pm 115$ BP for the overlying Gravel IV at Daiya (Jayaswal, 1989; Sharma, 1973a). Although little weight can be placed on such isolated dates, they are in keeping with dates for the Upper Palaeolithic to the west in Rajasthan (Agrawal et al., 1989). Further support for the presence of this facies of the Upper Palaeolithic may also be drawn from the occurrence of a number of assemblages of similar composition to those of Belan and Seoti at other sites in Uttar Pradesh (Pant, 1982).

At Ainchwara by the river Ohan, northeast of Mankikpur in Banda District, apart from a small percentage of microliths, most of the tools are said to be made on flakes and a number on blades (ibid.) Blade cores account for 76 per cent of the total number of cores and the tendency to use raw materials exhaustively noted by Jayaswal (ibid.) may account for the production of bladelets. Similar assemblages are also described from Kalinjar and Karwi in Banda District (ibid.; Pant, 1982) but all are undatable except by techno-typological comparison with the Belan and Seoti material. This also applies to the rockshelter assemblages that contain a higher proportion of microliths, as at Lahraidh (ibid.), which Jayaswal regards as a later facies with a wider distribution (ibid., p.252). Others (Sankalia, 1974; Ghosh (ed.), 1989) seem to regard this facies as an early stage of the Mesolithic to which it certainly relates. Even with more detailed analyses of assemblages, it may be impossible to draw a clear distinction between the Late Upper or Epi-Palaeolithic and Early Mesolithic but such differentiation should perhaps not be expected where, as Jayaswal (1989, p.252) notes, the techno-typological traits of toolkits may vary on a regional rather than a chronological or cultural basis.

This has posed certain problems in cataloguing the Carlyle material. Possible Upper Palaeolithic artefacts have been identified in Carlyle's collections from open sites around Banda (Catalogue entry 7), Kalinjar (26), Naro Hill (44) and in the Narmada Valley (43), as well as from Baghmara Pahar (6), Bhagatpura (9), Manohar Tali Pahar (35) and Moretha Pahar (39). In addition, recent excavations at Baghai Khor (5) and Morhana Pahar (38) have led to the suggestion that the basal assemblages in these sites may be Late Upper or Epi-Palaeolithic (Jayaswal, 1989; Pant, 1982; Sharmer, 1982), although no clearly diagnostic Upper Palaeolithic finds occur in Carlyle's collections from these rockshelters. As a result, the non-geometric microliths and bladelets from those and other sites have been referred to as Mesolithic in the Catalogue. This is not entirely satisfactory because some of these artefacts may well have originated from Upper Palaeolithic assemblages but, without distinctive types, dating evidence, detailed techno-typological descriptions or first-hand experience of recently excavated assemblages, it was not a problem that could be resolved in the context of a catalogue. Previously, all microliths would have been embraced under the terms Series III or Late Stone Age and it is to be hoped that as further regionally based research brings better definition and understanding of the Late Pleistocene-Early Holocene period, the significance of Carlyle's finds will become clearer.

THE MESOLITHIC

As discussed in Chapter I, Carlyle was the first to recognise 'pygmy implements' or microliths in India and these constitute by far the largest number of artefacts in his collection. Although microliths are known from Upper Palaeolithic contexts (see above) and persist into the Neolithic and, in some regions, recent times, they are nevertheless said to characterise the Mesolithic if they are not associated with pottery and generally antedate the earliest farming-based villages (Ghosh, 1989; Sankalia, 1974). For the purposes of cataloguing, this is not the easiest of definitions (Joshi, 1973, p.54) and may have led to some misattributions but, as many Mesolithic assemblages from Central India have come from stratified sites where it is possible to differentiate chronological variation in the types and proportions of artefacts present, reference to published material has provided a yardstick for general assessment.

New excavations at Baghai Khor and Morhana Pahar in Mirzapur District (Fig. 6;Catalogue entries 4, 38) during the early 1960s (Ghosh (ed.), 1965; Varma, 1965) produced a sequence of microlithic industries (Table 5) through the Mesolithic and Neolithic.

Table 5. The succession of microlithic industries in Central India.

Phase	Archaeology	Period
IV	Geometric & non-geomtric microliths with pottery. Microliths exceptionally small	NEOLITHIC
III	Geometric microliths including trapezes with pottery	
II	Geometric & non-geometric microliths without pottery	MESOLITHIC
I	Non-geometric microliths without pottery	

This general sequence has also been recognised *inter alia* at the rockshelter and open site of Lekhahia in Mirzapur District (Ghosh (ed.), 1965; 1973; Sankalia, 1974), at the open site of Chopani Mando (Deshpande (ed.), 1975; Ghosh (ed.), 1989; Thapar (ed.), 1980), on the left bank of the Belan, 69 km southeast of Allahabad (Fig. 4) and at Bhimbetka (Thapar (ed.), 1980; Misra, 1982), and Adamgarh I in Madhya Pradesh. At Chopani-Mando, the Early Mesolithic occurred above the Late Upper or Epi-Palaeolithic and is divided into two phases both associated with circular house structures (Thapar (ed.), 1980). The earlier assemblage (IIA) consists of non-geometric microliths, such as backed and truncated bladelets, borers and points, as well as lunates, all of which are smaller than those in the underlying Late Upper Palaeolithic levels. All of these forms persist in the subsequent phase (IIB) with the addition of geometric microliths. Among the geometric microliths, the triangle appears earlier than the trapeze. Diminution in the size of all these types characterises the Late Mesolithic phase (III) which is also associated with pottery and ringstones with hour-glass perforations.

The Early Mesolithic phase IIB assemblage at Chopani-Mando has been compared with and found similar to the artefacts associated with the occupation area and eight human burials found at Sarai Nahar Rai southwest of Pratapgarh in the Ganga Valley which was inhabited for the first time during the Mesolithic (Sharma, 1973b). The extended inhumations had an east-west orientation, the skulls lying towards the west. Each individual had one arm to the side with the other resting on the abdomen. A number of microliths were associated with the burials. Those associated with skeletons V, X and XIII occur in positions that suggest they formed the tips of weapons which killed or wounded the individuals (ibid.) whilst others may have been grave-goods. Similar burials associated with microliths occur at Mahadaha, also near Pratapgarh (Thapar (ed.), 1980), as well as in the rockshelters at Bhimbetka (Sankalia, 1974) and Baghai Khor (Varma, 1965). Noting the latter, Sankalia (1974) recalls Carlyle's remarks, quoted in V.A. Smith (1906), concerning the excavation of extended burials in the valleys of Vindhyas and suggests they might also have been Mesolithic.

In addition to a rare glimpse of human behaviour other than technological and economic activities, Sarai Nahar Rai has also provided a radiocarbon age estimate on calcified bone of 10,050 ± 110 BP (TF 1104; Dutta, 1971). This isolated date is still difficult to interpret (Sharma, 1973b) and it can only be noted that this assemblage appears to be older than the geometric microlith assemblages without pottery at Lekhahia which have associated radiocarbon age estimates of 2290 ± 115 bc (TF-419) and 1610 ± 110 bc (TF-417). If the latter dates are assumed to be reliable, they may reflect the persistence of hunter-gathers in the hill regions after the introduction of farming in the lowlands. This overlap is also seen in the occurence of hunted animals in association with querns and mullers and the microlithic assemblage at Mahadaha (Thapar (ed.), 1980), and domesticated and wild animal remains, as well as pottery, with the Late Mesolithic assemblage at Adamgarh I (Joshi, 1968) with a problematic radiocarbon age estimate on shell of 7450 ± 130 BP (TF-120; Ghosh (ed.), 1989). The absence of lithic raw materials in the Ganga valley, which was first settled during the Mesolithic (Sharma, 1973a, 1973b), must also have necessitated contact between the regions. Consequently, a chronological definition of this period is difficult to specify but in general the assemblages discovered by Carlyle probably accumulated between 10,000 and 4000 years ago. At Baghai Khor and Morhana Pahar they occurred in rockshelters decorated with paintings. Evidence of colouring materials in association with the microliths at Morhana Pahar led Carlyle and, subsequently, Cockburn (1899) to suggest that some of the paintings may be of the same antiquity (Chapter I). At the time, Vincent Smith in his footnotes to Cockburn's paper (ibid.) echoed general opinion in dismissing this idea and the view that most of the painting belonged to the historical period was later reiterated in a study by Gordon (1958). However, recent discoveries of green pigments in Upper Palaeolithic deposits as well as of red and yellow ochre, haematite and manganese in the Mesolithic and Chalcolithic levels at Bhimbetka (Misra and Mathpal, 1979; Thapar, 1985; Wakankar and Brooks, 1976) would seem to vindicate Carlyle and Cockburn's view of the age of some of the paintings.

Overall, Carlyle's material may be seen as fitting a view of the Mesolithic as a period characterised by artefacts with indigenous origins in the Late Pleistocene-Early Holocene. The increased use of microliths during this phase reflects hafting for composite tools and the introduction of the bow and arrow for hunting. Paintings and perhaps burials noted by Carlyle now provide a broader view of human behaviour in a period which saw the spread of settlement over a wider area of Central India.

THE NEOLITHIC AND CHALCOLITHIC

The evidence of incipient food production associated with hunting and gathering referred to above suggests a continuous indigenous transition from the Late Upper Palaeolithic to the Neolithic in Central India. This continuum is particularly well demonstrated at Chopani Mando where the Late Mesolithic or Proto-Neolithic levels (Table 5) show significant additions to the repertoire of artefacts (Sharma et al., 1989). These include ground stone tools such as hammerstones, querns, mullers, ringstones and stone discs (also referred to as palettes or anvils), as well as hand-made pottery. The appearance of querns and mullers would suggest cereal cultivation but the economy of the thirteen-hut settlement seems to have been based on hunting and gathering although impressions of wild rice grains and the presence of wild cattle and sheep bones in the faunal remains place the site just at the transition to food production (Thapar, 1985).

This Proto-Neolithic phase is thought to have occurred about 9000 years ago and, by about 7000 years ago, fully Neolithic settlements with domesticated rice and cattle are known from sites such as Koldhiawa (24° 54'N, 82° 2'E) and Mahagara (24° 54'N, 82° 3'E) in the Belan valley (Ghosh (ed.), 1989). At these sites, the microlithic toolkits are augmented by polished stone axes, parallel-sided blades and serrated blades and points. In the Carlyle collection such artefacts are rare or, in the case of stone axes, absent. There is also no pottery. This may indicate a collecting bias which might have been caused by Carlyle's interest in microliths or perhaps the division and disposal of his finds after his work. Unfortunately, there is no evidence either to confirm or refute such possibilities and in cataloguing the material it has been impossible to determine with any certainty whether geometric microliths together with ground stone implements indicate a Late Mesolithic/Proto-Neolithic or Neolithic phase.

The same problems accrue to the recognition of Chalcolithic material in the collection. Despite the introduction of metalworking, stone artefacts continued to play a significant role in the Chalcolithic toolkit. In the Indus Valley and areas where large nodules of cryptocrystalline silica such as chert could be quarried, these tools were made on long, parallel-sided blades as described from Maheshwar in Madhya Pradesh by Subbarao (1955) and from Nevasa in Maharashtra (Sankalia et al., 1960). Good examples of such blades are held in the Single collection, formerly in the Geological Museum, from the Rohri Hills, Pakistan (Appendix 2) but no such material diagnostic of the Chalcolithic occurs in the Carlyle collection. This is not due to collecting bias but reflects the continued use of small nodules of local raw materials in the area of Central India where Carlyle was working. Within this area, sites of the Kayathan, Banas and Malwa cultures spanning a period from about 4000 to 2000 years ago have been distinguished by their distinctive pottery types. Their lithic assemblages are, however, less diagnostic including backed and obliquely blunted blades and bladelets, lunates, borers, points and geometric microliths the same as those found in earlier periods. In the catalogue, the possibility that such artefacts may be Chalcolithic has been noted where the collection has come from an open site, surface scatter or is unprovenanced except to region. However, there would appear to be little material of this phase in the collection.

Summary

The Carlyle collection contains a representative sample of material from all periods of the Stone Age in Central India although approximately 80 per cent of the artefacts are probably Mesolithic. Although collected over a century ago, it remains relevant to many current lines of research and it is to be hoped that publication will help with future evaluations of some of the important sites which Carlyle discovered but lacked the means, ability or temerity to publish himself.

PART TWO

GLOSSARY AND CATALOGUE

III. GLOSSARY OF TERMS USED FOR THE DESCRIPTION OF CARLYLE'S FINDS

Introduction

In common with many Indian stone artefact assemblages, the Carlyle collection contains **tools** deliberately produced to carry out specific tasks, waste material or **debitage** from the production of tools and natural pebbles, cobbles and slabs modified by use in activities such as tool manufacture or food or pigment preparation and generally referred to as **utilised pieces**. All of the pieces in these categories are **artefacts** indicative of human activity. The many different types of stone artefact found by Carlyle are listed in the catalogue. Just as the categories of tools, debitage and utilised pieces are based on common usage standardised by Bordes (1961, 1972), the definitions of types are based on classifications devised by B. Allchin (1966), F.R. Allchin (1957), F.R. Allchin et al. (1986), Foote (1916), Ghosh (1989), Sankalia (1963, 1964), Sharma et al. (1980), Subbarao (1948), Tixier (1963) and Tripathy (1980). The glossary lists the type names and definitions as used by the present authors. As the Carlyle collection contains stone artefacts varying in age from Palaeolithic to Chalcolithic, and as many types may be common at different times throughout this period, the glossary is arranged on a technological basis by subdividing the artefacts into flakes and flaked artefacts, blades, microlithic and composite artefacts, ground, hammer-dressed and polished artefacts and utilised pieces. Descriptions of the raw materials used for tool-making in Central India appear at the end of the glossary. An index of glossary entries is included at the end of the volume.

FLAKED AND FLAKE ARTEFACTS

The artefacts in these categories are particularly characteristic of the Lower and Middle Palaeolithic although flakes and flaked tools are also known from later assemblages in which blades and microliths predominate. They include unmodified flakes, flakes struck from prepared cores, flake tools and pieces of rock reduced and shaped by the removal of flakes some of which are classified as cores or debitage and others as tools.

FLAKED ARTEFACTS

Unprepared cores/pebble tools. In northern India assemblages composed of flakes and pebble or core tools made by striking a few flakes from a pebble, cobble or similar chunk of rock, predominate over other Lower Palaeolithic assemblages containing handaxes and cleavers and persist into the Middle Palaeolithic. Following the work of de Terra and Paterson (1935) and Movius (1949), emphasis has always been placed on the flaked pieces in these assemblages (Dennell in Rendell et al., 1989), amongst which two types of tool have been recognised:

- **choppers**: cobbles or chunks of stone from which two or more flakes struck from a single platform have been removed from one face to form an edge (Fig. 8a).

- **chopping tools**: cobbles or chunks of stone from which flakes have been removed from both faces often by alternate flaking which produces a sinuous edge (Fig. 8b).

Flaked pebbles and chunks which do not fit either of these definitions are generally regarded as cores discarded after flakes have been obtained from them and consequently classified as debitage. This is an arbitrary distinction based on modern perceptions of form and function rather than on archaeological evidence. However, although it may be undesirable to perpetuate this functional assumption which probably discriminates against balanced assessment of assemblages, this particular problem cannot be properly addressed in a catalogue and the terms **chopper** and **chopping tool** have been retained in order to distinguish cobbles and chunks that have been modified unifacially and bifacially from a single platform from those pieces that have been reduced in different ways from one or more platforms. The latter are described by indicating the number and position of the striking platforms, the characteristics of the flaking and size and shape rather than by type names.

Handaxes/bifaces. These terms are used interchangeably to refer to pieces of stone or deliberately struck flakes which have been modified by the removal of flakes from both faces into a range of pointed and rounded shapes with a continuous edge around at least 50% of the perimeter (Fig. 8c). Although they are still often referred to as particularly characteristic of the **Acheulian** in Indian literature, the use of this term does not have the same definition as in France (Tuffreau 1984) and broadly implies the Lower Palaeolithic rather than a specific phase or aspect of that period. Bifaces, particularly smaller forms, also occur in the Middle Palaeolithic. They vary in size from 4 to 20cm and the terms used to describe their shapes follow those defined by Bordes (1961, 1972) but this should not be taken to mean that the technological or cultural implications that may apply to certain forms in Europe have any relevance in India.

Cleavers. Characteristic of the Lower Palaeolithic but also found occasionally in later assemblages, the distinctive feature of the cleaver is a straight axe-like edge parallel to the butt (Fig. 8d). In India, the majority of cleavers are made of large struck flakes or slabs which have split along a natural cleavage plane. They are usually unifacially flaked although there are some examples of bifacial cleavers reduced from cobbles or blocks and finished by a tranchet blow (Tixier et al., 1980) to form the transverse edge. The flakes or slabs selected as blanks for cleavers are usually broad and rectangular or, more rarely, triangular. They may be up to 18cm long and are often symmetrical in outline with thin parallelogram or lenticular cross-sections. The upper or dorsal surface frequently retains cortex or the natural stone surface although the parallel, divergent, convex or concave sides are flaked, possibly to facilitate holding or hafting. Sankalia (1964) distinguishes four types on the basis of butt, side and cross-sectional form but it has not been necessary to use this typology here.

Picks. Large, bifacially modified or trihedral rod-like pieces pointed at one or both ends. Some are plano-convex in cross-section but others are roughly flaked and less regular in outline.

Complex cores. These cores are distinct from the simple, randomly or expediently struck cores described above in that they are systematically reduced in particular ways. Two forms are common:

> - **discoidal cores:** approximately circular in outline as the name implies, these artefacts are produced by the alternate removal of flakes from a single platform which extends around the circumference of the piece (Fig. 9a). This technique produces a centripetal scar pattern on both faces, creating slightly domed surfaces and biconical-lozenge shaped cross-sections. The size of discoidal cores varies considerably and in some cases it is impossible to ascertain whether these bifacial artefacts are handaxes or cores discarded after a series of flakes has been struck from them. Although most commonly associated with the Middle Palaeolithic, discoidal cores occur in Lower Palaeolithic and, occasionally, in later contexts.

> - **Levallois cores:** these cores are the distinctive by-products of a particular technique of prepared flake production which involves preliminary flaking of a block of stone so as to predetermine the size and shape of a final removal which will require little or no further

modification before use. This is achieved by striking flakes from a single platform around the circumference of the piece which becomes disc-shaped to produce a convex upper surface with a centripetal removal pattern and a flatter lower surface on which the removal pattern may vary according to the desired end-product (Fig. 9b). Centripetal or opposed scar patterns may be achieved by alternate and bipolar flaking respectively if a flake is required, whereas long, broad blades are determined by parallel removals from one or both ends and points by a convergent scar pattern. The convexity of this lower surface is crucial as it determines where the shock waves travelling through the rock from the point of percussion will detach the flake, thus influencing its size and successful removal. The angle and position of the blow are also important and may be improved by the removal of a few small flakes from the point on the platform from which the final prepared flake is to be removed. Once the flake has been struck off the distinctive core may be discarded or reduced by the detachment of further unprepared flakes. Levallois cores are generally considered indicative of the Middle Palaeolithic but may also occur in the Lower Palaeolithic and in later periods.

FLAKE ARTEFACTS

Flakes are a common element in the assemblages of all periods in which stone artefacts were made and used. They are produced by striking larger pieces of rock or other flakes with a hammer. Deliberately manufactured flakes may be separated into three categories:

- **debitage flakes:** this category includes all unprepared flakes which were left unmodified after being struck. In European inventories all such flakes are regarded as waste products in the absence of any evidence that they were deliberately shaped or utilised. In India, this is true for all but pointed pieces which, owing to their frequent occurrence, are generally recognised as a distinct type (see Flake Tool Types below).

- **prepared or Levallois flakes:** the flakes in this category have been deliberately prepared so that they are suitable for use with little or no further modification after they have been struck from the core. They are oval, parallel-sided or pointed in shape and retain few, if any, remnants of cortex or natural rock surface on their dorsal faces which exhibit opposed, parallel or convergent scars produced by the preparatory flaking of the core to predetermine the size and shape of the required flake or point (Fig. 9b). Their butts are usually broad and often faceted and their edges regular and low angled (less than 35-40°). Prepared flakes are usually attributed to the Middle Palaeolithic but may also occur in the Lower Palaeolithic and later contexts.

- **flake tools:** after a flake has been struck from a core, the shape, angle and sharpness of its edges may be modified to suit a particular task by **retouching** which involves striking off a series of small flakes to obtain edges of the required angle and shape (Tixier et al., 1980). Different types of flake tool are distinguished by the nature of the retouch and its position in relation to the axis of percussion (see below and Figs. 10, 11). Right and left edges are determined with the flake orientated on its axis of percussion with the proximal end downwards and dorsal face uppermost (Fig. 10). A left edge may therefore appear on the right side if the ventral face is uppermost. **Retouch** is referred to as **direct** if the removal scars modify the dorsal surface and **inverse** if they occur on the ventral surface (Fig. 11). If retouch occurs on the dorsal side of one edge and the ventral face of the other, it may be referred to as **alternate**, or **alternating**, if it occurs alternately from face to face around the edges. It may be **marginal**, altering only the edge of the piece, **semi-invasive** if it extends across about half of one side of the piece or **invasive** if it modifies the entire surface. The types of retouch distinguished include **scalar, sub-parallel** and **abrupt** or **backing** (Fig. 12) following the definitions of Tixier et al. (1980). In addition, **micro-retouch** has been noted on a number of Mesolithic and Neolithic artefacts from Central India and consists of tiny removal scars with dimensions of less than 1mm which form a continuous and regular modification of the edge. Retouch may occur on one or two edges. If the retouched edges meet on the axis of percussion, they are referred to as **convergent**. If they converge off the axis of percussion they are said to be **offset**. Retouch on an edge parallel to the butt of the flake is referred as **transverse** (Fig. 11). Sporadic, discontinuous retouch is referred to as **edge damage** and may be produced accidentally during use or as a result of natural pressure or percussion before or during burial. The terminology used to describe such damage follows Keeley (1980).

FLAKE TOOL TYPES

Adze flakes. These are flakes with a triangular cross-section which resemble an orange segment in form. The thick edge is formed by steep retouch which may be bidirectional, having been struck both from the dorsal and ventral margins (Figs. 18:6.24, 19:7.20). Allchin (1966) suggested that such flakes are widespread in India (ibid., p.199) and compared their form and possible function to those of the Australian **eloura**. To avoid confusion with the Australian type, such pieces are referred to here as adze flakes. This name refers only to the form and should not be taken as an assumed function. In the catalogue, artefacts are distinguished as adze flakes only if the thicker side is formed by retouch. Core trimming flakes (see below) may have the same overall and cross-sectional form but their 'backing' is formed by a remnant of core surface rather than deliberate retouching. Where such flakes occur in the collection, their resemblance to true adze flakes is noted. Adze flakes occur only in Holocene assemblages, possibly attributable to the Neolithic-Chalcolithic periods.

Borers/awls. During the Middle Palaeolithic, borers were produced by retouching thick projections on flakes which lack the symmetrical pointed morphology of points and which protrude markedly from an angle or corner of the blank (Sankalia, 1964) (Fig. 13l).

Points. In some tool inventories it would appear that any flake on which the maximum width occurs at the proximal end is classified as a point. As a result, many debitage flakes with concave or convex sides converging to a rounded tip on or off the axes of morphology or percussion are incorporated as points, although there is no good reason other than a rough approximation in shape to suppose that they were used as such. This has probably led to an over-representation of this category of artefact in reports of some industries and although this problem cannot be dealt with in a catalogue of nineteenth-century finds, it should be noted that unmodified points are distinguished only if they exhibit the criteria defined below.

Unmodified, prepared and retouched points produced on flakes first appear in assemblages attributed to the Middle Palaeolithic and occur frequently after that time, occasionally predominating over points made on blades and vice versa. The following types have been distinguished:

- **unmodified triangular points:** unretouched, occasionally prepared flakes with straight sides converging to a point from a relatively broad butt on an axis of morphology which should be more or less coincident with the axis of percussion (Fig. 11a). These flakes usually have a pronounced central arête and two or three dorsal scars. Unprepared points were probably struck opportunistically from a natural ridge on the raw material.

- **unmodified leaf points:** thin in cross-section, these flakes have irregular, convex sides which converge to form points which resemble retouched forms (Fig. 11b).

- **single edge retouched points:** triangular or subtriangular flakes marginally retouched along one edge to improve the edge shape and overall form (Fig. 11c). Like the other retouched forms, these points are known from assemblages attributed to the Middle Palaeolithic.

- **double edge retouched points:** pointed flakes retouched along both edges. The retouch may or may not converge at the tip and the cross-section of these points may be steeply triangular.

- **alternately retouched points:** pointed flakes on which the edges and overall form have been modified by retouch which occurs alternately on the dorsal then the ventral surface.

- **bifacial points:** flakes modified by percussion removals from both faces to form a small, triangular or subtriangular biface. These are occasionally found in Middle Palaeolithic assemblages.

- **unifacial pressure flaked points:** small points rarely exceeding about 1.5cm in length from which long, narrow, approximately parallel-sided flakes have been removed from one face, usually the dorsal aspect, by pressure flaking. These points occur infrequently in late Mesolithic assemblages.

- **bifacial pressure flaked points:** triangular and convex-sided or **leaf-shaped** points pressure flaked on both faces with the result that the edges are sometimes finely serrated. These pieces vary from about 1 to 3cm in length, and occur in Late Mesolithic assemblages.

- **tanged points:** retouch may be applied to the proximal end of any type of point to reduce the butt and create a projection at the base which would assist in hafting the piece. Poorly formed or incipient tangs are known on a few points from Middle Palaeolithic assemblages (Sankalia, 1964) and in some Neolithic contexts (Fig. 16:2.2).

- **beaked points:** points on which the tips are steeply retouched along one or both sides to produce a recurved or beaked form (Allchin, 1966).

Saws/denticulates. Flakes from which tiny flakes have been removed directly or alternately (Tixier et al., 1980) at small, regular intervals to form an evenly serrated, usually straight edge (Figs. 13k, m). Saws are known in assemblages dating from the Mesolithic to the Chalcolithic but coarser, denticulate forms also occur occasionally on older sites.

Scrapers. This category includes a variety of retouched forms which are suggestive of scraping functions such as removing bark from trees or fat from bones or dressing wood, bamboo or hides. As in Europe, these basic tools were used from the Lower Palaeolithic to the Chalcolithic although in India they are generally less common. This variation probably reflects differences in the lithic raw materials available rather than in manufacturing technology because the chalcedonic silicas commonly used in India are less brittle and hold their edge better during use than chert or flint, which are easily damaged if not retouched. This would also imply that many unmodified flakes classed as debitage were used for tasks normally carried out by scrapers. Different types of scrapers are distinguished by the position and character of the retouched edges following the convention (Bordes, 1961) of orientating pieces with their axes of percussion perpendicular and the butts or proximal ends at the bottom (Fig. 10). The most common are:

- **side scrapers:** described as single, double or convergent according to whether retouch occurs on one or two sides or converges from two sides at the distal end, and as straight, convex or concave according to the shape of the retouched edges, following Bordes (1963, 1972). Like transverse and end scrapers, side scrapers are not diagnostic of a particular period although they are a more common element in Lower and Middle Palaeolithic assemblages than later ones.

- **transverse scrapers:** straight, convex or concave retouched edges occur parallel to the butt rather than on the sides of the flake (Fig. 11d).

- **end scrapers:** steep retouch occurs around the narrow, semicircular end of flake or blades (figure 13j).

- **round, semicircular or 'thumbnail' scrapers:** flat, round or semicircular flakes continuously retouched around most of the margin (Fig. 13j). This type may occur in the Middle Palaeolithic but is more common on small flakes found with microliths during the Mesolithic.

BLADE ARTEFACTS

Unmodified blades. In their primary form blades are at least twice as long as they are wide and have more or less parallel sides (Fig. 13h). The dorsal surfaces show parallel flake scars which may be opposed if the blade has been struck from a bipolar core. Butts are usually small and thin often showing only a point of percussion. Blades are relatively thin and may be triangular or trapezoidal in cross-section. They provide blanks for retouched tools and may also have been used without any secondary modification although unretouched blades without evidence of such use are regarded as debitage. In many reports on Indian lithic assemblages both retouched and unmodified blades are referred to as **Parallel-sided Blades** or **PSBs** (Fig. 13h) but this term has been avoided here because it did not seem to provide a useful differentiation of artefacts.

Blades were 'an essential basic element of all Upper Palaeolithic industries of the subcontinent, and of many of its later Mesolithic industries. Neolithic and Chalcolithic settlements almost always yield large numbers of blades...' (Allchin and Allchin, 1982, p.57). Joshi (1973) suggests that Neolithic and Chalcolithic assemblages can be distinguished by variation in the relative proportions of the different types of tool present. Some researchers also distinguish the Neolithic as represented by a **Neolithic Blade and Microlith Industry** (Ghosh, 1989) and the Chalcolithic by the term **Short Blade Industry** (ibid.).

Bladelets. Small blades less than 12mm wide produced during the Mesolithic and later prehistoric periods (Fig. 13i).

Blade cores. The size and shape of blade cores varies according to period and the techniques and raw materials used. During the Upper Palaeolithic broader blades, on average 8-10cm long, were produced from chert and basalt cores often started by simple flaking of the face from a platform at one end rather than by **cresting**. From the Mesolithic to the Chalcolithic, smaller nodules of cryptocrystalline silicas and quartzites were used with the result that blades were shorter and narrower. The discard form of all these cores varies according to whether the blades have been removed in decreasing circles around the entire perimeter of the striking platform reducing the core to a cylinder, or by working back and forth across one face leaving a semicircular or flat face. In general, blade cores have a more regular appearance than flake cores and two types may be recognised on the basis of platform characteristics:

- **single platform unipolar blade cores:** on these cores, blades have been struck from a single platform created at one end of a nodule (Fig. 26:27.2). According to the manner in which blades have been detached and the extent of use, the shape at discard may be pyramidal, prismatic or cylindrical.

- **double platform or bipolar blade cores:** these cores have two platforms which may be bipolar on opposite ends of the nodule or adjacent on an end and an edge (Fig. 16:8.2).

Crested blades. In order to set up the first arêtes which will act as guidelines in the detachment of blades, the edge of a nodule selected for use as a core may be crested by the alternate removal of flakes from each side (Fig. 13o). This bifacially modified edge is then struck off leaving arêtes which will enable the detachment of further blades. The resulting blade has a triangular cross-section and flake scar remnants which originate from the sinuous central ridge rather than the edges. This technique is well known in the Chalcolithic, but also occurs in the Mesolithic and Neolithic.

Core trimming flakes. During the course of removing blades from a core it is sometimes necessary to adjust the platform or distal end to provide a suitable striking position and prevent the detachment of outrepassé or plunging blades (Tixier et al., 1980). Two types of core trimming flake may be distinguished:

- **core tablets or rejuvenation flints:** to improve the quality of the striking platform and allow further blades to be removed, the old platform may be struck off producing a distinctive thick, polygonal flake with high-angled edges fluted by remnants of the scars left by previous blade removals.

- **distal end pieces:** the distal end of a core struck off after a series of blades have been removed in order to prevent blades curving and possibly plunging. The resulting flake is distinctive, having the shape and scar pattern of the distal end of the core.

On some core trimming flakes the remnants of the core surface occur along one margin, the piece forming the thicker side of a triangular or wedge-shaped cross-section. These flakes resemble and may have been used as adze flakes (see above).

Plunging blades. A plunging or **outrepassé** blade is markedly broad, thick and curved at the distal end because the distal end of the core has been detached as part of it (Tixier et al., 1980). Such blades are usually produced accidentally and may ruin the core.

BLADE TOOLS

Backed blades. A blade is described as backed if it has continous, steep, regular retouch along one edge (Figs. 11e, 17:5.15, 19:7.49). This retouch creates a high-angled, blunt or non-cutting edge which may make the pieces suitable for hafting because the broader surface provides contact for adhesive material such as mastic and cannot be pushed back into a shaft or handle when pressure is applied to the opposite edge of the blade during use. Such blades are also referred to as **blunted backed blades** or **BBB** and **straight backed blades** or **BSB**.

Backed blade points. Backing applied to an edge converging to a point on thin blades (Fig. 18:6.31). Such points are found in Mesolithic and later prehistoric contexts.

Borers. Usually made by accentuating a natural point or protrusion with steep retouch on one or both sides (Figs. 22:14.46, 14.47). These occur on blades with thick or triangular cross-sections.

Borers on bladelets. Small blades retouched to points which sometimes show some scalar retouch, possibly use damage, on one edge.

Burins. Blades and bladelets retouched by the removal of one or more spalls to produce a narrow, chisel-like edge at right angles to the side of the flake, blade or blade core fragment from which it was struck. Burins are known from Upper Palaeolithic and early Mesolithic contexts in India but they are not abundant and only two types recur:

- **simple angle burins:** this type of burin (Figs. 18:6.5, 6.6) exhibits a single burin facet produced by the detachment of a spall by a controlled burin blow (Tixier et al., 1980). The striking platfrom from which the spall is detached is often a natural fracture surface (Allchin and Allchin, 1982).

- **natural burins:** broken flakes or blades, or unmodified rock fragments with a narrow edge possibly utilised as a burin (Allchin and Allchin, 1982).

End scrapers. Blades retouched around the distal and, in some examples, also the proximal end (Figs. 13j, 18:6.15). The retouch may be steep and invasive. End scrapers occur in both the Upper Palaeolithic and the Mesolithic.

Obliquely truncated blades. These are blades which have been shortened by the removal of one or both ends. The truncation is usually placed diagonally across the blade and may be produced either by a break or retouch (Figs. 22:14.48, 35:41.1). Obliquely truncated blades are often referred to as **penknife blades** or **PKB**. If a backed edge meets an obliquely retouched truncation at a marked angle it may be called a scalene backed bladelet (Tixier, 1963). They are distinguished from **obliquely blunted points** because the axis of percussion and axis of morphology do not coincide. **PKB** are particularly common in Chalcolithic assemblages but also occur in the Mesolithic.

Obliquely blunted points. Artefacts formed by steep retouch on one edge of a blade, usually the left, to form or emphasise a point (Fig. 17:51). Such points are known from Mesolithic contexts in which they are similar to microlithic backed points and classed as non-geometric.

Saws. From the Upper Palaeolithic to the Chalcolithic saws were made on blades as well as flakes by the removal of tiny flakes, sometimes alternately, at regular intervals to produce a serrated edge (Figs. 13k, 20:12.1, 35:42.1).

Tanged blades. The tangs produced on blades as on flakes may be retouched on one or both sides of the end to produce a single- or double-shouldered tang (Fig. 13h). On some examples the tang is very slight or **incipient**. Tanged blades are known in some Neolithic and Chalcolithic assemblages but are rare.

Transverse arrowheads. Blade segments reduced to a trapezoidal form by steep retouch modifying more or less transverse breaks to form blunted edges tapering from a broad, sharp, unmodified end, which was previously part of the original blade edge. This type of retouched blade segment occurs during the Mesolithic and is usually assumed to be an arrowhead.

MICROLITHS

First described in India by Carlyle as 'pygmies' and also referred to as 'midgets', microliths are **bladelets** which have been retouched to produce a variety of geometric and non-geometric forms. They vary from 1 to 3cm in length and were probably set in hafts in groups to form a variety of projectile armatures, drills, knives, saws and sickles. Microliths are particularly associated with the Mesolithic period, the later part of which is characterised by an increased number of geometric forms. They also occur in Neolithic and Chalcolithic contexts (Allchin and Allchin, 1982).

Eight main types of microlith can be distinguished:

- **backed bladelets:** small, narrow blades blunted along one edge by steep backing retouch which may have facilitated hafting by providing a thicker surface on which to apply resin to stick the microliths in place (Figs. 17:5.15, 19:7.49). Backed bladelets may have been hafted as knives or, later, sickles or even as barbs in composite projectile tips. They occur during the Mesolithic, Neolithic and Chalcolithic and are classed as non-geometric microliths.

- **backed points:** blades or bladelets retouched along an edge converging to the tip (Fig. 18:6.31). The tip may also be formed by the detachment of a segment of the blade by microburin technique (Tixier et al., 1980) although this is rare in India. Occasionally, retouch may be applied to the edge opposite the backing just below the tip, to accentuate the point. Backed points are classed as non-geometric microliths and are particularly associated with the Mesolithic.

- **drill points/piercers:** non-geometric tools produced by steep retouching of edges converging to a point (Figs. 22:14.46, 14.47). Drills vary from 1 to 4cm in length and the tips sometimes show signs of modification resulting from use.

- **lunates:** these microliths are often very small and have a semi-ovoid form said to resemble the moon in its first quarter. Consequently, they have been called **lunates** or **crescents** (Fig. 13a). Produced on bladelets or blade segments, the convex edge is blunted by steep retouch (Fig. 23). The straight edge may also have small scalar retouch scars which in some cases may be the result of use damage. Lunates occur in both non-geometric and geometric Mesolithic assemblages and in some later contexts. They are sometimes difficult to distinguish from scalene triangles.

- **rhomboids:** geometric microliths made on blade or bladelet segments with blunting retouch on three sides of a rhombus or diamond-shaped form in which both pairs of sides are parallel (Fig. 13b).

- **trapezes:** four-sided geometric microliths made on blade or bladelet segments which have parallel edges and steeply retouched straight or concave, convergent or divergent sides (Figs. 13c, 24:14.87-14.95). This variable form may be associated with the later Mesolithic (Sankalia, 1964; Sharma, 1973).

- **trapezoids:** geometric microliths with a quadrilateral form blunted by retouch along three sides and with no two sides parallel (Fig. 13d).

- **triangles:** three-sided geometric microliths made on blade or bladelet segments with backing retouch along the two shortest edges and, occasionally, fine scalar retouch along the longest edge. The **isosceles** form has two equal sides and the less common **scalene** form known from later Mesolithic and Neolithic contexts has unequal sides (Figs. 13e, f, 24:14.98-14.105).

HAMMER-DRESSED, GROUND AND POLISHED STONE TOOLS

The technology of finishing flakes and flaked stone artefacts by reducing the scar arêtes by hammer dressing or **pecking** and smoothing the surfaces by grinding and/or polishing was developed during the Neolithic and led to the introduction of a distinctive new range of tools, some of which persisted into the Chalcolithic. The types distinguished are:

- **adzes:** roughly triangular in shape, adzes are usually produced on large flakes which provide a plano-convex cross-section. The broad end of the flake is bevelled by grinding on one or both faces to provide a working edge. Adzes were hafted so that the working edge was transverse to the handle. Narrow, steeply bevelled examples are occasionally referred to as shoe last celts (Fig. 14c).

- **axes:** probably the most common Neolithic tool, axes were produced by bifacial flaking of a block of raw material to obtain the required shape and then dressing the roughout to reduce the scar arêtes prior to grinding and/or polishing the whole piece or, more usually, the part of the surface adjacent to the working edge. The shape of axes is variable (Foote, 1916; F. R. Allchin, 1957). In central and southern India the most common form is subtriangular with narrow, rounded or straight butts and ovoid or lenticular cross-section (Fig. 14a). These may be ground all over or dressed all over and ground only at the edge. Rectangular forms may also occur, whilst in eastern India the butt of the **shouldered** axe may be elongated to provide a tang to assist hafting. In another type, the **splayed axe**, the concave sides turn out to provide a broad, convex cutting edge reminiscent of early metal axe forms (Sankalia, 1964). All forms of axe were hafted so that the cutting edge occurred parallel to the handle.

- **axe-hammers:** flaked and dressed axe forms lacking a sharp working edge and probably used for hammering or wedging.

- **celts:** synonym for axes still occasionally used in Indian archaeological literature.

- **chisels:** long, narrow, flaked, dressed and ground pieces, rectangular or cylindrical in cross-section with a working edge that is usually bifacially bevelled but occasionally splayed. The thickness and outline form may vary (Foote, 1916).

- **mullers:** hand-held grinding stones usually used with **querns** to grind cereals and other types of grain. Although natural pebbles could be used for this purpose, three types of deliberately shaped mullers have been recognised in the Neolithic and Chalcolithic (Sankalia, 1964). These include round mullers with surfaces which have either been dressed by pecking to remove large irregularities or roughened to improve their texture for grinding, round mullers with two naturally flat or deliberately flattened surfaces and plano-convex mullers with a lower face flattened for use. During the Iron Age, cylindrical mullers became common.

- **picks:** cylindrical flaked and occasionally dressed implements, pointed at one or both ends and suitable for hafting.

- **ringstones:** thick, round or squarish stones with dressed and ground surfaces and a central hole which has an hour-glass shape as a result of having been drilled from each face (Fig. 14d). These artefacts first appeared in the Mesolithic but became common in the Neolithic and Chalcolithic. They may have been used as weights for digging sticks or bow drills or even for weaving or fishing although some of the more carefully finished pieces may be maceheads with a symbolic or ceremonial function.

- **saddle querns:** large, roughly square or rectangular stone slabs with flat or concave upper surfaces which have been smoothed and/or dished by use in grinding cereals and other grains. The grinding surface may be circular as a result of the use of round mullers or elongated as a result of grinding back and forth with a plano-convex muller. Like mullers, these artefacts have been common from the Neolithic into recent times.

- **scrapers on ground stone flakes:** throughout the Neolithic and Chalcolithic flakes struck from ground stone tools, perhaps to resharpen them, were retouched and utilised as scrapers.

- **stone balls:** natural pebbles on average about 4cm in diameter and dressed to a spherical form. During the Chalcolithic these sometimes occur in caches and may have been used as sling or bolas stones (Sankalia, 1963).

- **wedges:** small pebbles shaped to a triangular or rectangular form, dressed and ground at the edge. These artefacts are relatively uncommon and occur during the Neolithic and Chalcolithic.

- **weights:** spherical or rounded stones, dressed and flattened on two opposite sides and usually assumed to be weights.

UTILISED PIECES

Most of the artefacts in this category are pieces which have been modified only by use during tool manufacture or pigment preparation but unmodified stones found in associaton with archaeological material as well as broken, deliberately modified pieces altered by secondary use are also included.

Anvils. Natural blocks of hard rock often round or oval in outline, sometimes as a result of flaking around the circumference (Fig. 15d). An anvil has at least one flat or slightly concave surface which exhibits pitting, scratches and small circular fissures known as **incipient cones** which result from the block being held immobile while other stone nodules or large bones are struck directly against it to cause fracture, or are rested on it while flakes or blades are struck off, or while the bone is splintered by percussion from a hammerstone. The battering tends to be localised, usually to the centre of the flat surface.

Fabricators. Small approximately cylindrical hammerstones with blunt ends which are usually chipped and battered by percussion. These artefacts were first described from Neolithic contexts in India by Foote (1916) and may have been used for reducing the uneven surfaces of axe roughouts by pecking prior to polishing (F.R. Allchin, 1957; Sankalia 1964). They are often natural stones but rod-like waste pieces and flakes with plano-convex cross-sections and some deliberately flaked rods are also known.

Grooved grinding surfaces. These may occur on natural rock surfaces (Foote, 1916) or on large concave or basin-shaped blocks, some of which may be portable (Allchin, 1957). Using sand and water as an abrasive, the edges of Neolithic axe roughouts were ground into shape by moving them up and down in the groove.

Hammerstones. Stones used to detach flakes and blades from other stone nodules, blocks or slabs by striking them either directly or indirectly by use of an intermediary such as a punch. Essential to the production of stone artefacts in all periods, hammerstones vary in size from 5 to 15cm in length and in form:

- **cylindrical hammerstones:** predominantly natural cylindrically shaped stones battered at one or both ends; in later sites (B. Allchin in Allchin, F.R. et al., 1986) some deliberately shaped examples occur (Fig. 15a). During the Neolithic grooved or waisted examples, possibly for hafting, also occur (ibid.; Sankalia, 1964). Small cylindrical hammerstones are usually referred to as **fabricators**.

- **spherical and cuboid hammerstones:** natural stones battered on some or all of the surface. In later sites, some spherical hammerstones which have been dressed and ground into shape before use are known (B. Allchin in Allchin, F.R. et al., 1986).

- **discoidal hammerstones:** usually made from flat river pebbles, occasionally flaked around the edge, discoidal hammerstones exhibit chipping and battering around the edge (Fig. 15c). They are known from later sites on which they may have been used for trimming axe roughouts prior to polishing (ibid.). Occasionally, fragments of ground stone artefacts may be reused as discoidal hammerstones.

- **pointed or stone-dressing hammerstones:** known from later sites (ibid.) hammerstones are mostly produced from naturally pointed stones which may show chipping and battering at both ends (Fig. 15b). These implements may have been used for roughing out the holes in **ringstones**, and possibly for trimming flaked surfaces before grinding and polishing took place.

Palettes. Flat or naturally dished slabs varying from 4 to 10cm in length with pigment residues, usually of red haematite, on the surface (Figs. 32, 33). Usually produced from tabular pieces of stone reduced to polygonal or roughly circular shapes by the removal of flakes around the margin. To date, palettes have been recorded only from Neolithic and later contexts.

Polishers (slickstones). In addition or as an alternative to smoothing down the edges of Neolithic and later axe roughouts by grinding them on an immobile block, polished surfaces were also achieved by rubbing with a hand-held polisher. These artefacts are recognised by the discrete flat, smooth areas on otherwise rough, irregular stones which vary in size and shape depending on the object to be polished and the degree of flatness or curvature required.

Projectiles, stone balls and sling stones. Usually natural stone balls averaging about 5cm in diameter and deliberately accumulated on sites, possibly for use as sling shot or bolas stones (Sankalia, 1963). Some examples have been partially modified by pecking off irregularities using a pointed hammerstone to make them more perfectly spherical.

Stone discs. Naturally flattish pebbles which may or may not be modified to a round or oval shape and show no signs of use.

RAW MATERIALS

In Central India, the range of raw materials used for making stone artefacts includes igneous and metamorphic rocks, as well as various forms of silica and other minerals. The descriptions given below indicate the criteria used in the hand identification of these materials into broad categories in the preparation of the catalogue. Although the list is probably not exhaustive for Central India, it is at least representative, as Carlyle collected over a wide geographical area.

Silicas. Fine-grained or **cryptocrystalline** silicas are the most common raw materials among Carlyle's finds. In many instances, the presence of cortex abraded and 'chattermarked' with numerous incipient cones caused by percussion during transport suggests the freqent use of pebbles and cobbles found in river beds. Five types of cryptocrystalline silica, as well as the coarse grained silica quartz, have been noted in the collection:

- **agate:** a variety of cryptocrystalline chalcedonic silica distinguished by its colour banding, which frequently occurs in concentric zones. The colours vary according to the nature of the mineral impurities which cause them (Pellant, 1990). The surface of agate has a glossy, somewhat 'soapy' appearance.

- **chalcedony:** the term used for white, grey-white, grey-bluish-grey, yellowish or light green cryptocrystalline silica, sometimes with fine banding which, like agate, has a glossy, 'soapy' appearance and forms from mineral-rich solutions in gas cavities within volcanic rocks and in fissures of sedimentary rocks. Geodes or hollow globular bodies of chalcedonic silicas are common in the basalts of the Deccan Plateau and as clasts in river gravels. (Allaby and Allaby, 1990; Pellant, 1990).

- **chert:** a cryptocrystalline silica which may form either in the same manner as the chalcedonic silicas or from organic silica such as the remains of sponges or microfossils (Allaby and Allaby, 1990; Pellant, 1990). This hard sedimentary rock may occur in cavities in lavas or as bands within limestone. It has a dull, opaque appearance varying in colour from dark grey to pinkish-brown, yellowish-brown and brown.

- **flint:** a variety of chert which occurs as nodules and bands in chalk. Commonly light grey through to black, it may contain fossils (Allaby and Allaby, 1990; Pellant, 1990). In the context of the catalogue, many of the artefacts identified as flint might be more strictly described as light grey, marbled grey or banded grey chert as the material is unlikely to be true chalk flint.

- **jasper:** a massive, fine-grained variety of quartz (see below), opaque and coloured by an admixture of iron oxides. The colours vary from red-reddish brown to brown-yellow and bluish-green. When the colours occur in bands they are broader than in agate and jasper lacks the microscopic banding of chalcedony. Deposited from silica-rich solutions in cavities, often associated with chalcedony, in all rock types (Allaby and Allaby, 1990; Pellant, 1990).

- **quartz:** hard, coarsely crystallised silica with grains visible to the naked eye and a jagged fracture. Quartz may be colourless, most commonly white or coloured purple (amethyst), pink (rose quartz), grey, green or yellow and has a glassy lustre. Common in many igneous and metamorphic rocks (ibid.).

Igneous rocks. Less commonly utilised for tool manufacture, the crystallised lavas noted among Carlyle's finds have been generally described in two broad categories:

- **basalt:** a dark-coloured, dull, fine-grained rock with an even texture which forms the plateax of the Deccan Traps.

- **granite:** a coarse-grained rock formed from a mass of interlocking crystals with a speckled appearance varying in colour according to the constituent minerals.

Metamorphic rocks. Like the igneous rocks, these recrystallised rocks are infrequent among Carlyle's finds and have been identified within four generalised groups:

- **gneiss:** coarse-grained, granular rock characteristically banded as a result of the segration of minerals (Allaby and Allaby, 1990).

- **marble:** metamorphosed limestone variously coloured or banded according to its chemical and mineralogical compositions.

- **quartzite:** fused mass of quartz rich sediment (ibid.). As the hand specimens are artefacts on which it is not possible to expose fresh break surfaces, it has not been possible to distinguish between metamorphosed or **metaquartzite** and sedimentary **orthoquartzites** (see below).

- **steatite (talc schist):** soft, white metamorphosed limestone with a dull surface (ibid.).

Sedimentary rocks. Artefacts made of sedimentary rocks are rare among Carlyle's finds. Two generalised groups have been noted:

- **sandstone:** lithified sands and silts varying in colour according to the minerals present. The grains may be rubbed off with the fingers.

- **quartzite:** sandstone composed of more than 95% quartz. Sedimentary or **orthoquartzite** may show bedding and other structures but for the catalogued artefacts, it has not been possible to distinguish from **metaquartzite** (see above).

Other minerals. Apart from the silicas, the only other utilised mineral among Carlyle's finds is haematite, an iron mineral which may be grey or black but more commonly ranges from bright red to duller brownish-red. Being relatively soft, its colour will rub off or it can be ground to a powder as a basis for paint.

IV. CATALOGUE OF STONE ARTEFACTS FOUND IN CENTRAL INDIA BY A. C. L. CARLYLE AND CURATED BY THE BRITISH MUSEUM

Introduction

The terminology used in the catalogue is given in the Glossary (Chapter III). The entries are arranged by locality. The localities are numbered in alphabetical order and each artefact is distinguished by the site number followed by an object number. The spelling of the locality names follows that of Carlyle; this appears to have been phonetic and sometimes varies from piece to piece. For example, Bharkach (see entry 11) is variously spelt Bharkachha, Bharkacha, Bharkaech, Bharkachka, Bharka, Bar Kachha and Bhar Khachh. In such cases, the current or most frequent orthography is used to denote the site and the alternative spellings are given in parenthesis. Occasionally, variation in spelling is the cause of some uncertainty as to whether pieces come from one or more sites. In these instances, the artefacts are listed under separate locality headings and cross-referenced.

General information concerning the location of the sites, subsequent excavations and the character of the assemblages precedes the inventory of artefacts. These introductions are based on late nineteenth- and early twentieth-century gazetteers and maps, as well as on more recent archaeological reports. However, establishing the location of some sites has been difficult and has sometimes been based on a process of elimination because, as Bridget Allchin (1958) also noted, the same village names occur repeatedly and the names of caves and hills do not usually appear on maps or in gazetteers at all.

The inventories are arranged so that the tools or retouched pieces appear first, followed by the unmodified artefacts, debitage and, finally, the modified stone implements. However, many of the artefacts are numbered or stuck onto numbered cards, the writing on which belongs to Charles Seidler. In a letter dated 29 July 1893, which accompanied a package of artefacts sold to Sturge, Seidler explained 'that the names given to each paper of specimens are mostly Mr Carlyle's' (PRBA QS archive). This suggests that the numbers may also relate to a list prepared by Carlyle and, although the archaeological relevance of this numbering is currently unknown, it was felt necessary to preserve the groupings in case further research should reveal their significance. Consequently, for some sites, the tools are not all listed consecutively at the beginning of the inventory but occur within each of the Carlyle/Seidler groups.

Each object is individually numbered except in instances where this is neither practical nor informative, as with the unprovenanced material or the large numbers of unmodified bladelets or debitage flakes. In these cases, a single number has been allotted to groups of pieces. Catalogue numbers are used to identify the pieces illustrated in Figs. 16-35.

Each entry includes the object identification followed by a length measurement, a description of any salient features, the raw material and its condition if other than fresh. The measurement given is the maximum length parallel either to the axis of percussion for modified and unmodified flakes, blades and bladelets (Fig. 10) or to the axis of morphology for bifacially modified pieces. For more complex forms, specified alternative or additional measurements are noted. Retouch is direct unless otherwise stated. Like the terms used in the categorising and description of the pieces, the criteria for the hand identification of raw materials are set out in the preceding glossary. It should be noted that without the benefits of a microscope, thin-sectioning or first-hand knowledge of the geology of Central India, the identifications are intended only as a guideline to the materials used.

Artefacts found by Carlyle and acquired as parts of the Christy, Franks, Sturge and Wellcome Collections are listed under separate headings at the end of the relevant site inventories. Carlyle acquisitions curated by the British Museum, Department of Oriental Antiquities are treated in the same manner. Material listed from the Christy Collection was originally acquired by the Department of Ethnography, where it was registered in 1926 before being transferred to the Department of Prehistoric and Romano-British Antiquities in 1939. The registration numbers for these pieces, beginning 1926, are quoted in brackets at the end of the relevant entries. Similarly, Carlyle pieces donated by the Royal Albert Memorial Museum, Exeter or as part of the Wellcome Collection are listed with their registration numbers, beginning P1993. 7-1 and P1982. 10-14 respectively, whereas items registered in the Department of Oriental Antiquities have numbers prefixed OA.

1. AMILA MORUHA

The location of this site is unknown. As *moruha* means cleft and *nala* a watercourse or depression, it is possible that Amila Moruha like Amila Nala (see 2 below) was a locality near Bhainsaur, Mirzapur District (Fig. 6).

1.1 Debitage flake, 27mm long. Flint. Heavily patinated.

2. AMILA NALA

Carlyle indicates on piece numbers 2.2, 2.3 and 2.4 that this site was near Bhainsaur (Fig. 6) and on 2.3 adds the note 'Vindyhas, Baghelkh'. The *Gazetteer of Mirzapur* (Drake-Brockman, 1911) states that there was a government encampment and inspection bungalow at Bhainsaur (Bhainswar/Bhainsod) situated on the Great Deccan Road, southwest of Mirzapur near the Rewa scarp, overlooking the Kaimur Plateau. This would probably have been a convenient place for Carlyle to break his journey, and at Amila Nala he collected eight stone artefacts. These pieces vary in raw material and condition and are not particularly diagnostic as to period, but the prepared or Levallois flake (2.3) and the three chert pieces may be Palaeolithic and the possibly tanged piece (2.2) Neolithic - Chalcolithic.

2.1 Levallois flake, 57mm long, with faceted butt and convergent edges. Flint. Patinated and abraded.

2.2 Blade, 45mm long, with a hinge termination and abrupt scalar retouch along the dorsal aspect of each edge. The slight curve on the left edge suggests a rudimentary single, shouldered tang. Chert. Heavily patinated, stained and abraded. Fig. 16.

2.3 Prepared core, 35mm long, with a single platform extending around the entire margin of the piece and a plano-convex cross-section. The convex face has been formed by the radial removal of small flakes, most of which were detached prior to the single flake struck from the plane face. However, the presence of small, scalar retouch scars on the distal end of the convex surface suggest that the piece may also have been a scraper. The fresh condition of this core-scraper, as well as its size and retouch suggest that it may be more recent than Palaeolithic. Chert.

2.4 Debitage flake, 40mm long, with plain butt and Siret fracture (Tixier et al., 1980). Flint. Heavily patinated and abraded.

2.5 Flake, 34mm long, struck from a discoidal core. Chert. Abraded.

2.6 Core trimming flake, 35mm long. Chalcedony.

2.7 Bifacially flaked pebble, 42mm long. Chert. Abraded.

2.8 Modified pebble, 35mm long, with possible conchoidal fracture scars. Crazed and slightly discoloured by burning. Flint. Patinated.

Wellcome Collection
2.9 Retouched bladelet, 37mm long. Abrupt scalar retouch at the proximal end of the right edge. Chert. Patinated. (P1982 10-4 4982)

3. ASHTBHUJA

Ashtbhuja (25° 10' N, 82° 30' E) is situated eight miles southwest of Mirzapur on a detached spur of Vindhyan tableland (Fig. 6). The *Gazetteer of Mirzapur* (Drake-Brockman, 1911) states that there was no village at this locality, just ancient shrines to Ashta-Bhuja Devi, an eight-limbed consort of Siva, tended by priests and temple-attendants. While visiting this place of pilgrimage, Carlyle found three stone artefacts. One of these (3.2) was presented to H.W. Seton Karr and is now in the Wellcome Collection. On a paper label stuck to the piece, Seton Karr wrote:

... from the high or oldest laterite deposits (denuded).... stained with the laterite of the laterite (*sic*) beneath which it was discovered. It is probably one of the oldest objects of human workmanship.

It is not possible to suggest an age for this context but the artefacts may be Lower Palaeolithic.

3.1 Flake, 100mm long, with a natural, high-angled butt and distinct ventral surface features. The dorsal surface is unmodified. Quartzite. Abraded.

Wellcome Collection
3.2 Flake, 118mm long. The flat facets on the surface are probably natural but the piece does appear to have been struck from a larger block. Quartzite. Abraded. (P1982.10-4.4983)

Department of Oriental Antiquities
3.3 Modified block, 80mm long, with a pitted depression formed by percussion on each of three surfaces. Possibly an anvil stone. Sandstone. (OA: 1880-1198)

4. BABURA

The location of this site is unknown.

4.1 Debitage flake, 28mm long. Flint. Patinated and slightly abraded.

5. BAGHAI KHOR
(Baghe-Khor Pahar, Bagha Kor Pahar, Baghakhor)

Carlyle did not record the precise location of his site at Baghai Khor although captions on cards to which some of the artefacts have been stuck or stitched refer to it as a rockshelter near Bhainsaur in the Vindhya Hills, Mirzapur District. Fortunately, the site was rediscovered in 1957 (Allchin, B., 1958) and is known to be one of a group of rockshelters including Morhana Pahar (see entry 38) on the edge of the Vindhyan Scarp at 24° 48'N; 82° 05'E (Fig. 6). In 1962 small excavations at the site by R.K. Varma (Ghosh, 1965; Varma, 1965) revealed a stratigraphy in which non-geometric microliths without pottery preceded assemblages which contain both non-geometric and geometric microliths as well as pottery, suggesting Mesolithic to Neolithic transition (see Chapter II). The thirty-two pieces in Carlyle's collection include non-geometric microliths and debitage but it is impossible to determine whether or not these artefacts derive from industries associated with pottery.

5.1 Distally truncated, partially backed bladelet, 47mm long. Chalcedony. Fig. 17.

5.2 Distally truncated and backed bladelet, 37mm long. Chalcedony.

5.3 Retouched bladelet, 28mm long, with fine, marginal retouch around the edges. Flint. Patinated.

5.4 Blade, 44mm long, retaining cortex at distal end. Chalcedony.

5.5 Blade, 46mm long, retaining cortex on the left side. Labelled 'scoop scraper' by Carlyle. Pale green jasper.

5.6 Single platform bladelet core, 57mm long, retaining chattermarked cortex on one face. The core is crested along both sides but shows only four bladelet scars. Chert. Fig. 17.

5.7 Bladelet core in preparation, 68mm long. A single platform has been created at one end and one side has been crested. The other retains cortex. No bladelets have been removed. Bluish-green jasper. Fig. 17.

5.8 Flake with thermally fractured ventral surface, 42mm long. Chert.

5.9 Debitage flake, 58mm long. Basalt.

5.10 Knapping fragment, 26mm long. Flint. Patinated.

The following artefacts (5.11 to 5.17) were glued to a card marked 981 and labelled as examples of double-edged knives in Seidler's handwriting:

5.11 Alternately retouched flake, 35mm long. Chalcedony. Patinated.

5.12 Flake with slight marginal, scalar retouch on the right edge, 33mm long. Chalcedony. Patinated.

5.13 Backed bladelet, 29mm long, with fine, marginal scalar retouch opposite the backed edge. Ancient breaks at proximal and distal ends. Chalcedony. Patinated. Fig. 17.

5.14 Backed bladelet, 31mm long. Chalcedony. Patinated.

5.15 Piercer on a narrow (4mm), backed bladelet, 25mm long, with inverse retouch at the tip of the proximal end forming the point. Ancient break at distal end. Chalcedony. Fig. 17.

5.16 Partially backed bladelet, 21mm long. Flint.

5.17 Unmodified point on a bladelet, 30mm long. Flint. Patinated.

Artefact numbers 5.18 to 5.29 were glued to a card marked 991 and labelled 'arrowpoints?' in Seidler's handwriting:

5.18 Blade, 32mm long. Agate.

5.19-5.22 Debitage flakes, 25, 27, 29 and 35mm long. Chalcedony.

5.23-5.24 Debitage flakes/unmodified points, 25 and 28mm long. Chalcedony.

5.25 Debitage flake/unmodified point, 21mm long. Chert.

5.26-5.27 Debitage flakes, 26 and 29mm long. Flint.

5.28 Proximal end fragment of a debitage flake, 25mm long. Retains chattermarked cortex on part of dorsal surface. Flint.

5.29 Debitage flake, 29mm long. Chalcedony.

Christy Collection
5.30 Single platform bladelet core, 24mm long. Chert. (1926-151). Fig. 7.

Sturge Collection
5.31 Bladelet fragment, 20mm long. Flint.

5.32 Debitage flake, 26mm long, lacking proximal end due to ancient break. Chert.

6. BAGHMARA PAHAR

Other than indicating that Baghmara Pahar was in Rewa District (Fig. 5), Carlyle provided no further information about the location of the site, from which he collected seventy-four artefacts. Although the majority of the pieces are debitage, the character of the few retouched pieces (6.5, 6.6, 6.15, 6.17, 6.32, 6.33) suggests an Upper Palaeolithic site with an admixture of more recent material. Carlyle sorted this material into numbered groups, the integrity of which has been retained in case further research should reveal their significance (see Introduction above).

Artefacts numbered 975 by Carlyle:
6.1 Denticulate, 37mm long, made on a flake struck from a bladelet core. Marginal, alternating retouch modifies right edge. Small patch of cortex remains on dorsal surface. Chert.

6.2 Core tablet/adze, 42mm long. This flake has been struck from the crested side of a bladelet core. The wedge-shaped cross-sectional form suggests an adze (see Glossary, Chapter III). Chert. Fig. 18.

6.3-6.4 Debitage flakes, 24 and 27mm long. Flint. Patinated.

Artefacts numbered 993 by Carlyle:
6.5 Burin on the distal end of a blade, 41mm long. Chert. Fig. 18.

6.6 Burin on an obliquely truncated blade, 38mm long. The burin occurs on the distal end and the retouched truncation modifies the proximal end. Chalcedony. Fig. 18.

6.7-6.8 Blades, 36 and 42mm long. Retain cortex on the left edge and along the medial arête respectively. Flint. Patinated.

6.9 Blade fragment, 32mm long, modified by burning. Flint

6.10 Nine debitage flakes, 25-42mm long, from blade/bladelet manufacture. Flint.

6.11 Debitage flake, 23mm long from a blade core. Jasper.

6.12 Debitage flake, 27mm long. Chert.

Artefacts numbered 1001 by Carlyle:
6.13 Bladelet, 40mm long, lacking proximal and distal ends. Chalcedony.

6.14　Debitage flake, 36mm long. Chert.

Artefacts numbered 1002 by Carlyle:

6.15　End scraper on the distal end of a blade, 30mm long. Broken in antiquity and lacking its proximal end. Flint. Fig. 18.

6.16　Retouched bladelet, 33mm long, lacking proximal end due to ancient break. Abrupt marginal retouch on left edge at the proximal end. Chert.

6.17　Retouched flake/point, 31mm long. The subtriangular shape of the flake has been accentuated by fine, marginal retouch around the pointed proximal end. Flint.

6.18　Unmodified point/flake with convergent shape, 30mm long. Flint.

6.19　Blade, 32mm long, lacking distal end. Chalcedony.

6.20　Six blades, 26-37mm long. Four pieces are broken at one or both ends. Flint. Patinated.

6.21　Bladelet, 21mm long. Flint. Patinated.

6.22　Bladelet, 34mm long. Flint.

6.23　Seven debitage flakes, 24-43mm long, from blade/bladelet manufacture. Flint.

6.24　Fragment, 52mm long, from a smoothed stone pebble or cobble, striated on both faces. The striations suggest possible utilisation as a retouching tool. Fig. 18.

Artefacts numbered 1012 by Carlyle:

6.25　Retouched notch, 55mm long. The marginal retouch forming the concavity on the left edge and slightly modifying the proximal right edge interrupts the patinated surface of the flake, indicating a secondary, possibly recent, origin. Chert. Patinated. Fig. 18.

6.26　Bipolar opposed bladelet core, 32mm long. Flint. Patinated. Fig. 18.

6.27　Crested blade, 52mm long. Flint.

6.28　Seven debitage flakes, 20-48mm long, from blade/bladelet manufacture. Chert-flint. Patinated.

Artefacts numbered 1014 by Carlyle:

6.29　Blade, 45mm long. Chert. Patinated.

6.30　Crested blade, 35mm long, lacking proximal end due to ancient break. Chalcedony. Patinated.

Unnumbered:

6.31　Backed point on a blade, 53mm long, retaining a small patch of cortex at the proximal end. Abrupt, marginal backing retouch on right edge. Flint. Fig. 18.

6.32　Retouched blade, 72mm long, retaining cortex at proximal and distal ends. Marginal micro-retouch, possibly edge damage, along left side. Flint.

6.33　Two blades, 32 and 40mm long. Flint. Patinated.

6.34　Blade, 53mm long. Flint. Corticated.

6.35　Two bladelets and a bladelet fragment, 11-27mm long. Chalcedony.

6.36　Five bladelets, 20-40mm long, lacking distal ends due to ancient breaks. The snap surface on one piece resembles a burin facet. Flint. Fig. 18.

6.37　Bipolar opposed bladelet core, 46mm long. Chert.

6.38　Single platform bladelet core, 31mm long. Chert.

6.39　Crested bladelet, 24mm long. Chalcedony.

6.40　Three debitage flakes, 29-30mm long. Chert.

6.41　Knapping fragment, 31mm long. Chert.

7. BANDA

Ninety-five artefacts in Carlyle's collection have no more specific provenance than Banda, Banda District or fields near Banda. Banda formed the most easterly district of British Bundelkhand within the Allahabad Division of the United Provinces (Drake-Brockman, 1909a), now the southern part of Uttar Pradesh (Figs. 3-6). The district included the large area of alluvial plain which stretches about 60 km from the Yamuna river in the north to the sheer sandstone escarpment or *ghats* of the first range of the Vindhyas in the south and about 150 km east from the Ken river (Fig. 4) which formed its western boundary (ibid.). As Carlyle distinguished the pieces he found in places such as Kalinjar and Marfa in the hilly southern part of this district by labelling them with village names, it is probable that those marked Banda were collected around the town of that name, situated at 25° 27'N, 80° 23'E close to the river Ken on the alluvial plain. With the exception of artefacts provenanced to a *nala* on the Kain (Ken) river and listed separately (see entry 27) which may be Palaeolithic, the tool types and technology of the Banda pieces indicate that they are from Holocene assemblages, probably attributable to the Mesolithic and Neolithic.

Artefacts numbered 983:
7.1　Lunate, 22mm long. Steep backing retouch along convex right edge. Chalcedony. Fig. 19.

7.2　Debitage flake with lunate morphology from the crested edge of a core, 25mm long. Chalcedony.

Artefacts numbered 983A:
7.3　Debitage flake from a bladelet core, 12mm long. Chalcedony.

7.4　Debitage flake with lunate morphology from a bladelet core, 23mm long. Chert.

Artefacts numbered 984 and labelled 'carefully worked at edges' (7.5 and 7.6) and 'borers etc.' (7.7 - 7.13) 'from fields near Banda':
7.5　Backed bladelet, 14mm long. Distal end fragment. Flint. Patinated. Fig. 19.

7.6　Backed bladelet fragment, 25mm long. Abrupt backing retouch occurs on the left side of the distal end. Chert. Patinated. Fig. 19.

7.7　Debitage flake, 14mm long. Chalcedony.

7.8　Three debitage flake, 12-24mm long. Two retain stained and chattermarked cortex. Flint. Patinated.

7.9 Debitage fragment, 18mm long, with Siret fracture (Tixier et al., 1980). Retains stained and abraded cortex at the distal end. Flint, patinated.

7.10 Two debitage fragments, 14-16mm long. Chalcedony.

Artefacts numbered 985:
7.11 Blade, 34mm long. Two small scar remnants on the ventral surface of the tip may be impact fractures. Chert.

7.12 Debitage flake, 15mm long. Chalcedony.

7.13 Debitage flakes, 23 and 31mm long. The smaller piece lacks its distal end, the larger retains some abraded cortex. Chert.

7.14 Debitage flake, 34mm long, lacking proximal end due to ancient break. Flint. Patinated.

Artefacts numbered 986:
These include pieces which were glued to two cards marked 'fields near Banda' and labelled 'wedge or chisel shape (*sic*) arrowheads' (7.20-7.23 and 7.28-7.29) and 'small double edged like spoke shaves' (*sic*) (7.15-7.18 and 7.24-7.28). Two further artefacts (27.4 and 27.7) marked 'Nala Kain R Banda' were glued to the latter card and have been listed under the entry heading Ken River. Another five pieces (7.30-7.31) have come loose from cards and their only identifying mark is the number 986.

7.15 Backed bladelet, 22mm long, with marginal abrupt retouch on the left side. Flint. Patinated. Fig. 19.

7.16 Backed bladelet, 19mm long with marginal, abrupt retouch on the left edge. Flint. Patinated. Fig. 19.

7.17 Retouched point, 22mm long, produced on a bladelet with bilateral marginal, abrupt retouch converging at the tip. Proximal end absent due to ancient break. Chert. Fig. 19.

7.18 Backed bladelet fragment, 12mm long, lacking both proximal and distal ends due to ancient breaks. Marginal abrupt retouch on the right edge. Flint. Patinated. Fig. 19.

7.19 Backed bladelet, 16mm long. Hinge terminated. Lacks proximal end due to ancient break. Fine backing retouch occurs on the right edge. Some small scalar edge damage scars on inverse side of opposite edge. Agate.

7.20 Core tablet/adze. Flake, 27mm long, struck from a bladelet core with abrupt retouch along the thicker margin, which exhibits bladelet scar remnants. The wedge-shaped cross-sectional form suggests an adze (see Glossary, Chapter III). Chert. Fig. 19.

7.21 Core tablet/adze. Flake, 23mm long, with wedge-shaped cross-sectional form. Steep edge exhibits surface of a quartz inclusion. Chert.

7.22 Core tablet/adze. Patinated chert, 14mm long, 30mm wide, with wedge-shaped cross-sectional form. The thick, abrupt edge exhibits remnants of opposed removal scars. The flake was struck from a point perpendicular to the previous platforms. Chert. Patinated.

7.23 Core tablet/adze, 18mm long, 33mm wide with wedge-shaped cross-sectional form. Chert. Patinated.

7.24 Six bladelets, 17-27mm long, one lacking proximal end due to ancient break. Agate-chalcedony.

7.25 Bladelet, 21mm long. Step terminated due to inclusion visible on dorsal surface. Flint.

7.26 Bladelet, fragment, 18mm long. Lacking proximal and distal ends due to ancient breaks. Chalcedony.

7.27 Debitage flake, 28mm long. Chalcedony.

7.28 Nine debitage flakes, 11-33mm long. Chert.

7.29 Debitage flake, 26mm long. Flint.

Artefacts numbered 986:
7.30 Three debitage flakes. 17-27mm long. Chalcedony.

7.31 Two debitage flakes, 19 and 23mm long. Flint.

Artefacts marked 'fields Banda':
7.32 Blade, 34mm long. Flint.

7.33 Debitage flake, 30mm long struck from the face of bladelet core. Chert.

7.34 Debitage flake from a flake core, 30mm long. Chert.

7.35 Debitage flake, 22mm long, struck from the face of a bladelet core. Jasper.

Artefacts numbered 1020:
7.36 Blade, 37mm long. Chert.

7.37 Bladelet, 29mm long. Flint.

7.38 Multi-platform bladelet core, 29mm long. Modified by the removal of flakes and bladelets from four platforms. Chert.

7.39 Single platform bladelet core, 30mm long. Retains about half of its natural surface area. Chert.

7.40 Plunging bladelet, 31mm long. Chalcedony.

7.41 Plunging blade, 23mm long, lacking proximal end due to ancient break. Flint.

7.42 Debitage flake, 21mm long. Chalcedony.

7.43 Debitage flake, 21mm long. Chert.

Artefacts on card labelled 'Banda district':
7.44 Blade, 28mm long, lacking distal end due to ancient break. Chalcedony.

7.45 Blade, 29mm long, lacking proximal end due to ancient break. Chert.

7.46 Blade, 40mm long, lacking distal end due to ancient break. Fresh cortex on proximal end of dorsal surface. Chert.

7.47 Blade, 21mm long, lacking proximal and distal ends due to ancient breaks. Chert.

7.48 Bladelet, 25mm long. Jasper.

Unlabelled artefacts from Banda:
7.49 Backed bladelet, 32mm long, lacking distal end due to ancient break. Abrupt backing retouch struck from the dorsal surface on the left edge. Small scalar marginal edge damage scars occur along the opposite edge on the ventral surface. Fig. 19.

7.50 Lunate, 22mm long. Abrupt backing retouch along the left convex edge. Flint. Patinated.

7.51 Lunate/drill bit, 17mm long. Flake with Siret fracture and abrupt marginal scalar retouch on the left convex edge. Points formed by Siret break may have formed drill points. Slight ancient damage at proximal end. Chalcedony.

7.52 Side and end scraper, 22mm long. Made on a flake. Semi-invasive, scalar retouch extends across the distal end and along the straight right edge. Chert. Fig. 19.

7.53 Denticulate, 40mm long. Made on a flake. Semi-invasive scalar retouch occurs on the convex right edge forming a partially serrated margin. Chert. Fig. 19.

7.54 Bladelet, 28mm long, lacking distal end due to subrecent break. Chert.

7.55 Bipolar opposed bladelet core, 44mm long. Chert. Patinated.

7.56 Bipolar opposed bladelet core, 27mm long. Quartz.

7.57 Single platform bladelet core, 34mm long. Retains two small patches of stained and chattermarked cortex suggesting the use of a river pebble. Chalcedony.

7.58 Single platform bladelet core, 25mm long, pyramidal form. Jasper.

7.59 Crested blade, 23mm long, with hinge termination. Chert.

7.60 Core trimming flake, 32mm long. Agate-chalcedony.

7.61 Debitage flake, 19mm long. Retains cortex on about 50% of the dorsal surface. Chalcedony.

7.62 Seven debitage flakes and a mid-section fragment, 18-30mm long. Chert.

7.63 Four debitage flakes and a mid-section fragment, 17-26mm long. Flint.

7.64 Debitage flake, 18mm long, lacking proximal end due to ancient break. Retains small area of chattermarked cortex at distal end. Chalcedony. Patinated.

7.65 Debitage flake, 30mm long, lacking proximal end due to ancient break. Chert-flint.

Christy Collection
7.66 Lunate, 18mm long. Chert. (1926-131). Fig. 7.

7.67 Lunate, 24mm long. Jasper. (1926-130). Fig. 7.

Royal Albert Memorial Museum, Exeter Collection
7.68 Lunate, 27mm long. Chert. Patinated. (P1993. 7-1. 1)

7.69 Lunate, 26mm long. Chert. Patinated and slightly stained. (P1993. 7-1. 2)

7.70 Lunate, 12mm long. Chert. Patinated. (P1993. 7-1. 3)

7.71 Trapeze, 20mm long. Chert. (P1993. 7-1. 4)

7.72 Trapeze, 13mm long, ancient break surface on the shorter of the parallel edges. Chert. (P1993. 7-1. 5)

7.73 Single platform bladelet core, 16mm long. Retains cortex on one side. Chalcedony. (P1993. 7-1. 6)

7.74 Single platform bladelet core, 30mm long. Retains abraded cortex on one face. Jasper. (P1993. 7-1. 7)

Sturge Collection
7.75 Crested blade, 30mm long. Flint. Patinated.

8. BARKOR
(Barkpura)

Carlyle provided little information concerning the location of this site. However, a caption written by Seidler on a card with artefacts attached to it in the Christy Collection refers to the site as west of Morhana Pahar (see entry 38). This suggests that the locality is probably a rockshelter on the Vindhyan escarpment near Bhainsaur (Fig. 6) in Mirzapur District, Uttar Pradesh. The four cores recovered by Carlyle are probably Mesolithic-Neolithic.

8.1 Bipolar opposed bladelet core, 48mm long, made on a flake. Retains some cortex along the crested edge. Pale green jasper. Patinated.

8.2 Bipolar bladelet core, 42mm long. The platforms occur on adjacent edges. Chert. Fig. 16.

8.3 Single platform bladelet core, 44mm long, retaining cortex on one face. The cortex shows chattermarks suggesting use of a river pebble. Chert.

Christy Collection
8.4 Bipolar opposed bladelet core, 41mm long. Chert. (1926-156). Fig. 7.

9. BHAGATPURA

The nature and location of this collecting spot is not known. All but one (9.16) of the sixteen artefacts were glued to a card marked 982 and labelled as 'rude crescent shape knives' (9.3, 9.12-9.15), 'small lances or knives' (9.1, 9.4 and 9.5) and 'double edge razor knives' (9.2, 9.3, 9.6-9.11). With the exception of the retouched bladelet (9.1), which in European terms might be regarded as Upper Palaeolithic, the debitage technique evident on the other items suggests that they come from a Holocene assemblage.

9.1 Retouched bladelet, 21mm long. The fine, semi-abrupt retouch is alternate, being direct on the left side and inverse on the right side. In Europe, bladelets with these characteristics appear in early Upper Palaeolithic, Perigordian assemblages and are referred to as *lamelle Dufour*. Whether such pieces have any diagnostic significance in India is unknown. Flint. Patinated. Fig. 16.

9.2 Retouched proximal end of a blade, 28mm long, with an ancient break interrupting fine, direct, marginal, semi-abrupt retouch on both edges. Chalcedony.

9.3 Retouched flake, 25mm long. Direct, marginal, semi-abrupt scalar retouch extends along the right edge. Chert.

9.4 Pointed flake fragment, 26mm long. The flake has an ancient lateral break along its axis of percussion giving it a pointed form and direct, invasive parallel retouch scars on the right side. It is impossible to determine whether this piece is a broken fragment of a larger artefact possibly utilised as a point or whether it was deliberately broken and modified for use as a projectile tip. Chalcedony.

9.5 Point/debitage flake, 18mm long. Orientated with the proximal end uppermost, this flake fits in the morphological category of unmodified points (see Glossary, Chapter III). Chalcedony.

9.6-9.7 Blades, 26 and 28mm long. 9.6 has an ancient break at the proximal end. Flint.

9.8-9.9 Bladelets, 15 and 19mm long. The former has a long step termination, the latter lacks its proximal end due to ancient break. Chalcedony.

9.10 Bladelet, 26mm long, lacking distal end due to ancient break. Chert.

9.11 Crested bladelet, 42mm long, lacking proximal end due to recent break. Flint. Patinated.

9.12 Three debitage flakes, 20-30mm long. Agate-chalcedony.

9.13 Debitage flake, 20mm long. Chert.

Numbered 1013:
9.14 Debitage flake from the crested edge of a chalcedony core, 36mm long. Small, scalar, marginal inverse retouch on right side resulting from subrecent edge damage. Agate.

10. BHAINSAWAR NALLA
(Nalla Bhainsawar, Bhainsaur)

A watercourse (*nala*) at or near Bhainsaur, southwest of Mirzapur (see entry 2 and Fig. 6).

10.1 Debitage flake from a bladelet core, 30mm long. Flat faceted butt. A thermal fracture has modified part of dorsal surface. Chert.

11. BHAISAND
(Bhaisaond)

Only two pieces (11.1 and 11.2) are labelled Bhaisand. The other thirteen pieces, all marked 1003, were stuck to a card captioned 'small razor knives from a cave near Bhaisand and as above at Mahrela Chacki, Riwa R.'. Unfortunately, it is impossible to distinguish with any certainty which artefacts come from the respective sites but, judging by the technology, it is possible that the bladelets (11.10-11.15) are from Mahrela Chacki (see entry 33) and the debitage pieces (11.3-11.9) from Bhaisand. Carlyle noted that Bhaisand was near Bhainsaur (Fig. 6) so the 'cave' may have been a rockshelter on the Rewa scarp. All of the pieces come from Holocene, probably Mesolithic-Neolithic, assemblages.

11.1 Blade, 15mm long, lacking proximal end due to ancient break. Flint. Patinated and abraded.

11.2 Debitage flake, 20mm long, lacking proximal and distal ends due to ancient breaks. Flint, patinated. Carlyle compared this piece to a transverse arrowhead from Urquhart, Scotland, illustrated in Evans, 1876 (fig. 342, p.352), mistaking the breaks for deliberate modification.

11.3 Retouched crested bladelet, 27mm long. Retains a small patch of abraded and stained cortex at distal end of the crested arête. Abrupt scalar retouch at distal end. Semi-abrupt, marginal scalar retouch on right edge. Chert.

11.4 Blade, 20mm long, with hinge termination. Chert.

11.5 Debitage flakes, 18-20mm long. One complete. All retain stained, abraded and chattermarked cortex. Chert.

11.6 Debitage flake, 18mm long. Flint.

11.7 Knapping fragment, 27mm long. Chert.

11.8 Retouched bladelet, 15mm long, lacking distal end due to ancient break. Inverse, semi-invasive, scalar retouch on both edges. Chert.

11.9 Retouched bladelet fragment, 14mm long, lacking distal end due to ancient break. Direct, marginal scalar retouch on right edge. Flint.

11.10 Two bladelets, 14mm long, lacking proximal ends due to ancient breaks. One retains stained and abraded cortex around end and on right margin. Chert.

11.11 Debitage flake, 17mm long. Retains stained and abraded cortex at distal end. Chert.

11.12 Knapping fragment, 18mm long. Chert.

12. BHARKACHA
(Barkacha, Bharkachha, Bharkacha, Bharkachka, Bharkaech, Bharka, Bar Kachha, Bhar Khachh)

Bharkacha is situated about 12 km southeast of Mirzapur on the road to Robertsganj in a region between the Vindhyan and Kaimur ranges (Figs. 4, 6) which also attracted the attention of Carlyle's contemporary, James Cockburn. The area was reinvestigated by G.R. Sharma (Ghosh (ed.), 1965; Sharma, 1973a) who, like Carlyle and Cockburn, recorded the occurrence of microliths which he attributed to the Mesolithic (ibid.). Carlyle's collection includes palettes and utilised stones which suggest a Mesolithic-Neolithic date but there is no information to relate the distribution of his finds to the cairn circles and dolmenoid cists which occur in the vicinity. Paper labels on 12.20 and 12.21 indicate that these pieces were collected from the 'surface' and 'scarp of the Vindhyas' respectively, while a faded label in Seidler's handwriting on 12.22 describes the artefact as a digging implement or root digger 'presented by Mr A.C. Carlyle who saw a hill man using one while at Dalai occasionally attached to a stick. He [the hill man] obtained it from one of the old sites...'. This suggests that finds marked Bharkacha may have come from more than one locality and illustrates the reuse of ancient artefacts into recent times.

12.1 Saw made on a bladelet, 30mm long, lacking distal end due to ancient break. Direct, denticulate retouch forms serrated edge on right side. Chert. Fig. 20.

12.2 Retouched flake, 28mm long. Direct, small scalar retouch scars at proximal end of left edge probably the result of ancient damage. Chert. Patinated.

12.3 Bipolar opposed bladelet core, 31mm long. Chert.

12.4 Two single platform bladelet cores, 23 and 35mm long. Both retain areas of stained and chattermarked cortex suggesting the use of river pebbles. Agate.

12.5 Four single platform bladelet cores, 27-30mm long. Two retain stained and chattermarked cortex on one side. Chert-flint.

12.6 Failed bladelet core, 40mm long, with scars of three bladelet removals from a platform formed by an edge and an attempt at cresting along another edge. Retains a small patch of stained and chattermarked natural surface. Flint.

12.7 Failed bladelet core, 51mm long, with a removal to start a platform at one end and attempts at cresting on both sides. Retains abraded and chattermarked cortex over more than 75% of its surface. Chert.

12.8 Unipolar, biconical core, 29mm across. Single platform extends around circumference. Scar remnants indicate the removal of small flakes from both faces to the point of exhaustion. Chert.

12.9 Core tablet, 39mm across. Retaining small patch of abraded and chattermarked cortex on side. Chalcedony.

12.10 Core tablet, 25mm long. Flint.

12.11 Debitage flake, 22mm long. Flint. Patinated.

12.12 Debitage flake, 50mm long. Flint.

12.13 Knapping fragment, 37mm long. Flint.

12.14 Flaked pebble, 65mm long. Flakes removed from both faces. Quartzite.

12.15 Rubber. Split chert pebble 41mm long, smoothed and polished on a flattened cortical face as a result of abrasion caused by rubbing or grinding against another material.

12.16 Palette. Sandstone tablet with sides trimmed to a polygonal outline, 58mm across. Fig. 20.

12.17 Palette. Sandstone tablet with sides trimmed to a polygonal outline, 59mm across. Fig. 20.

12.18 Utilised sandstone slab, 253mm long. Semi-circular in shape with an ancient break at one end, the slab is smoothed and polished as a result of abrasion on the upper, convex face along the straight edge. Numbered 945 by Carlyle. Fig. 21.

12.19 Natural sandstone pebble, 32mm long.

Wellcome Collection
12.20 Partially backed bladelet, 24mm long, with abrupt backing retouch on the distal end of the left edge interrupted by an ancient break. Flint. P1982.10-4.4628

Department of Oriental Antiquities
12.21 Hammerstone, 100mm long. Cylindrical cross-section, polished on one side, the remainder ground. One end has been modified by percussion which has resulted in bruising of the central area and the detachment of small flakes around the perimeter. Marked 947. Sandstone. (OA 1880-1192.1).

12.22 Ringstone roughout, 140mm long. Triangular outline formed by deliberate break surfaces. Two drilled depressions occur exactly opposite each other on the faces of the slab suggesting that an attempt to perforate the piece was abandoned because it was too thick. Marked 948. Sandstone. (OA 1888-1192.3)

12.23 Digging implement, 154mm long. Crescentic form thicker on the concave margin than on the convex outer edge and decreasing in thickness from one end to the other. Marked 942. Sandstone. (OA 1880-1192.2)

13. BHARKURA

The location of this site is unknown. Possibly the same locality as Barkor/Barkpura (see entry 8).

13.1 Backed bladelet, 29mm long. Flint. Fig. 16.

13.2 Bladelet, 36mm long. Modified by inverse scalar retouch, probably edge damage, along both edges. Chert. Patinated.

13.3 Single platform bladelet core, 28mm long. Chert.

13.4 Crested blade, 41mm long. Chert. Patinated.

14. BUNDELKHAND

Over one hundred artefacts in Carlyle's collection have no more precise provenance than Bundelkhand, a vast tract of country covering some 11,600 square miles (*Imperial Gazetteer of India*, Meyer and Cotton, 1908) across the southern part of the modern state of Uttar Pradesh and northern Madhya Pradesh (Figs. 3, 4). During the nineteenth century, this area southeast of the confluence of the Chambal and Yamuna rivers lay within the United Provinces and included, amongst others, the districts of Hamirpur, Banda and part of Allahabad where Carlyle was working. In modern terms, the absence of specific information about sites, the selection and possibly, the mixing of material is regrettable but it would appear that in putting this part of the collection together, Carlyle was trying to make a typological point (see Chapter I): the pieces grouped from Bundelkhand are all either microliths or bladelet debitage dating from the Late Mesolithic-Neolithic. The fresh condition of the material suggests that the pieces may derive from rockshelters hollowed out of the sandstones of the scarps of the northern range of the Eastern Vindhyas or *Bindhâchal* which stretch across the southern part of Bundelkhand, rather than the alluvium to the north. However, the presence of a single piece marked Morhana Pahar, a site in Mirzapur District (see entry 38 below) outside Bundelkhand and neighbouring Baghelkhand, might suggest that even Carlyle's broad terms are unreliable. His collection from Morhana Pahar contains few microliths although the site is known to have contained a great many (Ghosh 1965, 1989) and it is possible that some of the unmarked tools grouped as from Bundelkhand might account for this anomaly. Alternatively, the marked piece may have been misplaced. To avoid any further loss of information, the artefacts have been catalogued in groups according to the Roman numerals marked on them. However, these numerals would appear to reflect typological groupings rather than provenance.

Artefacts marked II and IIa respectively:
14.1 Backed bladelet, 20mm long. Abrupt retouch extends across an oblique truncation of the distal end forming a marked angle where it converges with semi-abrupt retouch along the straight left edge. This modification has produced a scalene form (see Glossary, Chapter III). Chert. Fig. 22.

14.2 Lunate made on a bladelet, 33mm long. Abrupt, marginal retouch extends along the left edge producing a convex back converging to a point at both ends with a straight unmodified opposite edge. Slightly abraded. Chert.

Artefacts marked III:
14.3 Backed bladelet, 23mm long. Abrupt retouch backing curved right edge. Chert. Fig. 22.

14.4 Backed bladelet, 30mm long. Abrupt retouch backing curved left edge. Chert.

14.5 Backed bladelet, 23mm long, lacking distal end due to ancient break. Abrupt retouch backing curved left edge. Chert.

14.6 Backed bladelet, 26mm long. Semi-abrupt retouch backing curved left edge. Flint.

14.7 Backed bladelet, 20mm long. Abrupt retouch backing straight left edge. Chert. Fig. 22.

14.8 Backed bladelet/point, 25mm long. Abrupt retouch backing straight right edge converges to a point at the distal end with the unmodified opposite edge. Chert.

14.9 Lunate, 17mm long, lacking proximal end point due to ancient break. Abrupt backing retouch extends along the right edge producing a crescentic form. Flint. Fig. 22.

Artefacts marked IV:
14.10 Bipolar opposed bladelet core, 18mm long. Pyramidal shape. Main platform at broad end faceted. Chalcedony.

14.11 Single platform bladelet core, 27mm long. Faceted platform. Agate.

14.12 Single platform bladelet core, 16mm long. Faceted platform. Chalcedony.

14.13 Single platform bladelet core, 25mm long. Faceted platform. Triangular shape with a plano-convex cross-section. The flat face retains stained and abraded cortex and shows remnants of cresting on the sides. Flint.

Artefact marked V:
14.14 Trapeze, 13mm long. Abrupt marginal retouch on left edge contiguous with oblique retouched truncations of the proximal and distal ends. Longest, right edge unmodified. Discoloured by burning with small thermal fractures on ventral surface. Flint. Fig. 22.

Artefacts marked VII:
14.15 Bladelet, 28mm long. Chalcedony.

14.16 Bladelet, 24mm long. Jasper.

14.17 Debitage flake, 31mm long. Chert.

Artefact marked X:
14.18 Backed bladelet, 21mm long. Abrupt marginal retouch occurs on the proximal and distal ends of the left edge. Chalcedony. Fig. 22.

Artefact marked XII:
14.19 Backed bladelet, 30mm long with a subrecent break at midpoint. Abrupt backing retouch along right edge and some scalar edge damage on the opposite side. Flint. Fig. 22.

Artefacts marked XV:
14.20 Triangular microlith, 17mm long. Isosceles shape. Chalcedony.

14.21 Triangular microlith, 16mm long. Isosceles shape. Chalcedony. Fig. 22.

14.22 Triangular microlith, 15mm long. Isosceles shape. Flint. Patinated. Fig. 22.

14.23 Triangular microlith, 13mm long. Scalene shape. Chalcedony. Fig. 22.

14.24 Triangular microlith, 14mm long. Scalene shape. Chert. Fig. 22.

Artefact marked XVII:
14.25 Single platform bladelet core, 24mm long. Chert.

Artefact marked XIX:
14.26 Point, 37mm long, produced by convergent, marginal abrupt denticulate retouch on both edges of a bladelet. A retouched notch at the proximal end of left edge narrows the base to suggest a tang. Chalcedony. Fig. 22.

Artefact marked XXI:
14.27 Lunate, 17mm long. Chalcedony. Fig. 22.

14.28 Lunate, 19mm long. Abrupt retouch around the curved back converges at the points with marginal, scalar retouch on the straight edge. Chalcedony. Fig. 22.

Artefact marked XXXIII:
14.29 Single platform bladelet core, 30mm long. Chert.

Artefact marked XXXVII:
14.30 Single platform bladelet core, 30mm long. Faceted platform. Chalcedony with a quartz inclusion.

Artefacts marked XXXIX:
14.31 Single platform bladelet core, 29mm long. Rectangular cross-section 5mm thick. Faceted platform. Remnants of cresting along one side. Chalcedony.

14.32 Single platform bladelet core, 19mm long. Faceted platform. Chalcedony.

14.33 Single platform bladelet core, 18mm long. Chalcedony.

14.34 Single platform bladelet core, 20mm long. Faceted platform. Chert.

14.35 Single platform bladelet core, 25mm long. Pyramidal. Flint.

Artefacts marked XL:
14.36 Backed bladelet, 20mm long lacking distal end due to subrecent break. Flint discoloured by burning.

14.37 Lunate, 19mm long. Chalcedony. Fig. 22.

14.38 Lunate, 21mm long. Agate. Fig. 22.

14.39 Triangular microlith, 16mm long. Scalene form. Chalcedony. Fig. 22.

14.40 Triangular microlith, 19mm long. Isosceles form. Chalcedony. Fig. 22.

14.41 Triangular microlith, 19mm long. Scalene form. Chalcedony.

Artefacts marked XLI:
14.42 Triangular microlith, 17mm long. Isosceles form. Chalcedony. Fig. 22.

14.43 Triangular. Microlith, 16mm long. Scalene form. Chalcedony. Patinated. Fig. 22.

14.44 Triangular microlith, 14mm long. Scalene form. Chalcedony.

14.45 Bladelet fragment, 15mm long, with fortuitous scalene triangle shape due to ancient breaks. Chalcedony.

Artefacts marked LI:

14.46 Point/drill bit made on a bladelet, 19mm long with an ancient break across the mid-point. The right edge of the bladelet is modified by abrupt marginal retouch. Similar retouch occurs on the left edge at the tip producing a thin, narrow tip. Chalcedony. Fig. 22.

14.47 Point/drill bit made on a distal end fragment of a bladelet, 17mm long. Abrupt, marginal retouch extends from an ancient break surface to the tip on the left side and along part of the right edge. A single, scalar scar occurs on the ventral surface of the tip. Flint. Fig. 22.

Artefact marked LII:

14.48 Scalene backed bladelet, 22mm long (Tixier, 1963). Abrupt, marginal retouch occurs along the left edge forming a marked angle with an oblique, retouched distal end truncation. Green jasper. Fig. 22.

Artefact marked LV:

14.49 Point/drill bit made on a distal end fragment of a bladelet, 20mm long, by abrupt marginal retouch along the right edge above an ancient break. Small, scalar edge damage scars occur on the ventral surface of the left edge below the tip. Flint. Fig. 23.

Unmarked artefacts:

14.50 Backed bladelet, 22mm long. Curved left edge modified by abrupt, marginal retouch. Flint.

14.51-14.67 Lunates varying from 11 to 23mm in length and from 4 to 6mm in width. All of the pieces have been modified to the more elongated segment form, as distinct from the broader, shorter semicircular type (see Glossary, Chapter III). Abrupt backing retouch forms the convex edges. The opposed edges are straight and unmodified. Chalcedony. Fig. 23.

14.68-14.72 Lunates varying from 16 to 20mm in length and from 4 to 5mm in width. Characteristics as for entry 14.51-14.67 above. Flint. 14.71 and 14.72 are patinated. Fig. 23.

14.73-14.81 Lunates varying from 17 to 23mm in length and from 6 to 7mm in width. Characteristics as for entry 14.51-14.67 above. Flint. Figs. 23, 24.

14.82-14.83 Lunates 17 and 20mm long respectively. Both are 5mm wide and exhibit the same characteristics as pieces 14.51-14.81 above. Chert and jasper. Fig. 24.

14.84 Point on a narrow (3mm wide) backed bladelet, 19mm long. Subrecent and ancient breaks across the mid-point and proximal end respectively. The proximal end break interrupts the abrupt backing retouch along the right edge. Flint.

14.85 Point on a curved backed bladelet, 24mm long. An inverse retouched notch on the side opposite the backed left edge suggests a tang. Flint. Fig. 24.

14.86 Point, 2mm long, made on a flake. Semi-invasive scalar retouch extends along the convergent edges. Rounded proximal end unmodified. Chalcedony. Fig. 24.

14.87 Trapeze, 19mm long. Isosceles form with abrupt retouch on the truncations. Chalcedony. Fig. 24.

14.88 Trapeze, 16mm long. Isosceles form with abrupt retouch on the truncations. Chalcedony. Fig. 24.

14.89 Trapeze, 15mm long. Isosceles form with abrupt retouch on the truncations. Chalcedony. Fig. 24.

14.90 Trapeze, 21mm long. Isosceles form with abrupt retouch on the truncations and shorter side. Chalcedony. Fig. 24.

14.91 Trapeze, 13mm long. Isosceles form with abrupt retouch on the truncations and shorter side. Chalcedony. Fig. 24.

14.92 Trapeze, 20mm long. Isosceles form with abrupt retouch on the truncations. Chert. Fig. 24.

14.93 Trapeze, 16mm long. Isosceles form with abrupt retouch on the truncations and shorter side. Chert. Fig. 24.

14.94 Trapeze, 19mm long. Isosceles form with abrupt retouch on the truncations and shorter side. Chert. Fig. 24.

14.95 Trapeze, 23mm long. Isosceles form with abrupt retouch on the truncations and longer side. Chert. Fig. 24.

14.96 Trapeze, 22mm long. Asymmetric form. Abrupt retouch occurs on the shorter truncation and shorter, concave side. Flint.

14.97 Trapeze/point, 23mm long. Asymmetric form. The proximal end is truncated and retouched whereas the distal end is obliquely retouched to form point. Flint. Fig. 24.

14.98 Triangle, 13mm long. Isosceles form. Chalcedony. Fig. 24.

14.99 Triangle, 18mm long. Isosceles form. Chalcedony.

14.100 Triangle, 13mm long. Isosceles form. Chalcedony.

14.101 Triangle, 15mm long. Isosceles form. Flint. Fig. 24.

14.102 Triangle, 16mm long. Elongated scalene form with an oblique, retouched truncation at the base and abruptly retouched sides converging to a point. Flint.

14.103 Triangle, 13mm long. Scalene form. Chalcedony. Fig. 24.

14.104 Triangle, 20mm long. Scalene form. Chalcedony. Fig. 24.

14.105 Triangle, 15mm long. Scalene form. Flint. Fig. 24.

14.106 Triangle, 20mm long. Scalene form retouched along an oblique basal truncation. Stained and abraded cortex interrupts the retouch on the left edge. Flint.

14.107 Unretouched trapeze, 18mm long. Mid-section of a bladelet with unmodified oblique breaks. Chert.

14.108 Unretouched trapeze, 18mm long. Mid-section of a bladelet with unmodified oblique breaks. Thermal fracture scars on the dorsal and ventral surfaces caused by burning. Flint.

14.109 Bladelet fragment lacking distal end due to ancient break, 11mm long. Chalcedony.

14.110 Debitage flake, 12mm long. Flint.

14.111 Core from which small flakes have been removed from at least two platforms, 28mm long. Retains cortex on one side and remnants of a positive fracture surface on the other suggesting reduction of a struck or thermal flake. Flint.

15. CHILÂHWA NÂLA

The location of this site is unknown. The one artefact collected is from a Holocene Neolithic-Chalcolithic assemblage.

15.1 Single platform bladelet core, 47mm long. Chert-flint.

16. CHITRAKOT

Chitrakot (25° 13'N, 80° 51' E) is a place of pilgrimage situated southeast of Banda on the road to Karwi in modern Uttar Pradesh (Fig. 6). The name is said to mean hill (*kut*) of various colours (*chitra*), referring to numerous different coloured stones found there (Drake-Brockman, 1909a) but Carlyle collected only two Neolithic-Chalcolithic artefacts there.

16.1 Crested blade, 35mm long. Flint. Patinated.

16.2 Debitage flake, 41mm long. Flint. Patinated.

17. DHIR

The register of The National Museums of Scotland refers to Dhir as situated east of Drummond Gar in Mirzapur District. Drummond Gar is presumably an alternative spelling for Drummondganj on the Great Deccan Road near Bhainsaur, southwest of Mirzapur (see entry 2). Dhir is not referred to by Drake-Brockman (1911) or in *The Imperial Gazetteer of India* (Meyer and Cotton, 1908) but Drummondganj is noted in the former as a government encamping ground with an inspection bungalow near the point where the road crosses the Seoti river at the foot of the Vindhyan escarpment (Fig. 6). The artefacts collected from this locality are Late Mesolithic-Neolithic bladelet cores. More recently, Ghosh (1965) has recorded microliths from this vicinity.

17.1 Bipolar opposed bladelet core, 27mm long. Considerably reduced, probably exhausted. Flint.

17.2 Single platform bladelet core, 41mm long. Retains stained, abraded and chattermarked cortex on one side suggesting use of river pebble. Flint. Patinated.

17.3 Single platform bladelet core, 31mm long. Retains stained and abraded cortex on one side of its pyramidal outline. Flint. Patinated.

18. GÂDUR HÂTA

The location of this site in the former native state of Rewa (Rewah), now part of northern Madhya Pradesh, is unknown. It does not appear in the published accounts of Carlyle's tours and no locality of this name is listed in the gazetteer for Rewa state (Luard, 1907) or in Ghosh (1989). However, in the register of the National Museums of Scotland an artefact is referred to as coming from Gâdur Hâta, Naogaon, Rewa. Naogaon may be an alternative spelling of Nowgain, a village on the Vindhyan escarpment (see entry 41). The nature and condition of the Late Mesolithic-Neolithic artefacts are commensurate with the possibility that they may have come from a rockshelter.

18.1 Backed blade, 40mm long. Direct abrupt retouch occurs along the left edge and the right edge is modified by inverse scalar subparallel scars which terminate in step fractures half-way across the ventral surface giving a 'mashed' or heavily utilised appearance. Flint.

18.2 Bipolar opposed blade core, 66mm long. Cresting still evident on two edges. Chert.

18.3 Bipolar opposed bladelet core, 51mm long. Cresting still complete on one edge, bladelets removed from opposite edge. Chert.

18.4 Single platform bladelet core, 36mm long. Chert.

18.5 Single platform bladelet core, 31mm long. Chert.

18.6 Single platform bladelet core, 32mm long. Faceted platform. Retains stained, abraded and chattermarked cortex on one side. Flint. Patinated.

18.7 Single platform bladelet core, 30mm long. Faceted platform. Flint. Patinated.

18.8 Single platform bladelet core, 30mm long. Faceted platform. The last removal plunged. Flint. Patinated.

18.9 Debitage flake, 40mm long. Chert.

18.10 Modified pebble/hammerstone, 59mm long. One face retains stained and abraded cortex, the opposite has been modified by invasive removals, the arêtes of which are heavily abraded. Localised battering on the narrower end suggests later reuse as a hammerstone. Bluish-green jasper.

19. GAUR RIVER

The Gaur river is a tributary of the Narmada (Fig. 4). It rises in the Mandla highlands of Madhya Pradesh and flows some 49 miles before it joins the right bank of the Narmada five miles south of Jabalpur, above the famous falls at Marble Rocks (Nelson, 1909). The character and abraded condition of all the artefacts marked Gaur river indicates that they were collected from exposures of Pleistocene and Holocene river gravels such as have been recorded from the Upper Narmada Valley (see Chapter II and entry 43 below). This is confirmed by paper labels stuck on 19.93 and 19.94 on which Carlyle has written 'Gaur R Gravels, same age as the Narbada (*sic*) gravels'. The absence of bifaces and debitage resulting from biface manufacture among the Palaeolithic artefacts is notable.

LOWER AND MIDDLE PALAEOLITHIC ARTEFACTS

19.1 Prepared flake, 85mm long, with step fractured, semi-invasive retouch scars on the ventral and dorsal sides of the right edge and inversely on the left edge. This modification resembles the edge damage probably caused by heavy use during an activity such as chopping on pieces described as *lame mâchuré*. Chert. Fig. 25.

19.2 Prepared flake, 72mm long, with semi-invasive, inverse scalar retouch on both edges and abrupt, marginal retouch along the transverse distal end. The retouch is probably edge damage caused by heavy usage as in the case of 18.1. Chert. Marked Mesolithic by Carlyle.

19.3 Straight side scraper, 61mm long, with direct semi-invasive retouch on a high-angled (>75°) edge. Chert.

19.4 Straight side scraper, 58mm long. The left side is modified by an inverse removal struck from the butt and direct, marginal scalar retouch along a high-angled edge. A small area of cortex remains at the distal end. The butt is faceted. Jasper. Fig. 25.

19.5 Transverse scraper, 41mm long, with subparallel retouch on the high-angled distal end. Chert.

19.6 End scraper on a flake, 31mm long. The abrupt, marginal retouch modifying the distal end is not patinated like the rest of the dorsal surface although it is similarly abraded. The blank may have been reutilised after having been discarded or the retouch may be natural edge damage. Flint.

19.7 End and side scraper on a prepared flake, 67mm long. Abrupt, marginal retouch extends around the distal end and along much of the right edge. Dihedral butt. Jasper. Marked Mesolithic by Carlyle. Fig. 25.

19.8 Denticulate on a prepared flake, 51mm long. Abrupt denticulate retouch modifies the right edge. Heavily abraded. Chert.

19.9 Retouched notch/awl, 44mm long. Scalar retouch accentuates the concavity of a notch on the left edge and the point at the distal end. Retains cortex over remainder of the dorsal surface. Jasper.

19.10 Point, 68mm long, made on a distal end fragment of a large hinge fractured flake. The round termination of the flake forms the left side of the point which is bifacially modified below the tip. Direct, semi-invasive scalar retouch also occurs on the right edge below the point. Chert.

19.11 Multipolar core with a conical-globular form, 72mm high. The margin of a flake scar forming a flat end to the core has been used as a platform for the removal of flakes around the circumference. Opposed removals have been made from the apex of the core and scar remnants suggest earlier removals from at least two further platforms. The core retains a small patch of abraded cortex. Chert.

19.12 Prepared core, 50mm long. A single platform extends around the margin of the pebble from which flakes were removed around the perimeter of the convex, natural surface. The final removal was struck from the opposite face after adjustment of the platform by faceting. Chalcedony.

19.13 Prepared core, 40mm long, plano-convex in cross-section with a single platform around the margin. The plane surface exhibits a single scar left by a flake struck off after a series of steep removals from the convex face. A small patch of cortex remains at the apex of the convex side. Jasper.

19.14 Single platform core, 42mm long, plano-convex in cross-section. The platform extends around the entire margin. The plane face exhibits step terminated semi-invasive scars which intrude on a previous removal surface suggesting continued working after the detachment of a prepared flake. Chalcedony.

19.15 Single platform core, 50mm long. One side exhibits remnant and complete removal scars struck from one end of the piece. The opposite face bears remnants of scars removed during a previous reduction phase. Chert.

19.16 Single platform, bi-convex core, 66mm long. The platform extends around most the margin of the core and flakes have been removed radially. One surface retains some cortex. Chert.

19.17 Single platform core, 55mm long, on a flake. The margin of the flake has been used as a platform to form a series of removals around the perimeter of the ventral surface prior to the removal of a single flake from the dorsal surface. The platform was adjusted by faceting prior to the final removal. Chert.

19.18 Single platform core, 73mm. The platform extends around the entire margin of the core and flakes have been removed radially from one side, which still retains some cortex, and then the opposite face. Flint.

19.19 Core/modified cobble, 82mm long. Flake scars and scar remnants struck from more than two platforms occur on each face of the cobble, which has a quadrangular cross-section. Jasper.

19.20-19.37 Debitage flakes, 31mm to 81mm long, complete. The largest pieces, 19.20 and 19.21, retain cortex over most of their dorsal surface whereas the remainder derive from later stages of reduction sequences, having several dorsal scars. None of the pieces are characteristic of biface manufacture. All appear to be the product of hard hammer flaking. 19.31 to 19.37 have edges more or less continuously modified by abrupt, marginal edge damage caused by fluvial transport. Chert. Abraded.

19.38-19.68 Debitage flakes. Complete with the exception of distal end fragment 19.67. Excluding the latter piece, the flakes vary from 35mm to 82mm in length. 19.38-19.42 retain large areas of cortex on their dorsal surfaces whereas the remaining flakes reflect the later stages of reduction sequences. None of the pieces are characteristic of biface manufacture and all appear to have been struck by hard hammer. 19.58-19.66 have edges modified by abrupt edge damage caused by fluvial transport. 19.67 might be regarded as a point in some classifications because of its convergent form. Red, green and banded/marbled jasper. Abraded. Fig. 26.

19.69 Debitage flake, 56mm long. Chalcedony. Labelled Mesolithic by Carlyle.

19.70 Debitage flake, 37mm long. Chert. Stained.

MESOLITHIC-CHALCOLITHIC ARTEFACTS

19.71 Adze, 39mm long. Modified by inverse stepped scalar retouch along the edge transverse to the butt. Rectangular form with wedge-shaped longitudinal section. Chert.

19.72 Awl, 39mm long. The pointed distal end of the flake has been improved by direct, scalar retouch on the right edge below the tip. Marked Neolithic by Carlyle. Chert. Fig. 26.

19.73 Retouched flake, 58mm long, with a steeply triangular cross-section. Shallow subparallel retouch scars left by removals struck from the ventral surface and the dorsal arête modify the dorsal face. Similar retouch occurs on the proximal and distal ends of the ventral surface reducing the bulbar swelling and modifying a hinge termination. Possibly intended as a pick-like form. Chert.

19.74 Flaked pebble, 70mm long, with trihedral cross-section. Jasper.

19.75 Bipolar opposed blade core, 48mm long. Chert.

19.76 Bipolar opposed bladelet core, 59mm long. The bladelet scars occur on one face of a natural flake. Chert.

19.77 Bipolar opposed bladelet core, 51mm long. The bladelet scars occur on one face of a flake. Banded jasper.

19.78 Single platform bladelet core, 53mm long, with cortex remaining on one end and most of one side. The corticated end has some flake scars and is battered, suggesting either previous or subsequent use of the core as a hammerstone. Chert.

19.79 Single platform core, 53mm long, with plano-convex cross-section. The platform extends around the equator of the piece and flakes have been removed alternately from both faces before the removal of a series of bladelets from one end. Chert.

19.80-19.81 Core tablets, 58 and 32mm long. Jasper.

19.82 Core rejuvenation flake, 45mm long.

19.83-19.84 Debitage flakes, 52 and 34mm long respectively. Both retain some cortex and derive from an early stage of bladelet core reduction. Both have small diffuse bulbs and lipped butts suggesting that they were struck using a soft hammer. Jasper. Slightly abraded.

AGE INDETERMINATE

19.85-19.88 Knapped pieces between 38 and 51mm maximum dimension. Reduced beyond recognition of knapping intention. Chert.

19.89-19.91 Knapped pieces. Jasper.

19.92 Knapped piece, 74mm maximum dimension. Cobble with random percussion removals originating from a natural fracture surface and edges on the upper part of the core. Chert.

Uncatalogued:
Thirty-four naturally fractured, heavily abraded pebbles and cobbles of chert and jasper.

Wellcome Collection

19.93 Retouched flake, 51mm long. Abrupt scalar retouch around the distal end and on the right side, probably edge damage. Chert. Stained and abraded. (P1982.10-4.4992)

19.94 Debitage flake, 84mm long. Retains cortex around distal end. Marked 582. Collected 28 September, 1884. Chert. (P1982.10-4.4992)

Department of Oriental Antiquities

19.95 Flake, 70mm long, naturally fractured. Marked 935. Chert. (OA 1880-1195)

20. GHARWA PAHÂRI

The only artefacts from this site curated by the British Museum were sold by Seidler on Carlyle's behalf to Sir Wilfred Peek, from whom they were acquired for the Christy Collection in 1926 (Fig.7). More recently the Royal Albert Memorial Museum in Exeter has donated additional microliths wrapped and labelled by Seidler. On the card to which the Christy Collection pieces were attached, Seidler refers to the site as a cave near Bhainsaur in the Vindhya hills (Fig. 6). This suggests that the site is in a similar location to those of Baghai Khor, Barkor and Morhana Pahar (see entries 5, 8 and 38 respectively). The occurrence of geometric microliths suggests that the pieces come from a Late Mesolithic-Neolithic assemblage.

Christy Collection

20.1 Backed bladelet, 29mm long. Flint. (1926-107). Fig. 7.

20.2 Backed bladelet, with small scalar retouch on the edge opposite the backing, 20mm long. Flint. (1926-108). Fig. 7.

20.3 Lunate, 15mm long. Chalcedony. (1926-149). Fig. 7.

20.4-20.6 Lunates, 16, 15 and 17mm long. Flint. (1926-146, 147, 150). Fig. 7.

20.7-20.8 Lunates, 17 and 18mm long. Jasper. (1926-145, 148). Fig. 7.

20.9 Trapeze, 14mm long. Chalcedony. (1926-135). Fig. 7.

20.10 Trapeze, 22mm long. Flint. (1926-132). Fig. 7.

Royal Albert Memorial Museum, Exeter Collection

20.11-20.12   Lunates, 15 and 12mm long. Chalcedony. (P1993. 7-1. 8-9)

20.13-20.14   Lunates, 19 and 18mm long. Chert. (P1993. 7-1. 10-11)

20.15   Lunate, 16mm long. Flint. (P1993. 7-1. 12)

20.16   Triangular microlith, 18mm long. Isosceles form. Chalcedony. (P1993. 7-1. 13)

20.17   Triangular microlith, 16mm long. Scalene form. Flint. (P1993. 7-1. 14)

21. JABALPUR
(Jabul pur, Jubbulpore, Jubalpur)

In labelling artefacts as from Jabalpur, Carlyle did not specify whether he was referring to collecting localities in the vicinity of the town (23° 10'N, 79° 51'E), now in Madhya Pradesh (Fig. 3) or to the entire 3912 square miles of the eponymous district (Fig. 5), a long narrow alluvial plain running northeast-southwest between 22° 49' and 24° 8'N and 79° 21' and 80° 51'E (Nelson, 1909). Judging by the condition and raw materials of the artefacts, some mixing from different localities has occurred. The larger, more abraded flakes (21.9-21.22) may come from the Pleistocene gravels/Holocene alluviums of the Narmada or Gaur rivers (see Chapter II), whereas the fresher debitage and tools (21.1-21.8) could possibly have been collected at sites on the sandstone cliffs of the Vindyhan outliers to the northwest of the plain.

21.1   Backed and retouched bladelet, 36mm long. The left edge is backed by abrupt retouch struck from the flake margin and a dorsal arête. The opposite convex edge is modified by invasive subparallel retouch which extends around the distal end. Flint. Patinated.

21.2   Bipolar opposed bladelet core, 35mm long. Faceted platform. Chalcedony.

21.3   Single platform bladelet core, 28mm long. Pyramidal form. Chalcedony.

21.4   Single platform bladelet core, 23mm long. Retains stained and abraded cortex around one side. Chalcedony.

21.5   Blade, 31mm long. Chalcedony. Patinated.

21.6   Blade, 33mm long. Chert.

21.7   Debitage flake from blade/bladelet manufacture, 37mm long, lacking proximal end due to ancient break. Curled ventral surface. Chalcedony. Patinated.

21.8   Debitage flake, 14mm long. Chalcedony. Patinated.

ABRADED ARTEFACTS

21.9   Prepared flake, 40mm long. The dorsal surface exhibits a radial scar pattern produced from a single platform. The plain butt is lipped along the ventral edge and the cone of percussion is dispersed. Abrupt, marginal retouch occurs sporadically around the dorsal margin and there is a retouched notch on the distal end, transverse to the butt. The retouch is probably the result of post-depositional damage rather than deliberate modification. Jasper.

21.10 Retouched flake, 48mm long. Abrupt, marginal scalar retouch occurs around the entire perimeter of the flake producing denticulations. The surface condition of the retouch scars contrasts with that of the rest of the flake, suggesting the modification is probably the result of edge damage. Chert.

21.11 Globular core, 43mm maximum dimension, with more than two platforms at different heights on the core. Jasper.

21.12 Core rejuvenation flake, 55mm long, with remnants of cresting and abraded cortex. Jasper.

21.13-21.14 Debitage flakes, 40 and 57mm long. The latter retains cortex on right side. Chert.

21.15-21.16 Debitage flakes, 48 and 66mm long. The latter derives from blade manufacture. Flint. Patinated.

21.17 Debitage flake, 69mm long. Abrupt, marginal stepped edge damage scars occur on the distal end. Jasper.

21.18 Debitage flake, 69mm long. Abrupt, marginal stepped edge damage scars occur on the distal end. Jasper.

21.19 Debitage flake, 58mm long. The conical dorsal surface is modified by radial flake scars struck from a single platform and retains some cortex. Two small removals struck from proximal end of ventral surface. Basalt.

21.20 Debitage flake, 63mm long. Dorsal surface retains a large area of cortex. Basalt.

21.21 Debitage flake, 54mm long. Basalt.

21.22 Knapping fragment, 63mm long. Jasper.

Royal Albert Memorial Museum, Exeter Collection
21.23 Single platform bladelet core, 28mm long, with faceted platform. One face retains remnants of flake removals from a previous reduction sequence. Chert. (P1993. 7-1. 15)

Sturge Collection
21.24 Bladelet, 33mm long. Flint.

22. JATHI, REWA

The location of this site is unknown. No place of this name is listed in the *Rewah State Gazetteer* (Luard, 1907) or the *Imperial Gazetteer of India* (Meyer and Cotton, 1908), although the former work has a reference to a village called Jatri at 25° 3'N, 81° 24'E, southeast of Karwi on the edge of the Vindhyas. Jatri is within an area explored by Carlyle but it has been impossible to determine whether Jathi and Jatri are the same. The artefacts come from a Mesolithic assemblage.

22.1 Bipolar opposed bladelet core, 26mm long. Both platforms faceted. Retains stained, abraded and chattermarked cortex of a river pebble on one side. Flint. Patinated.

22.2 Single platform bladelet core, 23mm long. Pyramidal form. Flint. Patinated.

23. JOGRAN DARI

The location of this site is unknown.

23.1 Single platform bladelet core, 27mm long. Faceted platform. Retains natural surface on one side. Jasper.

24. JONOA PAHAR

The location of this site is unknown.

24.1 Debitage flake, 38mm long. Abraded and edge damaged. Flint. Patinated.

25. KABRAI

Kabrai (25° 23'N, 80° 4'E) is near the road from Maholoa to Banda in the modern state of Uttar Pradesh (Fig. 6). In the gazetteer for Hamirpur (Drake-Brockman, 1909b), a district of British Bundelkhand (see entry 14 above) it was described as an unremarkable amalgam of four villages and shown on the map as situated adjacent to one of the numerous rock outcrops which cluster in a low range in this area. On a paper label glued to the single artefact he found there, Carlyle noted that this find, numbered 1018, came 'from a gravel slope of a hill' adding 'probably Palaeolithic'. Unfortunately, the flake is not diagnostic of any particular period.

25.1 Debitage flake, 42mm long. Slight ancient damage to the distal end. Flint. Patinated.

26. KALINJAR

The hillfort and town of Kalinjar (Fig. 6) is situated at 25° 00'N, 80° 29E, 35 miles south of Banda on the old high road to Nagod in Madhya Pradesh (Drake-Brockman, 1909a). The fort is built on an isolated hill of the Vindhyan Range. This hill, composed of Archaean gneiss overlain by Kaimur sandstone, towers some 700 feet above the southeastern edge of Bundelkhand plain. Carlyle records his finds as coming from south of Kalinjar, which suggests that they may derive from a site or sites on the slopes of the Vindhyas. The fresh condition of the pieces and the mixture of Upper Palaeolithic and Holocene material is commensurate with this. Pant (1982) reports an Upper Palaeolithic site located on a hillock 3 km west of Kalinjar on the right bank of the river Baghain. The large assemblage contains a range of artefacts which may be comparable to those recovered by Carlyle (ibid.). Seven artefacts collected from Kalinjar by Carlyle and marked in his handwriting were acquired as part of the A.W. Franks collection and are listed as number 26.36.

Artefacts numbered 988 and mounted on a card labelled 'arrow points' by Seidler:
26.1 Backed bladelet, 19mm long, lacking proximal end due to ancient break. Chalcedony.

26.2 Nineteen debitage flakes, 14-31mm in length, from blade/bladelet manufacture. Only one retains a small area of cortex on the dorsal surface. Flint and chalcedony. Patinated.

Artefacts numbered 1004:
26.3 Blade, 42mm long, lacking distal end due to ancient break. Possibly Upper Palaeolithic. Chert.

26.4 Eight debitage flakes, varying from 26 to 49mm in length, from blade manufacture. Agate and patinated flint.

Artefacts numbered 1006:

26.5 Four debitage flakes, 33-49mm long, from blade/bladelet manufacture. Two pieces retain some cortex and one has a Siret fracture. Chert.

Artefacts numbered 1011:

26.6 Retouched flake, 47mm long. Fine, direct marginal scalar retouch occurs on the proximal part of the left edge and scalar retouch scars also occur on the proximal end of the ventral surface. Chert.

26.7 Four blades, 36-43mm long. Flint and chert.

26.8 Five debitage flakes, 30-43mm long. One is modified by small thermal fractures on the ventral surface. Flint and chert.

26.9 Debitage flake, 39mm long. Chalcedony.

Artefact marked VII:

26.10 Debitage flake, 22mm long. Chalcedony.

Artefacts marked IX:

26.11 Three debitage flakes, 26-38mm long, from bladelet production. Chert.

Artefacts marked X:

26.12 Retouched blade, 37mm long, modified by abrupt, marginal scalar retouch, possibly edge damage, along both edges and ends. Chert. Patinated.

26.13 Three debitage flakes, 33-38mm long. Chert. Patinated.

Artefacts marked XXVII:

26.14 Two debitage flakes, 22 and 30mm long. Chert. Patinated.

Artefacts marked XXIX:

26.15 Three debitage flakes, 34-37mm long. Chert.

Artefact marked XXXIV:

26.16 Debitage flake, 38mm long. Chert.

Artefacts marked XLIX:

26.17 Two bladelets, both 40mm long. Chert.

26.18 Two bladelets, 38 and 40mm long, both lacking distal ends due to ancient breaks. Chert.

Unmarked artefacts:

26.19 Flake, 45mm long. Struck from a discoidal core. Quartzite.

26.20 Four blades, 50 and 58mm long. One retains stained, abraded and chattermarked cortex at the proximal and distal ends. Chert.

26.21 Two blades, 40 and 43mm long, proximal ends absent due to knapping breaks. Chert.

26.22 Bladelet, 13mm long. Proximal end fragment. Chalcedony.

26.23 Bladelet, 21mm long. Chert.

26.24 Seven bladelet fragments, 9-29mm long. Ancient breaks. Flint.

26.25 Bipolar opposed bladelet core, 45mm long, cylindrical form. Flint.

26.26 Two single platform bladelet cores, 38 and 53mm long. Faceted platforms. Flint and chalcedony.

26.27 Two crested blades, 47 and 53mm long, from blade cores. Chert.

26.28 Four crested blades, 28-48mm long, from bladelet cores. Chert and flint.

26.29 Plunged bladelet, 25mm long, retaining distal end of single platform bladelet core. Chalcedony.

26.30 Two core rejuvenating flakes, 23 and 27mm long, from the faces of bladelet cores. Agate and chalcedony.

26.31 Thirty-eight debitage flakes, 12-18mm long, from bladelet core production. Chalcedony.

26.32 Twenty-nine debitage flakes, 15-60mm long. Only one flake retains a small area of cortex and flakes indicative of the initial stages of core preparation are not represented. Chert and flint.

26.33 Five debitage flakes, 11-35mm long, from bladelet core production. Flint.

26.34 Five knapping fragments. Chert and flint.

26.35 Two natural fragments. Sandstone.

Franks Collection
26.36 Seven debitage flakes, 31-73mm long, from blade production. Chert.

Wellcome Collection
26.37 Three debitage flakes, 25-32mm long, from blade/bladelet production. Chert. (P1982 10-4 4993)

27. KEN RIVER
(Kain, Kanya, Kayan River)

The river Ken rises near Jabalpur in Madhya Pradesh and flows generally north through the Vindyhas to its confluence with the Yamuna in Uttar Pradesh (Fig. 4). Carlyle does not record where along its course he recovered the Mesolithic-Neolithic artefacts in his collection, noting only that he found them in a *nallah* or small watercourse. This may refer to a tributary stream or an ox-bow of the main river which had exposed alluvial deposits in its banks and is commensurate with the abraded condition of the evidently derived artefacts. None of them is made of the agate well known from the Ken in historical times (Nelson, 1909). Artefact numbers 27.2, 27.4, 27.6 and 27.7 are numbered 1028, 986, 985 and 986 respectively.

27.1 Denticulate, 28mm long. Direct denticulate retouch along the shortest, left edge of a flake. Chert. Fig. 26.

27.2 Single platform bladelet core, 33mm long. One end of split tabular pebble utilised for removals. Chert. Fig. 26.

27.3 Split pebble with two flakes removed from dorsal side, 36mm long. Quartzite.

27.4 Debitage flake, 26mm long. Retains small area of cortex. Chalcedony. Fig. 26.

27.5 Debitage flake, 35mm long. Retains small patch of stained, abraded and chattermarked cortex at the distal end. Chert.

27.6 Debitage flake, 33mm long. Retains small area of natural surface at distal end. Flint.

27.7 Debitage flake, 36mm long. Denticulate retouch on the right edge results from subrecent edge damage. Jasper.

28. KODAILI PAHAR

The location of this site is unknown. The artefacts derive from a Holocene assemblage.

28.1 Single platform bladelet core, 26mm long. Retains an area of unworked surface and stained and abraded cortex on one face. Faceted platform. Chert.

28.2 Single platform bladelet core, 40mm long. Removals made around one face only. Opposite face retains patches of stained and abraded cortex and cresting scars, along one edge. Faceted platform. Flint.

28.3 Plunging core rejuvenation flake, 43mm long. Struck from the distal end of the core, the thickened distal end of the flake has detached an area of striking platform. Attempts to rejuvenate this platform from the face of the core had resulted in the removal of small, step terminated flakes. Flint. Patinated.

28.4 Knapping fragment, 38mm long. Heavily abraded with some subrecent edge damage. Chert.

29. LIKNAYA PAHAR
(Laknahar, Likhniya Pahâr)

The location of this site is unknown. A note in Seidler's handwriting wrapped around 29.9 refers to it as a rockshelter in the Vindhya Hills. The artefacts probably derive from a Mesolithic-Neolithic assemblage.

29.1 Bipolar opposed bladelet core, 21mm long. Chalcedony.

29.2 Bipolar opposed bladelet core, 35mm long. Bladelet removals extend around one face. Opposite side modified by a single flake scar. Retains small patches of stained, abraded and chattermarked cortex. Flint.

29.3 Bipolar opposed blade core, 48mm long. Retains cresting along one edge. Faceted platform. Flint.

29.4 Blade, 44mm long, struck from a preparatory ridge of a core. Retains chattermarked cortex at distal end. Chert.

29.5 Debitage flake, 34mm long. Chert.

29.6 Palette, maximum width 41mm, thickness 8mm. Quartzitic sandstone tablet trimmed to a polygonal outline shape by the removal of flakes around its margin.

Christy Collection
29.7 Bipolar opposed bladelet core, 26mm long. Chalcedony. (1926-155). Fig. 7.

29.8 Single platform bladelet core, 18mm long. Jasper. (1926-154). Fig. 7.

Royal Albert Memorial Museum, Exeter Collection
29.9 Single platform bladelet core, 25mm long. Retains cortex on one face. Chert. Patinated. (P1993. 7-1. 16).

Sturge Collection
29.10 Core tablet, 35mm long. Marked Laknahar P. Flint.

30. LURHWÛRU PAHAR, KARWI
(Lurwara pahar, Lurnwara Pahâr)

The gazetteer for Banda District (Drake-Brockman, 1909a) does not list or mention Lurhwûru Pahar, a hill (*Pahar*) at or near Karwi in modern Uttar Pradesh. Karwi is situated near the Paisani river at 25° 12'N, 80° 54'E, on the road between Allahabad and Banda (Fig. 6). It was the main residence of the Maratha chieftain and boasts several temples which may have been of interest to Carlyle. The artefacts he collected here come from a Neolithic or later prehistoric assemblage.

30.1 Palette, maximum width 92mm, thickness 21mm. Quartzitic sandstone tablet trimmed to a polygonal outline shape.

Department of Oriental Antiquities
30.2 Saddle quern, 80mm long. Marked 946. Sandstone. (OA 1880-1194)

31. MAGARDAR
(Magahdah, Magardah)

The location of this site is unknown. Carlyle notes that it was situated in the southeast of Mirzapur District, now in Uttar Pradesh, but no locality of this name is listed in the *Gazetteer of Mirzapur* (Drake-Brockman, 1911). Paper labels in Carlyle's handwriting on 31.6 and 31.7 refer to a 'terrace on scarp' and a 'laterite deposit ... N scarp of Vindhyas', whereas 31.5, a curiously named 'crocodiles tool', was collected from a hill man 'who obtained it from one of the old sites' (see also entry 11). These vague provenances suggest that the artefacts are surface finds from various places around a village. With the exception of the bladelet cores (31.5 and 31.6) which may be Neolithic-Chalcolithic, the other artefacts are not diagnostic of a particular period.

31.1 Flake, 54mm long. Ventral surface shows characteristics of percussion fracture. A percussion fracture scar also occurs on the long axis of the dorsal surface, intruding into an otherwise natural surface. Granite.

31.2 Flake, 66mm long. Deliberate percussion fractures difficult to discern. Probably natural. Quartzite.

31.3 Flake, 78mm long. Natural spall with fortuitous pointed shape. Quartzite.

31.4 Pebble, 60mm long. Natural.

Royal Albert Memorial Museum, Exeter Collection
31.5 Bipolar opposed bladelet core, 20mm long. Chalcedony. (P1993. 7-1. 17)

31.6 Single platform bladelet core, 25mm long. Flint. Patinated. (P1993. 7-1. 18)

Department of Oriental Antiquities

31.7 Digging implement, 125mm long, with crescentic form. Marked 939. Quartzite sandstone. (OA 1880-1193.1)

31.8 Naturally fractured flake, 125mm long. Marked 940. Quartzite. (OA 1880-1193.2)

31.9 Naturally fractured flake, 80mm long. Quartzite. (OA 1880-1197)

32. MAHARAJAPUR, NAGOD

The provenance of this artefact is unknown. Neither the *Imperial Gazetteer of India* (Meyer and Cotton, 1908) nor the gazetteers covering the districts grouped within the nineteenth-century political agency of Baghelkhand list a locality called Maharajapur in Nagod state. Nagod, capital of the former Nagod state, now part of Madhya Pradesh, is situated at 24° 34'N, 80° 31'E on the Amran river. Nagod state covered about 500 square miles and included hills of the Kaimur Range (Fig. 5).

32.1 Rejuvenating flake, 40mm long, struck from the face of a blade core. Previous atttempts to remove blades or rejuvenating flakes resulted in a series of step fractures at the proximal end giving a tanged appearance. Marginal scalar retouch, probably edge damage, extends around the distal end and right edge. Flint. Patinated.

33. MAHRELA CHACKI

On the card to which these artefacts were glued (see entry 11), Seidler indicates that Mahrela Chacki was near Bhainsaur (see entry 2), which is in the modern state of Uttar Pradesh (Fig. 6). No further information about the nature or location of the site is given but the artefacts probably derived from a Mesolithic-Neolithic assemblage.

33.1 Curved backed bladelet, 18mm long, lacking proximal and distal ends due to ancient breaks. Direct, abrupt backing retouch on left side. Flint. Patinated. Fig. 16.

33.2 Curved backed bladelet, 17mm long, lacking proximal end due to ancient break. Direct, abrupt backing retouch on left side. Flint. Patinated.

33.3 Straight backed bladelet, 22mm long, lacking proximal end due to ancient break. Direct, abrupt backing retouch on left side. Flint. Patinated.

33.4 Modified bladelet, 19mm long, lacking distal end due to ancient break. Inverse, marginal retouch consisting of half-moon edge damage scars resembling crushing on the left edge. Chalcedony.

33.5 Bladelet, 18mm long, lacking distal end due to ancient break. Chalcedony.

33.6-33.7 Bladelets, 22 and 21mm long. The latter lacks its proximal end due to an ancient break. Chalcedony and jasper.

33.8-33.10 Bladelets, 17, 20 and 16mm long. The two latter pieces lack distal ends due to ancient breaks. Flint.

34. MANGAWAN

All but one (34.4) of these pieces are labelled 'Mangawan, Paisani River' in Carlyle's handwriting. This indicates that the artefacts were collected around the Mangawan in the southern part of Banda District, southeast of Marfa (see entry 36) on the road from Jabalpur to Karwi (Fig. 6). Carlyle may have stopped here to visit the famous Paisani falls where the river drops over the edge of the Vindhyan Plateau in two cascades before flowing into a deep gorge. The artefacts he recovered appear to have been surface finds, probably of the Neolithic-Chalcolithic period.

34.1 Bipolar opposed bladelet core, 34mm long. One side retains natural pebble surface. Flint. Stained and abraded.

34.2 Debitage flake, 58mm long, struck from the edge of a blade core. Flint. Patinated and slightly abraded.

34.3 Debitage flake, 36mm long. Chert.

34.4 Debitage flake, 38mm long. Flint. Patinated.

34.5 Debitage flake, 39mm long, lacking proximal end due to ancient break. Chert. Patinated.

35. MANOHAR TALI PAHAR

The location of this site is unknown. Ten of the pieces (35.1, 35.3-35.6, 35.8-35.12) were stuck to a card numbered 995 and marked 'Manchar Tali Pahâr near Lauring Par' by Seidler. Neither of these locality names are listed in the *Imperial Gazetteer of India* (Meyer and Cotton, 1908), and they do not appear in the gazetteers for districts of the Central and United provinces or in Ghosh (1989). A paper label on 33.14 refers to the site as a rockshelter. The artefacts appear to derive from an Upper Palaeolithc-Mesolithic assemblage.

35.1 End scraper on the distal end of a blade, 22mm long, lacking proximal end due to ancient break. Flint.

35.2 Partially backed and distally truncated blade, 52mm long. Abrupt backing retouch extends around the butt forming a curved end and straight left edge to the point of a protrusion caused by an inclusion in the flint just below the distal end. The distal end is also modified by abrupt retouch, straightening and partially truncating it. The right edge is modified by minute scalar edge damage scars and slight rounding, suggesting that this may be a knife form. Flint. Fig. 35.

35.3 Straight backed bladelet, 18mm long, lacking proximal and distal ends due to ancient breaks. Chert.

35.4 Modified bladelet, 16mm long, lacking proximal and distal ends due to ancient breaks. Inverse marginal retouch consisting of half-moon crushing edge damage on right edge. Agate.

35.5 Blade, 45mm long, step terminated. Chert.

35.6 Bladelet, 15mm long. Chalcedony.

35.7 Single platform bladelet core, 26mm long. Bladelet scars extend around two-thirds of the circumference. The remaining area shows the scar remaining from the removal of a rejuvenating flake which failed, owing to a large inclusion in the flint. Faceted platform.

35.8 Crested blade, 40mm long, lacking distal end due to ancient break. Retains small patch of stained, abraded and chattermarked cortex. Agate.

35.9 Crested blade, 43mm long. Flint.

35.10 Three debitage flakes, 17, 24 and 21mm long. Only one is complete, the others being damaged by ancient breaks. Flint.

35.11 Natural fragment of ironstone, 36mm long, with a triangular form. Described by Seidler/Carlyle as a spearpoint and numbered 1019.

Department of Oriental Antiquities
35.12 Natural fragment, 63mm long. Marked 576. Sandstone. (OA 1880-1196)

36. MARFA
(Marpha)

The fortified town of Marfa lies just inside Uttar Pradesh at 25° 07'N, 80° 45'E (Fig. 6). Like Kalinjar (see entry 26), 16 miles to the southwest, it is situated on an outlying portion of the Vindyhan Plateau which towers above the surrounding plain (Drake-Brockman, 1909a). The main part of the collection provenanced to Marfa (36.1-36.54) consists of Lower-Middle Palaeolithic artefacts including bifaces, flake tools, and Levallois flakes and debitage. These artefacts are probably made from Archaean gneiss, a metamorphic rock which forms the base of the plateau below the Kaimur sandstone. Although their surfaces have an alteration crust, the edges are fresh and they appear to come from a discrete primary context. This is confirmed by the paper labels written by Carlyle and stuck to pieces 36.63-36.65 provenancing the implements to 'the workshop site - foot of Marpha Hill' and in the case of the 36.69 to the 'oldest bed'. It suggests that Marfa was an important, perhaps stratified locality (see Chapter II) but unfortunately, the site does not seem to have been rediscovered (Ghosh, 1989). By contrast, the artefacts made on blades from cryptocrystalline silicas (36.55-36.61) are abraded, suggesting that they may derive from a different, Holocene source, probably from Mesolithic-Neolithic assemblages. Confirmation of this comes from the labels written by Carlyle on two ringstones (36.67-36.68) of the same period which are provenanced to the Marpha plain, as opposed to Marfa hill.

PALAEOLITHIC ARTEFACTS MADE FROM GNEISS (see also 36.62-36.66)
36.1 Triangular biface, 88mm long, made on a flake. Fig. 27.

36.2 Subtriangular biface, 62mm long.

36.3 Biface, 80mm long. Slightly elongated limande form with a lenticular cross-section but an irregular outline suggesting a pick.

36.4 Partial biface, 92mm long. Subtriangular form made on a flake bifacially flaked around its margins, retaining a large area of natural surface on the dorsal face and unmodified detachment surface on the ventral side. Fig. 27.

36.5 Partial biface, 72mm long. Subtriangular form retaining a large area of natural surface on one face but having a carefully reduced point.

36.6 Bifacial pick, 94mm long. Fig. 28.

36.7 Bifacial pick, 108mm long. Fig. 28.

36.8-36.11 Levallois flakes, 58-86mm long, points of percussion only.

36.12-36.14 Levallois flakes, 64, 87 and 88mm long. Plain butts. Fig. 29.

36.15-36.16 Levallois flakes, 88 and 102mm long. Dihedral butts.

36.17 Levallois flake, 90mm long. Faceted butt.

36.18-36.19 Levallois blades, 135 and 141mm long. Plain butts.

36.20-36.21 Atypical Levallois blades, 97 and 154mm long. Retain areas of natural surface. Plain butts. Fig.30.

36.22-36.32 Atypical Levallois flakes, varying between 53 and 110mm long. Each retains an area of natural surface and has fewer dorsal removals than the typical product. 34.25 has an irregular outline shape and like 34.26 has plunged, causing a slightly curved and thickened distal end. Plain butts.

36.33-36.34 Atypical Levallois flakes, 93 and 118mm long. Both retain areas of natural surface. Dihedral butts.

36.35 Atypical Levallois flake, 119mm long. Retains natural surface, irregular outline shape. Faceted butt.

36.36-36.38 Levallois points, 44, 62 and 97mm long. Show convergent dorsal scar pattern. 36.36 has a faceted butt, the others are plain. Fig. 30.

36.39 Retouched point, 82mm long. Morphological point produced by bifacial, semi-invasive scalar retouch of the proximal end of a divergent, atypical Levallois flake.

36.40 Single, straight side scraper, 83mm long. Marginal scalar retouch on left edge.

36.41 Single, convex side scraper, 98mm long. Marginal scalar retouch on right edge of an atypical Levallois blade. Fig. 29.

36.42 Single convex side scraper, 85mm long. Marginal scalar retouch along right edge of flake from a prepared core.

36.43 Convergent convex side scraper, 85mm long. Marginal, scalar retouch on both edges converging at the tip on the coincident axes of morphology and percussion of a Levallois flake.

36.44 End scraper, 45mm long. Marginal, scalar retouch occurs around the end and right side of a round flake.

36.45 Side and end scraper, 57mm long. Direct marginal scalar retouch around the rounded end of a flake. Inverse scalar retouch on left side.

36.46 Debitage flake, 50mm long, which has removed the conical face of a core produced by the removal of flakes around a single, equatorial platform.

36.47 Six debitage flakes, 45-65mm long, struck from prepared cores. Fig. 31.

36.48 Nine debitage flakes, 66-90mm long, struck from prepared cores. Fig. 31.

36.49 Three knapping fragments. The two latter pieces may be natural. Fig. 31.

ARTEFACTS MADE FROM CRYPTOCRYSTALLINE SILICAS
Palaeolithic:
36.50 Levallois flake, 76mm long. Intermittent, marginal retouch at the distal end, probably edge damage. Faceted butt. Chert. Patinated.

36.51 Atypical Levallois point, 48mm long. Convergent scar pattern. Retains cortex along left edge. Plain butt. Chert. Patinated.

36.52 Failed Levallois flake/blade, 49mm long. Terminated short in a hinge-step fracture. Plain butt. Flint. Patinated.

36.53 Three debitage flakes, 48, 64 and 66mm long. Chert.

36.54 Natural flake or cobble modified by thermal fracture on one face and retaining cortex on the other. Chert.

Mesolithic and later:
36.55 Blade, 37mm long. Jasper.

36.56 Bipolar opposed bladelet core, 29mm long. Removals made around one side of a pebble. Chert. Patinated.

36.57 Debitage flake, 39mm long. From a blade core. Flint. Patinated.

36.58 Three debitage flakes, 32, 36 and 38mm long. Chert.

36.59 Modified pebble 49mm long. Two opposed percussion removals on one face. Another has removed most of the opposite side. No edge or shape has resulted from the removals. Rosey quartz.

36.60 Rubber, 45mm maximum dimension. Plane face of a split pebble worn and slightly polished. Convex side naturally rounded but unmodified. Jasper.

ARTEFACTS MADE FROM OTHER RAW MATERIALS
36.61 Utilised pebble, 46mm maximum dimension. The flat, probably natural facets are abraded and particles of haematite are trapped in interstitial spaces suggesting that it may have been utilised for grinding colouring material. Granite.

Franks Collection
36.62 Three debitage flakes, 40, 42 and 69mm long, from prepared cores. Palaeolithic. Gneiss.

Department of Oriental Antiquities
Palaeolithic:
36.63 Biface, 61mm long, butt absent due to ancient break across the mid-section. Alternate, bifacial removals have detached most of the natural surface. Gneiss. (OA. 1880-1190.1)

36.64 Biface, 59mm long, butt absent due to ancient break across the mid-section. Bifacial removals have detached most of the natural surface and created a triangular tip, with straight, regular edges and a lenticular cross-section. Gneiss. (OA 1880-1190.2)

36.65 Pick, 78mm long, butt absent due to ancient break. Trihedral cross-section formed by the removal of flakes from the perimeter and from each side of a natural arête. Most of the natural surface has been removed. The perimeter edge is regular and high angled (>60°). The tip is rounded. Gneiss. (OA 1880-1190.4)

36.66 Blade, 129mm long, struck from a prepared core. Gneiss. (OA 1880-1190.3)

Neolithic:
36.67 Ringstone fragment, 99mm diameter. An ancient break occurs across the perforation, which has an hour-glass form. Marked 950. Possibly steatite. (OA 1880-1189.1)

36.68   Ringstone fragment, 84mm diameter. An ancient break across the perforation. Marked 951. Possibly steatite. (OA 1880-1189.2)

Wellcome Collection
36.69   Biface, 128mm long. Limande form with a slightly irregular outline and twisted profile. Retains a small patch of natural surface on one side of tip. Marked 550. Gneiss. (P1982.10-4.5009)

37. MIRIR GAON, REWA
(Misitagaon, Misirgaon)

The location of this site is unknown. On a card of artefacts sold to Sir Wilfred Peek and subsequently acquired to form part of the Christy Collection, Seidler records the site as south of Naon in Rewa District.

37.1   Single platform bladelet core, 24mm long. Retains a small area of stained and abraded cortex on one side. Flint.

Christy Collection
37.2   Bipolar opposed bladelet core, 30mm long. Chalcedony. (1926-152). Fig. 7.

Franks Collection
37.3   Bipolar opposed bladelet core, 49mm long. Flint.

38. MORHANA PAHAR
(Morahna Pahar, Morahana Pahar)

The cave or deep rockshelter at Morhana Pahar discovered by Carlyle in 1880 or 1881 was relocated by Bridget Allchin in 1957. It is one of a group of sites on the Vindhyan escarpment overlooking the Ganga Valley about five miles north of Hanmana village near Bhainsaur (Fig. 6) in Mirzapur District, Uttar Pradesh (Allchin, B., 1958). In addition to collecting at the site, Carlyle recorded the rock-paintings (Carlleyle 1885 and see Chapter I) and possibly intended to carry out further work there (Cockburn, 1899). In 1962, R.K. Varma excavated a 1.8 x 1.2 m trench through 60cm of deposit (Varma, 1965). Preliminary reports of this excavation (ibid.; Ghosh, 1965) draw brief comparisons with the findings at Baghai Khor (see entry 5 and Chapter II) noting that no non-geometric microliths were recovered from Morhana Pahar. By contrast, the Carlyle material curated at the British Museum includes only a few geometric microliths (see inventory below), suggesting the possibility of a pre-pottery lithic assemblage at the site. Unfortunately, it is probable that the Carlyle material acquired by Sturge has suffered some mixing. Consequently, only marked pieces are included in this entry, the remainder being listed as unprovenanced (see entry 50).

38.1   Backed bladelet with rounded base, 29mm long, lacking distal end due to ancient break. Flint. Patinated.

38.2   Backed bladelet, 19mm long, lacking distal end due to ancient break. Flint

38.3   Backed bladelet, 21mm long, lacking proximal end due to ancient break. Flint.

38.4   Backed bladelet, 18mm long, lacking proximal end due to ancient break. Flint.

38.5   Backed bladelet, 25mm long, lacking proximal end due to ancient break. Flint.

38.6 Backed bladelet, 18mm long, mid-section fragment. Flint

38.7 Backed bladelet, 16mm long, with ancient damage at the proximal and distal ends. Narrow (<4mm) with triangular cross-section. Flint.

38.8 Curved backed bladelet. 21mm long with slight ancient damage at the distal end. Flint.

38.9 Backed and obliquely truncated bladelet, 17mm long, lacking proximal end due to ancient break. Chalcedony.

38.10 Backed bladelet with retouched distal truncation, 16mm long, lacking proximal end due to ancient break. Flint.

38.11 Backed bladelet with marginal scalar retouch on the edge opposite the backing. 51mm long. Flint.

38.12 Backed bladelet with marginal scalar retouch on the edge opposite the backing. 17mm long. Chalcedony.

38.13 Backed bladelet with alternating, semi-invasive scalar retouch on the edge opposite the backing. 22mm long. Flint.

38.14 Backed bladelet with semi-invasive scalar retouch on the edge opposite the backing. The backed right edge is partially retouched at the proximal end but the backing is otherwise natural, being formed by heavily stained and abraded cortex. 24mm long, lacking distal end due to ancient break. Flint. Patinated.

38.15 Backed bladelet with inverse marginal scalar retouch on the edge opposite the backing. The backed right edge is partially retouched at the proximal end but the backing is otherwise natural, being formed by heavily stained and abraded cortex. 24mm long, lacking distal end due to ancient break. Flint. Patinated.

38.16 Truncated bladelet, 21mm long. The retouched truncation occurs across the proximal end. The distal end is modified by an ancient break. Flint.

38.17 Bladelet with bilateral inverse retouch, 31mm long. Continuous, semi-invasive scalar retouch occurs on both edges of the ventral surface of the parallel-sided bladelet but is not convergent at either end. Chalcedony. Patinated.

38.18 Bladelet with bilateral inverse retouch, 23mm long, with slight ancient damage at the distal end. Semi-invasive scalar retouch along both edges of the ventral surface. Chalcedony.

38.19 Bladelet with bilateral inverse retouch, 20mm long, lacking proximal and distal ends due to ancient breaks. The retouch on the left edge is invasive, that on the right edge, marginal. Flint.

38.20 Bladelet with unilateral inverse retouch, 27mm long. Chalcedony.

38.21 Bladelet with unilateral inverse retouch, 29mm long. Marginal scalar retouch restricted to distal end. Flint.

38.22 Bladelet with unilateral inverse retouch, 30mm long. Flint. Patinated.

38.23 Bladelet with unilateral inverse retouch continuous to ancient break at distal end, 26mm long. Flint.

38.24 Bladelet with unilateral inverse retouch continuous to an ancient break at the distal end, 19mm long. Flint. Patinated.

38.25 Bladelet with unilateral inverse retouch, 35mm long, lacking proximal and distal ends due to ancient breaks. Flint. Patinated.

38.26 Bladelet with unilateral inverse retouch, 17mm long, lacking proximal and distal ends due to ancient breaks. Flint.

38.27 Bladelet with unilateral inverse retouch, 21mm long, lacking proximal and distal ends due to ancient breaks. Flint.

38.28 Bladelet with unilateral inverse retouch, modifying mid-section of right edge. 31mm long, lacking distal end due to ancient break. Flint. Patinated.

38.29 Bladelet with alternate retouch, 20mm long, lacking distal end due to an ancient break. Both the direct and the inverse retouch is semi-invasive and scalar. Chalcedony.

38.30 Bladelet with direct marginal micro-retouch on the distal end, 25mm long. Chalcedony.

38.31 Bladelet with alternate inverse and direct micro-retouch on the left edge and around the distal end respectively, 17mm long, lacking proximal end due to ancient damage. Chalcedony.

38.32 Bladelet with alternate inverse and direct micro-retouch on the left edge and across a proximal end truncation, 52mm long. Flint. Patinated.

38.33 Bladelet with alternate inverse and direct marginal retouch on the left edge and distal end respectively, 18mm long, lacking proximal end due to subrecent break. Flint.

38.34 Bladelet with unilateral micro-retouch, 31mm long, lacking distal end due to ancient break. Flint.

38.35 Bladelet with direct bilateral micro-retouch, 18mm long, lacking proximal and distal ends due to ancient breaks. Retouch may have converged at the distal end. Flint.

38.36 Bladelet with inverse bilateral micro-retouch, 21mm long, lacking distal end due to ancient break. Chalcedony.

38.37 Bladelet with inverse bilateral micro-retouch continuous along the left edge but modifying only the central part of the right side, 29mm long, lacking distal end due to ancient break. Flint. Patinated.

38.38 Bladelet with inverse bilateral micro-retouch on the proximal end of the left edge and the distal end of the right edge, 26mm long, with slight ancient damage at the proximal end. Chalcedony.

38.39 Bladelet with discontinuous inverse bilateral micro-retouch, 28mm long. Flint. Patinated.

38.40 Bladelet with unilateral inverse micro-retouch, 31mm long. Flint. Patinated.

38.41 Bladelet with unilateral inverse micro-retouch, 32mm long, with slight damage at the distal end. Flint.

38.42 Bladelet with alternate micro-retouch, 28mm long. Flint. Patinated.

38.43 Bladelet with alternate micro-retouch, 15mm long, mid-section fragment. Chalcedony.

38.44 Bladelet with bilateral micro-retouch, direct at the narrower proximal end and inverse below the distal end, 25mm long. The ventral surface exhibits opposing conchoidal rings suggesting the core was struck against an anvil. Chalcedony.

38.45 Bladelet with shallow retouched notch at the distal end of the right edge, 34mm long. Flint. Patinated.

38.46 Bladelet with shallow retouched notch at the distal end of the right edge below and interrupted by an ancient break. 27mm long. Flint. Patinated.

GEOMETRIC MICROLITHS

38.47 Scalene triangle/piercer, 13mm long. The point is accentuated by retouch opposite the backing. Flint. Patinated.

MODIFIED BLADES

38.48 Blade with alternating micro-retouch continuous around its margins, 34mm long. The retouch has not modified the irregular outline form of the piece. Chert.

38.49 Blade with sporadic micro-retouch on both edges, 33mm long, mid-section fragment. Chalcedony.

MODIFIED FLAKES

38.50 Simple end scraper, 22mm long. Chert. Heavily patinated and abraded.

38.51 Nosed scraper, 54mm long, on the proximal end of a flake struck from a blade core. Retains stained and abraded cortex along one edge and around the distal end. Flint.

38.52 Retouched point, 26mm long. Direct marginal scalar retouch occurs on the left edge. A shallow retouched notch at the proximal end suggests a rudimentary tang. Flint.

38.53 Retouched point, 24mm long. Direct marginal scalar retouch occurs on the left edge. Chert.

38.54 Retouched point, 15mm long. Direct backing retouch occurs on the left edge and part of the base. Lacks proximal end. Probably the tip of a large backed piece, broken off and reworked. Flint.

38.55 Flake with bilateral micro-retouch at the proximal end, 40mm long. Retains stained and abraded cortex at the distal end. Flint.

38.56 Backed flake, 32mm long. Backing retouch extends along the convex right edge of a flake struck from the face of a bladelet core. Flint.

UNMODIFIED BLANKS

38.57 Blade, 32mm long. Chalcedony.

38.58 Five blades, 28-60mm long, the smallest piece is a proximal end fragment. The longest piece is extremely thin (1.7mm). Chalcedony. Patinated.

38.59 Two blades, 35 and 57mm long, the smaller, patinated piece is a proximal end fragment. Flint.

38.60 Blade, 34mm long, distal end fragment. Chert.

38.61 Two bladelets, 25 and 36mm long. Chalcedony.

38.62 Bladelet, 63mm long. Slightly curled in long profile. Retains a small area of stained and abraded cortex at the distal end. Flint.

38.63 Seven bladelets, 15-36mm long. Flint.

38.64 Six bladelets with slight ancient damage at the distal ends, 23-33mm long. Chalcedony.

38.65 Two bladelets 18 and 30mm long, with slight ancient damage at the distal end. Chert.

38.66 Twenty-three bladelets, 20-35mm long, with slight ancient damage at the distal ends. Flint.

38.67 Two bladelets, 19 and 43mm long, lacking distal ends due to ancient breaks. Jasper.

38.68 Three bladelets, 24, 33 and 38mm long, lacking distal ends due to ancient breaks. Chert.

38.69 Five bladelets, 22-36mm long, lacking proximal ends due to ancient damage. Flint.

38.70 Bladelet, 16mm long, distal end fragment. Chalcedony.

38.71 Bladelet, 21mm long, distal end fragment. Chert.

38.72 Two bladelets, 16mm and 18mm long, distal end fragments. Flint.

38.73 Six bladelets, 17-20mm long, proximal end fragments. Flint.

38.74 Bladelet, 12mm long, proximal end fragment. Green jasper.

38.75 Bladelet, 16mm long, proximal end fragment. Chert.

38.76 Five bladelets, 22-32mm long, lacking proximal and distal ends due to ancient damage. Flint.

38.77 Fifteen bladelets, 8-20mm long, mid-section fragments, including one burnt piece. Flint.

38.78 Bladelet, 18mm long, mid-section fragment. Jasper.

38.79 Bladelet, 21mm long, mid-section fragment. Chert.

DEBITAGE
38.80 Bipolar opposed bladelet core, 31mm long. Faceted platforms. Chert.

38.81-38.84 Bipolar opposed bladelet cores, 25-41mm long. Faceted platforms. Flint.

38.85-38.86 Bipolar opposed bladelet cores, 25mm and 30mm long. Faceted platforms. Jasper.

38.87 Single platform bladelet core, 39mm long. Narrow, elongated form with small platform (5mm wide, 2mm thick). Chalcedony.

38.88-38.89 Single platform cores, 28mm and 31mm long. The latter piece is crazed by burning. Small platforms. Flint.

38.90 Single platform bladelet core, 25mm long. Small platform. Jasper.

38.91-38.92 Single platform bladelet cores, 16 and 21mm long, with markedly pyramidial form. Flint.

38.93-38.100 Single platform bladelet cores, 27-40mm long. Chert.

38.101 Single platform bladelet core, 32mm long. Faceted platform. Jasper.

38.102 Single platform bladelet core, 34mm long. Corticated flint. Chert.

38.103 Single platform bladelet core, 16mm long. Faceted platform and distal end modified by the removal of a core tablet. Flint.

38.104 Single platform bladelet core, 42mm long, with plano-convex cross-section. The plane surface is not fluted by bladelet removals and suggests the use of a split pebble. Faceted platform. Chert.

38.105-38.110 Single platform bladelet cores, 30-48mm long, retaining cortex or unmodified natural surfaces on one side. All have faceted platforms. The staining and abrasion of the cortical faces indicates the use of river pebbles for raw material. Flint.

38.111 Single platform bladelet core, 30mm long. Retains chattermarked cortex on one face. Jasper.

38.112 Single platform core, 40mm long. The platform extends around the margin of the pebble. Blades have been removed from one face and flakes detached around the circumference of the opposite side. Chert.

38.113 Single platform core 43mm long. The platform extends around the margin of the piece. Flakes have been removed from both faces and at least four bladelets from one side. Chert.

38.114 Two core tablets. 14 and 35mm long. Flint.

38.115 Six crested blades, 20-47mm long. Agate-chalcedony.

38.116 Fourteen crested blades, 21-33mm long. Flint.

38.117 Four crested blades, 24-52mm long. Chert.

38.118 Eight plunged blades, 25-43mm long. Flint.

38.119 Plunged bladelet, 32mm long. Chert.

38.120 Flake, 34mm long, struck from the face of a bladelet core. Chalcedony.

38.121 Four flakes, 21-56mm long, struck from faces of blade cores. Chert.

38.122 Five flakes, 28-50mm long. Struck from the faces of blade cores. Flint.

38.123 Flake, 48mm long, struck from the face of a blade core. Corticated flint.

38.124 Flake, 60mm long, struck from the face of a blade core. Chert.

38.125 Thirty-six debitage flakes, 18-41mm long. Only four pieces retain small areas of cortex. All complete. Agate-chalcedony.

38.126 Fifteen debitage flakes, 19-48mm long. One retains approximately 50% cortex on dorsal surface. All complete. Distinctive pink-white banded agate-chalcedony.

38.127 Twelve debitage flakes, 20-50mm long. Only two pieces retain cortex and one of these is an *entamé* flake (Tixier et al., 1980) with an entirely cortical dorsal surface. All complete except for a distal end fragment. Chert.

38.128 Seventy-nine flakes, 15-25mm long, including twelve fragments. Only two pieces retain small areas of cortex, all of the rest derive from the later stages of reduction sequences. Flint.

38.129 Ninety-five debitage flakes, 26-35mm long, including six fragments. Twenty-one pieces retain small areas of cortex. Flint.

38.130 Forty-two debitage flakes, 36-45mm long. Eighteen pieces retain small areas of cortex. Flint.

38.131 Four debitage flakes, 46-55mm long. One piece retains cortex. Flint.

38.132 Thirty-eight debitage flakes, 10-54mm long. Heavily patinated-corticated flint.

38.133 Four debitage flakes, 19-38mm long, including a burnt fragment. The largest piece retains cortex at the distal end and has been struck from a bladelet core. Jasper.

38.134 Thirty-three debitage flakes, 22-50mm long. Chert.

38.135 Debitage flake, 35mm long, struck from a polished implement. Chert.

38.136 Fourteen knapping fragments. Flint.

ARTEFACTS MADE FROM QUARTZITE
38.137 Two blades, 121 and 76mm long.

38.138 Two single platform blade cores, 58 and 77mm long.

38.139 Discoidal flake core, 58mm long. A single platform extends around the entire margin of the piece and flakes have been removed alternately from both faces. Lenticular cross-section.

38.140 Core tablet, 32mm long, with a wedge shape. The thicker end of the wedge exhibits proximal end remnants of blade removal scars.

38.141 Three plunging blades, 39, 88 and 95mm long.

38.142 Twenty-two debitage or knapped fragments, 22-80mm long.

38.143 Three debitage flakes, 27, 40 and 45mm long. Grey quartzite.

OTHER IMPLEMENTS
38.144-38.150 Palettes varying from 38-77mm diameter and from 10-22mm in thickness. The faces of tabular pieces of quartzite provided opposed platforms from which flakes have been removed to give a circular shape. Figs. 32, 33.

38.151-38.152 Palettes, 85 and 92mm long, 50 and 47mm wide respectively. These artefacts have a semicircular form produced in the same manner as the circular and polygonal types. Quartzite. Fig. 33.

Christy Collection
38.153 Backed bladelet, 30mm, lacking distal end due to ancient break. Chalcedony. (1926-140). Fig. 7.

38.154 Curved backed bladelet with abrupt marginal retouch on the opposite edge. 20mm long. Flint. (1926-137). Fig. 7.

38.155 Curved backed bladelet with retouch on the opposite edge at the distal end tip forming a point. 22mm long, with slight ancient damage at the proximal end. Flint. (1926-136). Fig. 7.

38.156 Backed and obliquely truncated bladelet with small scalar retouch on the opposite edge, 17mm long. Chalcedony. (1926-139). Fig. 7.

38.157 Obliquely truncated bladelet, 19mm long. Flint. (1926-138). Fig. 7.

38.158 Lunate, 14mm long. Chalcedony. (1926-133). Fig. 7.

38.159 Lunate, 15mm long. Chalcedony (1926-141). Fig. 7.

38.160 Lunate, 22mm long. Chert. (1926-132). Fig. 7.

38.161 Triangle, 18mm long, isosceles form. Chalcedony. (1926-142). Fig. 7.

38.162 Triangle, 18mm long, scalene form. Chalcedony. (1926-143). Fig. 7.

38.163 Nineteen bladelets, 18-31mm long. Chalcedony and flint. (1926.112-129 and 144). Fig. 7.

38.164 Single platform bladelet core, 31mm long. Chert. (1926-153). Fig. 7.

Franks Collection

38.165 Backed bladelet, 34mm long. Abrupt backing retouch on leading edge. Flint. Patinated.

38.166 Bipolar opposed bladelet core, 57mm long. One platform retains stained and chattermarked cortex. Flint. Patinated.

Royal Albert Memorial Museum, Exeter Collection

38.167 Backed bladelet, 22mm long, lacking proximal end due to ancient break. Chalcedony. (P1993. 7-1. 19)

38.168 Backed bladelet, 23mm long. Flint. Patinated. (P1993. 7-1. 20)

38.169 Bladelet with bilateral inverse micro-retouch, 26mm long. Chalcedony. (P1993. 7-1. 21)

38.170 Bladelet with bilateral inverse retouch, 24mm long, lacking proximal end due to ancient break. Chalcedony. (P1993. 7-1. 22)

38.171 Bladelet with unilateral inverse micro-retouch, 22mm long. Chalcedony. (P1993. 7-1. 23)

38.172 Bladelet with unilateral inverse retouch, 26mm long. Chalcedony. (P1993. 7-1. 24)

38.173 Bladelet with unilateral inverse retouch, 24mm long. Chert. (P1993. 7-1. 25)

38.174 Bladelet with unilateral inverse retouch, 35mm long, lacking distal end due to ancient break. Chert. (P1993. 7-1. 26)

38.175-38.176 Lunates, 16 and 18mm long. Flint. (P1993. 7-1. 27-28)

38.177 Lunate, 14mm long. Jasper. (P1993. 7-1. 29)

38.178-38.179 Triangular microliths, 14 and 15mm long. Isosceles form. Chalcedony. (P1993. 7-1. 30-31)

38.180 Triangular microlith, 16mm long. Scalene form. Chalcedony. (P1993. 7-1. 32)

38.181 Triangular microlith, 26mm long. Scalene form. Chert. (P1993. 7-1. 33)

38.182 Triangular microlith, 21mm long. Scalene form. Flint. Patinated (P1993. 7-1. 34)

38.183 Seven bladelets, 18-28mm long, one lacking distal end due to ancient break. Chalcedony (P1993. 7-1. 35)

38.184 Two bladelets, 22 and 27mm long. Flint. Patinated (P1993. 7-1. 36)

38.185 Three bladelets, 22-27mm long. Flint (P1993. 7-1. 37)

38.186 Five bladelet fragments, less than 5mm long. Chalcedony and flint. (P1993. 7-1. 38)

Sturge Collection

38.187 Backed bladelet with inverse scalar retouch on the left edge opposite the backing, 24mm long, lacking distal end due to subrecent break. Flint. Patinated.

38.188 Bilaterally backed bladelet, 23mm long, lacking proximal and distal ends due to ancient breaks. Flint. Patinated.

38.189 Obliquely truncated and retouched bladelet, 30mm long, lacking the proximal end due to an ancient break. The retouched truncation occurs at the distal end and the left edge is modified by micro-retouch. Flint. Patinated.

38.190 Bladelet with unilateral inverse retouch, 28mm long. Flint.

38.191 Bladelet with bilateral inverse retouch, 24mm long, lacking distal end due to ancient break. Flint.

38.192 Triangular microlith, scalene form, 13mm long, with slightly damaged points. Chalcedony.

38.193 Eleven bladelets, 20-30mm long. Five complete, the remainder lack proximal or distal ends due to ancient breaks. Chalcedony and flint.

38.194 Five debitage flakes, 26-30mm long, from bladelet manufacture. Flint.

Wellcome Collection

38.195 Bladelet with unilateral inverse retouch, 26mm long, lacking proximal end due to ancient break. (P1982. 10-4.5010)

38.196 Eleven bladelets, 23-28mm long, all but one with ancient breaks at the proximal and/or distal ends. Chert and flint. (P1982.10-4.5010)

38.197 Ten debitage flakes, 20-32mm long, from bladelet manufacture. Chert and flint. (P1982.10-4.5010)

Department of Oriental Antiquities

38.198 Modified stone, 232mm long, struck or split from a larger block. Semicircular outline, thicker at centre than at perimeter. Described by Carlyle as a digging implement and although the weight, form and absence of edge damage would seem to preclude this, it is similar to a smaller example (12.22) from Bharkhach which he saw in use (see entry 12). Marked 938. Quartzite. (OA 1880-1191.1)

39. MORETHA PAHAR

The location of this site is unknown. The artefacts appear to come from an Upper Palaeolithic assemblage. 39.1 is marked XIII.

39.1 Backed bladelet, 50mm long, distal end absent due to ancient break. Marginal, abrupt backing retouch on right edge. Slight edge damage on the left edge. Flint. Fig. 35.

39.2 Blade, 55mm long, lacking distal end due to ancient break. Retains small area of stained and abraded cortex at distal end. Flint.

39.3 Bipolar opposed bladelet core, 47mm long. Retains a small area of stained and abraded cortex and cresting on one side. Flint. Patinated.

39.4 Bipolar opposed bladelet core, 37mm long. Retains stained and abraded cortex on one side. Chert.

39.5 Bipolar opposed bladelet core, 28mm long. Flint.

40. NAGRI KA PAHAR, REWA

The location of this site is unknown. No place of this name is listed in Luard (1907) or the *Imperial Gazetteer of India* (Meyer and Cotton, 1908). The two artefacts probably came from a Holocene context.

40.1 Bipolar opposed bladelet core, 41mm long. Retains stained and abraded cortex and cresting scars on one face. Chert.

40.2 Single platform bladelet core, 35mm long. Chert.

41. NAO GAON

The location of this site is uncertain. The *Imperial Gazetteer of India* (Meyer and Cotton, 1908) lists Naogaon as a village in East Bengal and Assam which also lent its name to the surrounding subdivision. However, this is unlikely to be the source of the Upper Palaeolithic-Mesolithic artefact found by Carlyle because it is off the track of his tours. More probably, the name may be a misspelling of Nowgain, a village in Rewa State (Luard, 1907) situated at 24° 29'N, 82° 23'E, 10 miles south of Sihawal on the Vindhyan escarpment forming the southern edge of the Son Valley (Fig. 6). Nowgain was within Carlyle's reach. Naogaon, Rewa is also referred to as the location of Gâdur Hâta (see entry 18) in the register of the National Museums of Scotland.

41.1 Backed and obliquely truncated bladelet, 38mm long. Marginal abrupt backing retouch on left edge and truncating distal end. Small scalar retouch on the proximal end of the right edge. Flint. Fig. 35.

42. NAON KA PAHAR
(Naon Paka)

The provenance of the Neolithic artefacts labelled Naon Ka Pahar is unknown.

42.1 Saw, 30mm long, lacking proximal and distal ends due to ancient breaks. Marginal abrupt retouch on left edge. Right edge denticulated by a series of retouch notches. Flint. Patinated. Fig. 35.

42.2 Bipolar opposed bladelet core, 44mm long. Faceted platforms. Flint.

43. NARMADA VALLEY
(Narbada, Nerbuda)

The Narmada river is one of the major rivers of peninsular India (Figs. 1, 4). It rises on the Armarkantak Plateau in Madhya Pradesh and flows some 1300 km in a generally westerly direction to reach the Arabian Sea near Bharuch on the Gulf of Cambay (Ghosh, 1989). The river occupies a tectonically formed rift in which deep alluvial deposits have accumulated (ibid.). Stone artefacts and mammalian fossils have been reported from many sites in the valley (ibid. and Chapter II). A flake (43.17) found by Carlyle and given to the British Museum by Edward Bidwell (1905. 10-23.2) is recorded as having been found with a fossil jawbone of an ox but the latter has not survived. Unfortunately, Carlyle does not specify where he collected but it is most likely to have been in the region of Jabalpur where he also found artefacts in the Gaur Valley (see entry 19 above). The abraded tools and debitage in the collection include Lower and Middle Palaeolithic pieces which must have been derived in Middle-Late Pleistocene gravels, as well as Upper Palaeolithic-Mesolithic blades and bladelets from Late Pleistocene-Early Holocene contexts.

43.1 Biface, 66mm long. Discoidal form, made on a flake. Irregular outline and edge. Jasper. Slightly patinated. Fig. 34.

43.2 Pick, 88mm long. Trihedral form converging to a point from a thicker butt. Chert. Abraded.

43.3 Bifacially modified cobble, 60mm long, with flakes removed from two platforms: one extending around the perimeter of the object, the other formed by the removal of a flake from one end of the cobble. Retains small area of cortex on one face. Chert. Abraded.

43.4 Flake from a prepared core, 73mm long. Chert. Patinated and stained. Fig. 34.

43.5 Flake from a prepared core, 63mm long. Chert.

43.6 Flake from a prepared core, 45mm long. Convergent dorsal scar pattern. Faceted butt. Jasper.

43.7 Two debitage flakes, 38 and 47mm long. The latter retains cortex on the dorsal surface. Agate. Abraded.

43.8 Debitage flake, 43mm long. Chalcedony.

43.9 Four debitage flakes, 46-67mm long, modified by marginal abrupt scalar retouch, resulting from natural edge damage. Chert. Heavily abraded.

43.10 Four debitage flakes, 26-45mm long, from prepared cores. Includes one flake given to Edward Bidwell and registered 1905. 10-23.2. Chert. Abraded.

43.11 Six debitage flakes, 37-65mm long. Flint. Patinated and heavily abraded.

43.12 Three debitage flakes, 46-56mm long. Jasper. Heavily abraded.

43.13 Debitage flake, 57mm long. Retains cortex over most of dorsal surface which shows remnants of two previous removals. Fine silt still adheres to dorsal face. Flint. Fresh.

43.14 Knapping fragment, 45mm long. Pebble partially modified by percussion. Chalcedony. Abraded.

43.15 Single platform bladelet core, 46mm long. Retains part of the ventral surface of the flake from which it has been reduced and cortex at the distal end. Chalcedony. Abraded.

43.16 Single platform bladelet core, 50mm long. Retains abraded and chattermarked cortex of the pebble from which it has been reduced on one side and around the distal end. Cresting scars present on one side. Flint. Patinated and slightly stained.

43.17 Single platform bladelet core, 36mm long. Retains abraded and chattermarked cortex of the pebble from which it has been reduced. Flint. Patinated.

43.18 Core tablet, 60mm long. Struck from the platform of a blade core. Chert. Abraded.

43.19 Crested blade, 73mm long. Jasper. Abraded.

43.20 Debitage flake, 63mm long. Struck from the side of a blade core. Retains large area of cortex and a series of bladelet removal scars. Flint. Abraded.

43.21 Rubber, 53mm long. Pebble with an unmodified convex surface retaining cortex and a plane face worn smooth and flat by deliberate abrasion. A slight polish has developed around the plane surface margin. Haematite.

43.22 Four naturally modified stone flakes.

Wellcome Collection
43.23 Debitage flake, 86mm long. Collected 28 September 1887. (P1982.10-4.5011)

43.24 Debitage flake, 72mm long. Marked 581. Marble. (P1982.10-4.5011)

44. NARO, REWA
(Naro Hill, Riwa)

The provenance of this collection of Upper Palaeolithic artefacts from an apparently unmixed assemblage is unknown. Luard (1907, p.10) refers to Naro Fort in his historical introduction to the *Rewah State Gazetteer* but he notes only that this place was seized by the Parihars in the fourteenth century and gives no location. One of the artefacts is marked 'Naro Hill Kaimurs' in Carlyle's handwriting but no more precise reference to the whereabouts of this site has been traced. Artefact number 44.9 is marked XVI, numbers 44.24, 26 and 27 are marked XXXIV and 44.4 and 44.8 are marked XLIII and LVII respectively. 44.3 and 44.13 are numbered 1007a and 1008 in the manner used on Seidler's cards.

44.1 Backed blade, 52mm long, lacking proximal end due to ancient break. Abrupt backing retouch on the left edge. Chert. Fig. 35.

44.2 Backed blade, 55mm long. Abrupt backing retouch on the right edge extending from pointed proximal end, possibly the morphological tip, to the distal end. Chert. Fig. 35.

44.3 Backed blade, 64mm long. Struck from a bipolar opposed core. A remnant of one of the platforms forms the distal end of the blade, as well as forming the butt. Abrupt backing retouch on the left edge. Chert.

44.4 Backed blade, 48mm long, lacking proximal end due to ancient break. Abrupt backing retouch on the right edge. Chert. Fig. 35.

44.5 Backed bladelet, 47mm long, lacking distal end due to subrecent break. Abrupt backing retouch on the left edge. Chert. Fig. 35.

44.6 Backed and truncated bladelet, 55mm long. Abrupt backing retouch truncates narrow (4mm) proximal end and extends along the right edge, slightly truncating the distal end. Recent edge damage notch on left edge. Chert.

44.7 Bilaterally backed bladelet, 50mm long, lacking distal end due to ancient break. Abrupt backing retouch extends from the pointed proximal end to just above the mid-point of the blade. Chert. Fig. 35.

44.8 Modified blade, 53mm long, lacking distal end due to subrecent break. Sporadic marginal scalar retouch on both edges, probably edge damage. Chert.

44.9 Blade, 48mm long. Flint.

44.10 Blade, 47mm long, lacking proximal and distal ends due to ancient breaks. Flint.

44.11-44.12 Blades, 60 and 64mm long. Flint. Stained.

44.13-44.15 Blades, 47, 64 and 70mm long. Chert.

44.16 Bipolar opposed bladelet core, 36mm long. Chert.

44.17 Core tablet, 33mm long. Detached platform of bipolar opposed bladelet core. Chert.

44.18 Crested blade, 73mm long. Chert.

44.19-44.20 Crested blades, 38 and 51mm long, lacking distal and proximal ends respectively due to ancient breaks. Chert.

44.21 Plunged flake, 38mm long, from a blade core. Chert.

44.22 Debitage flake, 28mm long. Chalcedony.

44.23 Debitage flake, 35mm long. Flint. Patinated.

44.24-44.26 Debitage flakes, 30, 30 and 48mm long. Chert.

44.27-44.29 Debitage flakes, 47, 40 and 52mm long. Chert.

44.30 Knapped fragment, 37mm long, with at least one percussion removal. Granite.

Franks Collection
44.31 Blade, 56mm long. Chert.

45. PARARI, PATHAR-KACHHAR
(Patur Kachar, Pâtur ka)

The provenance of these few derived Mesolithic artefacts lies in the rugged country on the edge of the Vindhyas, about 10 miles north of Kalinjar near Baraunda (see entry 24) at 25° 03'N, 80° 33'E (Fig.6). In Carlyle's day, Parari was in the petty state of Baraunda, administered by the political agent of Baghelkhand. This state, now part of Madhya Pradesh, was also known as Pathar-Kachhar, a name derived from its position on the skirts of the Vindhyas (*Imperial Gazetteer of India*, Meyer and Cotton, 1908, volume 6).

45.1 Debitage flake, 69mm long, from a prepared core. Slightly stained. Chert. Patinated.

45.2 Debitage flake, 55mm long. Retains area of stained and abraded cortex. Chert.

45.3 Core tablet, 23mm long, step terminated. Struck from the faceted platform of a bladelet core. Chert.

46. PARTAP GANJ, REWA
(Partap Gang, Partupgunj, Pertap Ganj, Pratapganj)

This locality was situated in the eastern part of Rewa state at 24° 43'N, 82° 06'E (Fig. 6). The fresh condition of the Mesolithic/Neolithic artefacts suggest that the site may have been a rockshelter.

46.1 Bipolar opposed blade core, 70mm long. Retains patch of stained, abraded and chattermarked cortex on one face. Flint.

46.2 Single platform blade core, 64mm long. Retains stained, abraded and chattermarked cortex on distal end. Flint.

46.3 Bipolar opposed bladelet core, 23mm long. Chalcedony.

46.4 Bipolar opposed bladelet core, 28mm long. Chalcedony.

46.5-46.7 Bipolar opposed bladelet cores, 18-38mm long. Flint.

46.8-46.11 Single platform bladelet cores, 30-49mm long. All have a markedly pyramidal shape. Flint.

46.12 Crested blade, 46mm long. Chalcedony.

Franks Collection
46.13 Retouched point, 47mm long. Made on a blade with bilateral convergent marginal scalar retouch. Jasper.

47. RAJAPUR/RAJPURA REWA

The provenance of these artefacts is unknown. There are several towns and villages of this name in Uttar and Madhya Pradesh but Carlyle provides no clues as to the source of his finds.

47.1 Core rejuvenation flake, 40mm long, struck from platform of a bladelet core. Inverse, marginal edge damage on right side. Flint.

Franks Collection
47.2 Single platform bladelet core, 42mm long. Chalcedony.

48. SARSI
(Pathar-Kachhar, Pâtur Kacha)

The exact location of this site is unknown but Carlyle's handwriting on the artefact records it as being in Patur Kachur (Päthar Kachār) or Baraunda, a petty state of 218 square miles on the edge of the Vindhyas, just north of Kalinjar (Fig. 6, and see entry 45 above).

48.1 Debitage flake, 67mm long. Chert.

49. VINDHYA HILLS

The Vindhya Hills stretch for some 1000 km across Central India from Jobat in Gujarat to Sassarem in Bihar, forming a divide between the Ganga Basin and the Deccan Plateau (Fig. 4). Carlyle was particularly active in the eastern part of this area around Mirzapur, Allahabad, Banda and Rewa where cave, rockshelter and open sites occur along the scarps formed by the denudation of a series of plateaux. Many of the sites already listed fall within this region and it is unfortunate that in apparently attempting to establish a typology for the region, Carlyle, or perhaps Seidler, seems to have erased the provenances of this material. The artefacts numbered 49.1-49.15 are in a fresh condition and appear to come from a discrete Upper Palaeolithic context. They are made from a distinctive, fawn-coloured chert. The remaining material probably derives from Mesolithic-Neolithic assemblages, with the exception of 49.21, which is probably Lower-Middle Palaeolithic, possibly from Marfa (see entry 36). The artefacts are made from cryptocrystalline silicas unless otherwise stated.

49.1 Single convex side scraper, 82mm long. Made on a flake. Semi-invasive subparallel retouch extends along the left edge. Retains cortex on the right edge.

49.2 Transverse scraper, 57mm long. Made on a flake retaining cortex along each margin. Semi-invasive scalar retouch extends across the broad distal end.

49.3-49.8 Single platform blade cores, 60-88mm long. Four retain fresh cortex on one face whereas on 49.7 this has been removed by the detachment of flakes. On 49.8, the surface not utilised for blade removals exhibits remnants of the ventral surface of a flake.

49.9 Single platform flake core, 55mm wide, 40mm high. Flakes removed alternately from a marginal platform extending around the diameter of the piece producing a conical form. Retains cortex at its apex.

49.10 Plunging blade, 67mm long, with cortex around the distal end.

49.11 Debitage flake, 57mm long, 36mm thick struck from a flake core with more than one platform.

49.12 Seven debitage flakes, 45-102mm long. Struck from flake cores.

49.13 Modified pebble, 42mm long. Retains cortex except at one end from which a small number of flakes have been detached.

49.14 Modified pebble, 66mm long. Retains cortex around margin. Flakes have been randomly detached from both faces. Abraded.

49.15 Natural fragment.

OTHER PROVENANCES

Marked 1023:
49.16 Three bladelet cores.

Marked 1027:
49.17 Eight bladelet cores.

Marked 1028:
49.18 Three bladelet cores.

Unnumbered:
49.19 Ten variously retouched flakes.

49.20 Five bladelets with micro-retouch.

49.21 Blade, 124mm long, from a prepared core. Possibly Middle Palaeolithic. Quartzite.

49.22 Twenty-two unmodified bladelets.

49.23 114 bladelet cores.

49.24 Sixty-three debitage flakes deriving from bladelet manufacture.

49.25 Thirty debitage flakes.

49.26 Sixteen knapping fragments.

49.27 Three debitage flakes, a knapping fragment and a natural pebble. Quartzite.

49.29 Palette, 24mm across with plano-convex cross-section. Unmodified around margin.

49.29 Pebble, polished and striated by abrasion on one face.

49.30 Four polished red pebbles.

Sturge Collection
49.31 Bladelet core.

Wellcome Collection
49.32 Four debitage flakes from bladelet manufacture. P1982.10-4.4654

50. UNPROVENANCED

Due to the break-up of Carlyle's collection, many pieces have lost their provenances. It is also evident that collectors such as Sturge liked to form display case groups of particular types of tool or raw material regardless of provenance. Regrettably, this has caused mixing and, although many of the retouched tools and microliths probably come from stratified sites such as Morhana Pahar and Baghai Khor, there is no certainty as to their source and much archaeological information has consequently been lost. The artefacts concerned are predominantly Upper Palaeolithic and Mesolithic and are all made of cryptocrystalline silicas.

Marked 997:
50.1 Two microliths and a debitage flake.

Marked 980:
50.2 Microlith and two bladelets.

Marked 989:
50.3 Retouched blade and debitage flake.

Marked 990:
50.4 Two bladelet fragments.

Marked 992:
50.5 Two microliths, bladelet core, core tablet and one debitage flake.

Marked 996:
50.6 Debitage flake.

Marked 1005:
50.7 Debitage flake.

Marked 1010:
50.8 Three debitage flakes.

Marked 1012:
50.9 Debitage flake.

Marked 1013:
50.10 Three debitage flakes.

Marked 1017:
50.11 Core tablet and three debitage flakes.

Marked 1021:
50.12 Bladelet core and nine debitage flakes.

Marked IIb:
50.13 Two microliths and a debitage flake.

Marked VIII:
50.14 Microlith and nine bladelets.

Marked XII:
50.15 Three microliths and four bladelets.

Marked XXVI:
50.16 Four bladelets.

Marked XLIV:
50.17 Nine bladelets.

Marked LIV:
50.18 Microlith and five bladelets.

Unmarked:
50.19 Nine microliths.

50.20 Sixteen bladelets.

50.21 Seven blades.

50.22 Ninety-six debitage flakes.

Christy Collection
South of Mirzapur District:
50.23 Three lunates. (1926-109, 110, 111). Fig. 7.

Franks Collection
50.24 Three bladelets and ten bladelet cores including pieces marked III, XI, XXV and LVI.

Royal Albert Memorial Museum, Exeter Collection
Wrapped in paper labelled 'south Mirzapur District, fields' by Seidler:
50.25 Two backed bladelets. (P1993.7-1.39 and 44)

Sturge Collection
These artefacts were mixed with marked material from Baghai Khor (see entry 5) and Morhana Pahar (see entry 38):
50.26 Microlith and 122 bladelets and debitage flakes.

50.27 376 microliths and retouched blades.

50.28 139 geometric microliths.

50.29 154 bladelets and bladelet fragments.

50.30 Three bladelet cores.

50.31 Twenty-eight crested blades.

50.32 315 debitage flakes from bladelet manufacture.

APPENDIX I: CARLYLE MATERIAL IN OTHER MUSEUMS IN BRITAIN AND IRELAND

As described in Chapter I, Carlyle's collection was split up and sold to various collectors and museums in England, Scotland, Ireland and North America. Efforts have been made to trace material in museums in Britain and Ireland based on references to buyers in Seidler's letters. The following appendix refers to collections located in this way but may not be exhaustive because there is no record of artefacts sold or given away by Carlyle himself or by Charles Seidler. The numbers in brackets are those given to sites listed in this catalogue.

Cambridge University Museum of Archaeology and Anthropology

Number of objects: 20 and 44
Accession numbers: 1922. 1362-1371; Z37689, Z38190-38196, Z38495-38496, Z38498-38499
Collection: Sir C. H. Read and unknown.
How obtained: Sold by Seidler to Read, donated by Read.
Sites represented: Banda (7), Gâdur Hata (18), Ghârwa Pahari (20), Jabalpur (21), Kalingar (26), Kottirah (-), Karwi (-), Liknaya Pahar (29), Morahna Pahar (38), Naro Hill (44).

Dublin: The National Museum of Ireland

Number of objects: 51
Accession numbers: 693-1892. 1-27
Collection: Carlyle.
How obtained: Purchased from Seidler.
Sites represented: Baghi Khor (5), Banda (7), Bharkhacha (12), Ghârwa Pahari (20), Morahna Pahar (38), Vindhya Hills (49).

Edinburgh: The National Museums of Scotland

Number of objects: 220
Accession numbers: 1890-1. 1-26
Collection: Carlyle.
How obtained: Purchased from Seidler.
Sites represented: Baghai Khor (5), Dhir (17), Gâdur Hata (18), Kalinjar (26), Manohar Tali Pahar (35), Morahna Pahar (38), Naro (44).

Liverpool: Liverpool Museum

According to a letter dated 1892 from Seidler to Colonel MacEnery in Dublin (see Chapter I), some Carlyle material had been sold to an unspecified purchaser in Liverpool. These objects were not purchased by or deposited in Liverpool Museum and their whereabouts are unknown (C. Baird, pers. comm.).

Oxford: Ashmolean Museum

Number of objects: uncertain.
Accession numbers: 1927. 6114 and 1927. 6115
Collection: Sir John Evans.
How obtained: Some of the microliths and micro-debitage in the Evans collection may have been purchased from Carlyle through Seidler (see Chapter I). However, it is now impossible to differentiate objects collected by Carlyle from those which Evans may have obtained from other sources because he amalgamated them into typological groups, apparently without keeping a record of their origins.
Sites represented: Banda (7); Vindhya Hills (49).

Oxford: Pitt-Rivers Museum

Number of objects: 50
Accession numbers: Not numbered.
Collections: Carlyle; H. Balfour and S. G. Hewlett.
How obtained: Purchased from Seidler in 1892; purchased from Seidler by Balfour and donated in 1901; purchased from Seidler by Hewlett, who sold them on in 1907.
Sites represented: Baghai Khor (5); Banda (7); Bharkacha (12); Gâdur Hata (18); Ghârwa Pahâri (20); Morahna Pahar (38).

Salisbury: Salisbury and South Wiltshire Museum

In a letter dated 1892 to Colonel MacEnery in Dublin (see Chapter I), Seidler refers to artefacts having been sold to Salisbury. During the last quarter of the nineteenth century, interest in stone implements was such that there may have been several actual or potential purchasers. Amongst these the strongest contenders may have been E.T. and/or F. Stevens, successive curators of the Blackmore Museum, which opened in 1868. However, E.T. Stevens' descriptions of the Blackmore collections (Stevens, 1868, 1870) refer only to artefacts from Jabalpur collected by Lieutenant Swiney. Other records of Indian artefacts incorporated from the Blackmore into the Salisbury and South Wiltshire Museum relate to material collected outside Carlyle's territory and transferred in 1975 to Birmingham City Museum and Art Gallery (P. R. Saunders, pers comm.).

Sheffield: Sheffield City Museum

Artefacts sold, according to Seidler, to Sheffield were not purchased by or deposited in the City Museum and their whereabouts are unknown (J. Parsons, pers. comm.).

APPENDIX 2: STONE AGE COLLECTIONS FROM INDIA, PAKISTAN AND SRI LANKA IN THE BRITISH MUSEUM

Compiled by Tracy Newman

The following list of collectors and sites is provided as a reference to the collections from India, Pakistan and Sri Lanka held in the Department of Prehistoric and Romano-British Antiquities of the British Museum.

The inventory is arranged alphabetically with the name of the collector preceding listings by site. Each site entry records the site name and the district and state in which it is located. This is followed by the name of the collector, excavator or original source when applicable, and the archaeological period of the material. If the material has been assigned a British Museum registration number this is included at the end of the site entry. The registration number consists of the year, month and day of the month when the material was accessioned, followed by the artefact number, for example 1933.7-6.83. The registration number does not always indicate the total number of objects in the collection as groups of artefacts such as debitage flakes are sometimes assigned a single bulk number. References to published work relating to the collectors and their sites or collecting areas are given at the end of each inventory.

The site names recorded for each entry are those given by the collector; whenever possible these have been given a full provenance to district and state or province. The sources used to locate these sites are the same as those mentioned in the introduction to the catalogue. If a site has not been located, this is stated and if necessary explanatory comments have been added. This relates most commonly to site names that are ambiguous or that are too vague to be provenanced to a specific location. In some cases it has been possible to suggest the general area in which the site may be located, based upon knowledge of the collectors and their collecting areas. The spelling of some unlocated site names may be incorrect or antiquated. In some of these cases, localities within the general area which have similar names have been suggested as possible provenances but these remain to be checked by more detailed local research.

INDIA

Breeks, J. W.
    Tripati. Specific location unknown but may be North Arcot district, Tamil Nadu. Lower/Middle Palaeolithic.

Bruce Foot, R.
    Madras, Tamil Nadu. Lower/Middle Palaeolithic.

    Nellore. Specific provenance unknown, may refer to the town or district of Nellore in Andhra Pradesh. Lower/Middle Palaeolithic.
    (See also: entries listed under *Geological Museum Transfer*.)

Cammiade, L. A.
    Attamtangal, Chingleput District, Tamil Nadu. Lower/Middle Palaeolithic. 1933.7-6.83

    Dhone, Kurnool District, Andhra Pradesh. Lower/Middle Palaeolithic. 1933.7-6.32-47

Giddalur, Kurnool District, Andhra Pradesh. Lower/Middle Palaeolithic. 1933.7-6.18-31

Gundla-Bhramhesvaram, Kurnool District, Andhra Pradesh. Lower/Middle Palaeolithic. 1933.7-6.48-61

Isukka-Gundham. Specific location unknown but may be in Madras Presidency. Lower/Middle Palaeolithic. 1933.7-6.81

Kollegal, Mysore District, Karnataka. Lower/Middle Palaeolithic. 1933.7-6.73-76

Mambakkan, Chingleput District, Tamil Nadu. Lower/Middle Palaeolithic. 1933.7-6.89

Manjankarani, Chingleput District, Tamil Nadu. Lower/Middle Palaeolithic. 1933.7-6.62-65,77-80

Perumuchi-chi. Specific location unknown but may be in Madras Presidency. Lower/Middle Palaeolithic. 1933.7-6.87

Puliyamangalam. Unable to locate under this spelling. An alternative may be Paliamangalam, located in the North Arcot District of Tamil Nadu. Lower/Middle Palaeolithic. 1933.7-6.88, 90

Rajahmundry, East Godavari District, Andhra Pradesh. Lower/Middle Palaeolithic. 1933.7-6.85

Red Hills, Chingleput District, Tamil Nadu. Lower/Middle Palaeolithic. 1933.7-6.84

Timampuram. Unable to locate under this spelling. An alternative may be Timmapuram, located in the Kurnool District of Andhra Pradesh. Lower/Middle Palaeolithic. 1933.7-6.82

Yerra-Konda-Palem. Located near the eastern entrance of the Dornala-Atmakur Pass, across the Nallamalla Mountains, Andhra Pradesh. Lower/Middle Palaeolithic. 1933.7-6.1-17,86

Unprovenanced. Lower/Middle Palaeolithic. 1933.7-6.67-72

(For further reference to collecting area see Cammiade and Burkitt, 1930; Richards, Cammiade and Burkitt, 1932.)

Cardew, Colonel
South India. No further provenance. Middle/Upper Palaeolithic.

Cockburn, J.
Banda. Specific provenance unknown, may refer to the town or district of Banda in Uttar Pradesh. Mesolithic.

Bundelkhand. Specific provenance unknown, Madhya Pradesh/Uttar Pradesh. Mesolithic/Neolithic.

Mirzapur. Specific provenance unknown, may refer to the town or district of Mirzapur in Uttar Pradesh. Lower Palaeolithic.

Singrauli Valley, Mirzapur District, Uttar Pradesh. Lower Palaeolithic.

Cole, R.S.
Lodai (Island of Kutch), Kutch District, Gujurat. Mesolithic/Neolithic. 1926.10-9.1-5,7

Fawcett, F.
   North Arcot District. Specific provenace unknown, Tamil Nadu. Lower/Middle Palaeolithic. 1909.12-13.1-8

   Cuddapah. Specific provenance unknown, may refer to the town or district of Cuddapah in Andhra Pradesh. Lower/Middle Palaeolithic.

Geological Museum Transfer
   Bundelkhand. Specific provenance unknown, Madhya Pradesh/Uttar Pradesh. H. F. Blandford collection. Neolithic. P1989.3-1.132-133

   Jabalpur, Jabalpur District, Madhya Pradesh. J. Evans collection. Mesolithic/Neolithic. P1989.3-1.183-250

   Madras District. Specific provenance unknown, Tamil Nadu. R. Bruce Foot collection. Lower Palaeolithic. P1989.3-1.256-257

   Nagpur. Specific provenance unknown, may refer to the town or district of Nagpur in Maharashtra. J. Fedden collection. Mesolithic/Neolithic. P1989.3-1.134-143

   Panur, North Arcot District, Tamil Nadu. R. Bruce Foot collection. Lower/Middle Palaeolithic. P1989.3-1.251-253

   Penganga Valley (near Sinkeir), Hyderabad District, Andhra Pradesh. J. Fedden collection. Mesolithic/Neolithic. P1989.3-1.144-182

   near Vaniembuddy (River Palur), North Arcot District, Tamil Nadu. Lodwick collection. Lower/Middle Palaeolithic. P1989.3-1.254

   Woodcotta, Chingleput District, Tamil Nadu. R. Bruce Foot collection. Lower/Middle Palaeolithic. P1989.3-1.255

   Unprovenanced. Neolithic. P1989.3-1.269

Gordon, D.H.
   Adamgarh, Hoshangabad District, Madhya Pradesh. Mesolithic/Neolithic. 1935.12-17.111-130

   Ellora, Aurangabad District, Maharashtra. Mesolithic/Neolithic. 1935.12-17.131-132

   Pachmarhi, Hoshangabad District, Madhya Pradesh. Mesolithic/Neolithic. 1935.12-17.1-70

   Singanpur, Raigarh District, Madhya Pradesh. Holocene. 1935.12-17.143-160

   Tamia, Hoshangabad District, Madhya Pradesh. Mesolithic/Neolithic. 1935.12-17.71-83,88-91,93,97-110

   (For further reference to collecting area, see Gordon, D.H., 1938, 1950.)

Gowan, H.C.
   Nagpur, Nagpur District, Maharashtra. Lower/Middle Palaeolithic, Mesolithic/Neolithic. 1929.7-12.1-38

Grieg, A.W.
Jhansi. Specific provenance unknown, may refer to the town or district of Jhansi in Uttar Pradesh. Mesolithic/Neolithic. 1928.4-11.1-8

Joyner, R.B.
Malprabha Basin (River Malprabha), no further provenance, Karnataka. Lower Palaeolithic. 1959.10-4.1-8, 11

Keatinge, G.
Ghotawada, Poona District, Maharashtra. Holocene. 1910.3-8.1-14

Jambdha. Specific location unknown but original artefact labels refer to Khandeish, Bombay Presidency. Non-diagnostic. 1915.11-10.1-9

Wadagaon, Poona District, Maharashtra. Mesolithic. 1919.11-15.1-12

Knox, H.T.
Bellary Fort Hill, Bellary District, Karnataka. Mesolithic/Neolithic. 1893.12-15.45

Tripati Hills. Specific location unknown but may be North Arcot District, Tamil Nadu. W.H.R.P. Carter Collection. Lower Palaeolithic. 1893.12-15.1-19

Macleod, B.
Cuddapah (River Penner). Specific provenance unknown, may refer to the town or district of Cuddapah in Andhra Pradesh. Lower/Middle Palaeolithic. 1902.11-10.1-101

Maries, C.
Gwalior. Specific provenance unknown, may refer to the town or district of Gwalior in Madhya Pradesh. Lower/Middle Palaeolithic. Non-diagnostic.

Raipur. Specific provenance unknown, may refer to the town or district of Raipur in Madhya Pradesh. Lower Palaeolithic, Lower/Middle Palaeolithic, undiagnostic. 1894.11-15.1-5

Marston, A.T.
Bandari. Specific location unknown, but may be in Banda District, Uttar Pradesh. Neolithic/Chalcolithic.

Chipni, Banda District, Uttar Pradesh. Neolithic/Chalcolithic.

Mangawan (River Paisani), Banda District, Uttar Pradesh. Neolithic/Chalcolithic.

Marta (or Marpha), Banda District, Uttar Pradesh. Neolithic/Chalcolithic.

Turri. Specific location unknown but may be in Banda District, Uttar Pradesh. Neolithic/Chalcolithic.

Unprovenanced. Neolithic/Chalcolithic.

Mitchell, T.J.
    Mehgaon. Specific provenance unknown, Madhya Pradesh. Mesolithic/Neolithic. 1946 2-1 1-33

Murray, E.F.O.
    Hartopa, Dhalbhum region, Bihar. Mesolithic/Neolithic. 1928.1-11.1-19

Rivett Carnac, J.H.
    Darsenda, Banda District, Uttar Pradesh. Neolithic. 1883.9-1.51, 73, 77-78, 80-85

Ryder
    Jabalpur. Specific provenance unknown, may refer to the town or the district of Jabalpur in Madhya Pradesh. Mesolithic/Neolithic. 1883.7-9.1-43

    River Narmada. No further provenance. Mesolithic/Neolithic.

Sainty, J.E.
    Unprovenanced. Mesolithic/Neolithic.

Seton Karr, H.W.
    Cazeepet. Unable to locate under this spelling. An alternative may be Kazipet, located in the Warangal District of Andhra Pradesh. Lower/Middle Palaeolithic.

    Cuddapah, Cuddapah District, Andhra Pradesh. Lower/Middle Palaeolithic.

    River Gaur (tributary of the Narmada), Uttar Pradesh. Lower Palaeolithic.

    Madras and **Madras Presidency.** Specific provenance unknown, probably Tamil Nadu. Lower/Middle Palaeolithic. 1903.3-19.2-5

    Unprovenanced. Lower Palaeolithic.

Smith, W.G.
    Madras, Tamil Nadu. Given to W.G. Smith by Doctor George Bidie and dispersed to various collectors prior to donation to the British Museum. Lower/Middle Palaeolithic.

    Tirupati, Chittoor District, Andhra Pradesh. Given to W. G. Smith by Doctor George Bidie and dispersed to various collectors prior to donation to the British Museum. Lower/Middle Palaeolithic.

Sturge, W.A.
    Cuddapah, Cuddapah District, Andhra Pradesh. Collected by H.W. Seton Karr and Valentine MacCleod. Lower/Middle Palaeolithic.

    Lingala, Cuddapah District, Andhra Pradesh. Non-diagnostic.

    Manneru Valley, Nellore District, Andhra Pradesh. Collected by H.W. Seton Karr. Lower Palaeolithic.

Unprovenanced. Lower/Middle Palaeolithic.

(For further reference to the Sturge collections, see Smith, 1937.)

Swiney, Lieutenant
Jabalpur. Specific provenance unknown. May refer to either the town or district of Jabalpur in Madhya Pradesh. Mesolithic/Neolithic. 1865.3-2.1-151

Swynnerton, C.
Gwalior. Specific provenance unknown, may refer to the town or district of Gwalior in Madhya Pradesh. Naturally modified material from river gravels.

Raipur. Specific provenance unknown. May refer to the town or district of Raipur in Madhya Pradesh. Naturally modified materal from river gravels.

Todd, K.R.U.
River Amba (Kasu Shoal), Konkan region, Maharashtra. Mesolithic/Neolithic, Neolithic. 1950.7-1.82-92

Bald Hill (Salsette Island), Thana District, Bombay, Maharashtra. Mesolithic/Neolithic. 1950.7-1.51-59

Calicut, probably Calicut District, Kerala. Original artefact labels refer to Calicut-Madras area. Mesolithic/Neolithic. 1950.7-1.107-120

Hog Island, Bombay harbour, Maharashtra. Mesolithic/Neolithic. 1950.7-1.60-62, 65-76

Jalahalli, Bangalore District, Karnataka. Mesolithic/Neolithic. 1950.7-1.98-106

Khandivili (Salsette Island), Thana District, Bombay, Maharashtra. Lower/Middle Palaeolithic, Upper Palaeolithic, Mesolithic/Neolithic. 1937.11-13.19-32, 34-40, 46-54, 56-88, 92-94

Mahableshwar, Satara District, Maharashtra. Mesolithic/Neolithic. 1950.7-1.93-97

Manori Point (Salsette Island), Thana District, Bombay, Maharashtra. Mesolithic/Neolithic. 1950.7-1.23-32

Marve (Salsette Island), Thana District, Bombay, Maharashtra. Mesolithic/Neolithic. 1950.7-1.14-22

Mhar Fort (Salsette Island), Thana District, Bombay, Maharashtra. Mesolithic/Neolithic. 1950.7-1.33-35

Pali Hill (Salsette Island), Thana District, Bombay, Maharashtra. Mesolithic/Neolithic. 1950.7-1.1-13

Pokhran, Thana District, Bombay, Maharashtra. Mesolithic/Neolithic. 1950.7-1.77-81

Varsova (Bald Hill, Salsette Island), Thana District, Bombay, Maharashtra. Mesolithic/Neolithic. 1950.7-1.51-59

Yerangal Point (or Erangal, Salsette Island), Thana District, Bombay, Maharashtra. Mesolithic/Neolithic. 1950.7-1.36-50

Unprovenanced. Neolithic.

(For further reference to collecting area, see Todd, 1939, 1948 and 1950.)

Trechmann, C.T.
River Narmada. No further provenance. Lower Palaeolithic. P1964.12-6.1508

University College London, Institute of Archaeology
Ahmadnagar, Ahmadnagar District, Maharashtra. Mesolithic/Neolithic.

Amritamam Galam. Specific location unknown but may be in Madras Presidency. Lower/Middle Palaeolithic.

Anagwadi, Bijapur District, Karnataka. Excavated by Professor Sankalia. Non-diagnostic debitage.

Attantangal, Chingleput District, Tamil Nadu. Lower/Middle Palaeolithic.

Attirambakkam, Chingleput District, Tamil Nadu. Lower/Middle Palaeolithic.

Aurangabad. Specific provenance unknown, may refer to either the town or district of Aurangabad in Maharashtra. Mesolithic/Neolithic.

Ayappadi. Specific location unknown but may be in Madras Presidency. Lower/Middle Palaeolithic.

Bagalkot, Bijapur District, Karnataka. Excavated by Professor Sankalia. Non-diagnostic debitage.

Banabasa (Rakha Mines), Dhalbhum region, Bihar. Mesolithic/Neolithic.

Bangalore, Bangalore District, Karnataka. Mesolithic/Neolithic.

Bangalore to Sarjapur road site, Bangalore District, Karnataka. Mesolithic/Neolithic.

Barapedi Cave, Belgaum District, Karnataka. Mesolithic/Neolithic.

Belpandhari, Ahmadnagar District, Maharashtra. Excavated by Professor Sankalia. Lower/Middle Palaeolithic.

Bheraghat, Jabalpur District, Madhya Pradesh. Lower/Middle Palaeolithic.

Brahmagiri, Chitradurga District, Karnataka. Mesolithic/Neolithic.

Chandargi, Belgaum District, Karnataka. Lower/Middle Palaeolithic, Mesolithic/Neolithic.

Chedhari, Hyderabad District, Andhra Pradesh. Lower/Middle Palaeolithic.

Chingleput. Specific provenance unknown, may refer to the town or district of Chingleput in Tamil Nadu. Lower/Middle Palaeolithic.

Chintaladevi. Unable to locate under this spelling. An alternative may be Chintalavadi, located in the Tiruchirapalli District of Tamil Nadu. Lower/Middle Palaeolithic.

Cuddapah. Specific provenance unknown, may refer to the town or district of Cuddapah in Andhra Pradesh. Lower Palaeolithic, Lower/Middle Palaeolithic.

Dharwar. Specific provenance unknown, may refer to the town or district of Dharwar in Karnataka. D.H. Gordon Collection. Mesolithic/Neolithic.

Dholakia (on the Orsary, Chhata Udaipur), Varanasi District, Uttar Pradesh. D.H. Gordon Collection. Mesolithic/Neolithic.

Dighi Hill (Poona), probably Poona District, Maharashtra. Mesolithic/Neolithic.

Dudheshwar (River Narmada), Rajpipla area, Broach District, Gujurat. D.H. Gordon Collection. Mesolithic/Neolithic.

Ellora, Aurangabad District, Maharashtra. Professor Codrington Collection. Neolithic and later.

Erumaivetti Palaiyam, Chingleput District, Tamil Nadu. Lower/Middle Palaeolithic.

Forest sites (Jabalpur), Jabalpur District, Madhya Pradesh. Probably Neolithic.

Ganasidu (River Narmada), specific provenance unknown, Madhya Pradesh. D.H. Gordon Collection. Mesolithic/Neolithic.

Hampasagara, Bellary District, Karnataka. Lower/Middle Palaeolithic.

Haritero. Unable to locate. Lower/Middle Palaeolithic, Neolithic.

Hindustan Aircraft Factory Site (Bangalore), Bangalore District, Karnataka. Mesolithic/Neolithic.

Ichchputtur. Specific location unknown but may be in Madras Presidency. Lower/Middle Palaeolithic.

Jabalpur. Specific provenance unknown, may refer to the town or district of Jabalpur in Madhya Pradesh. D.H. Gordon Collection. Mesolithic/Neolithic.

Jambu Dwip (Pachmarhi), Hoshangabad District, Madhya Pradesh. Mesolithic/Neolithic.

Jamshedpur, Dhalbhum region, Bihar. Lower/Middle Palaeolithic.

Jamuldara, Hyderabad District, Andhra Pradesh. Lower/Middle Palaeolithic.

Kalegaon, Ahmadnagar District, Maharashtra. Excavated by Professor Sankalia. Lower/Middle Palaeolithic.

Kanapur, Hyderabad District, Andhra Pradesh. Lower/Middle Palaeolithic.

Karnataka State, no further provenance. Non-diagnostic debitage.

Keslapur, Adilabad District, Andhra Pradesh. Lower/Middle Palaeolithic, Upper Palaeolithic.

Khaladgi, Bijapur District, Karnataka. Lower/Middle Palaeolithic.

Khyad, Bijapur District, Karnataka. Lower/Middle Palaeolithic.

Kilkuppam, Salem District, Tamil Nadu. Lower/Middle Palaeolithic.

Kootam Puli, Tirunelveli District. Tamil Nadu. Mesolithic/Neolithic.

Langhnaj, Mahesana District, Gujurat. Neolithic.

Mahadeo Hills (Pachmarhi), Hoshangabad District, Madhya Pradesh. Mesolithic/Neolithic.

Maharashtra State, no further provenance. Lower/Middle Palaeolithic.

Manjankaranai, Chingleput District, Tamil Nadu. Lower/Middle Palaeolithic.

Marble Rocks (Jabalpur), Jabalpur District, Madhya Pradesh. Lower/Middle Palaeolithic, Mesolithic/Neolithic.

Marlavai, Hyderabad District, Andhra Pradesh. Lower/Middle Palaeolithic.

Menasgi, Dharwar District, Karnataka. Lower/Middle Palaeolithic.

Navda Toli, Nimar District, Madhya Pradesh. Excavated by Professor Sankalia. Neolithic/Chalcolithic.

Nevasa, Ahmadnagar District, Maharashtra. Excavated by Professor Sankalia. Lower/Middle Palaeolithic.

Nisila. Unable to locate. Neolithic.

Pachmarhi, Hoshangabad District, Madhya Pradesh. Mesolithic/Neolithic.

Pachmarhi Plateau, Hoshangabad District, Madhya Pradesh. Mesolithic/Neolithic.

Pedhamli, Ahmadabad District, Gujarat. Lower/Middle Palaeolithic.

Perumuch-chi. Specific location unknown but may be in Madras Presidency. Lower/Middle Palaeolithic.

Piranvadi, Belgaum District, Karnataka. D.H. Gordon Collection. Probably Mesolithic/Neolithic.

Polur, Nellore District, Andhra Pradesh. Lower/Middle Palaeolithic.

Puliyamamgalam. Unable to locate under this spelling. An alternative maybe Paliamangalam, located in the North Arcot District of Tamil Nadu. Lower/Middle Palaeolithic.

River Sabarmati, no further provenance, Gujarat. Lower/Middle Palaeolithic.

Satyavedu (River Korttalayar), Chingleput District, Tamil Nadu. Lower/Middle Palaeolithic.

Singarpur, Mandla District, Madhya Pradesh. Mesolithic/Neolithic.

Sirkonda, Karimnagar District, Andhra Pradesh. Lower/Middle Palaeolithic.

Ulliyam Bakkam. Specific location unknown but may be in Madras Presidency. Lower/Middle Palaeolithic.

Vada Mambakkam. Specific location unknown but may be in Madras Presidency. Lower/Middle Palaeolithic.

Varjaput site (Bangalore), probably Bangalore District, Karnataka. Mesolithic/Neolithic.

Unprovenanced. Mesolithic/Neolithic.

(For further reference to material collected by D.H. Gordon see Gordon, 1938, 1950. For the site of Lanhnaj, Mahesana District, Gujarat, see Zeuner, 1952. For Attirambakkam, see Bannerjee, 1965.)

Warren, S.H.
   Basim. The present-day name for this site may be Washim, Akola District, Maharashtra. Modern.

Wellcome, H.
   Cazeepet. Unable to locate under this spelling. An alternative may be Kazipet, located in the Warangal District of Andhra Pradesh. Lower/Middle Palaeolithic. P1982.10-4.4985-4988

   Cuddapah, Cuddapah District, Andhra Pradesh. Acquired by purchase from various collectors, predominantly H. W. Seton Karr. Lower/Middle Palaeolithic. P1982.10-4.4989-4991

   Madras, Tamil Nadu. Acquired by purchase from various collectors, predominantly H.W. Seton Karr. Lower/Middle Palaeolithic. P1982.10-4.4994-5008

   Pondi. Specific location unknown but may be Madras area, Tamil Nadu. Lower/Middle Palaeolithic. P1982.10-4.5012

Unknown Collector
   River Mahanadi. No further provenance, Madhya Pradesh/Orissa. Mesolithic/Neolithic.

   Nagpur. Specific provenance unknown, may refer to the town or district of Nagpur in Maharashtra. Collection comprises Palaeolithic and Neolithic material.

   Unprovenanced. Mesolithic/Neolithic.

PAKISTAN

Christy, H.
   Anmadabad fort. Specific location unknown. Original artefact labels refer to Khairpur, but this place-name is found in more than one area of Pakistan as for example in Punjab Province and also in Sind Province where it is a town and a district. J. Burgess Collection. Non-diagnostic.

   Bhakkar (River Indus), Sind sagar Doab (interfluve) region, northwest Punjab. J. Burgess Collection. Chalcolithic.

   River Indus. No further provenance. J. Burgess Collection. Chalcolithic.

   Rohri Hills, Sukkur District, Sind Province. T.R. Jones Collection. Chalcolithic.

   Sukkur. Specific provenance unknown, may refer to the town or district of Sukkur in Sind Province. J. Burgess Collection. Chalcolithic.

Collyer, H.O.
   Khajuri (Near Bannu), probably Bannu District, Northwest Frontier Province. Neolithic and later.

Geological Museum Transfer
   Rohri Hills (left bank of River Indus), Sukkur District, Sind Province. J.G. Single Collection. Neolithic/Chalcolithic. P1989.3-1.258-268

Greenwell, J.
   Sukkur. Specific provenance unknown, may refer to the town or district of Sukkur in Sind Province. W.R. Dickinson Collection. Chalcolithic.

Gordon, D.H.
   Jamal Garhi Cave, Mardan District, Northwest Frontier Province. Mesolithic/Neolithic.

   (For further reference to collecting area, see Gordon, 1938, 1950.)

Lubbock, J.
   Rohri Hills, Sukkur District, Sind Province. Neolithic/Chalcolithic. 1883.11-9.2-4

   Sind Province. No further provenance. Neolithic/Chalcolithic. 1883.11-9.1, 5

Morris, T.O.
   Akbari, Marwat Kundi Hills area, Northwest Frontier Province. Non-diagnostic. 1935.10-13.8

   Banda Shak Nowaz, Marwat Kundi Hills area, Northwest Frontier Province. Non-diagnostic. 1937.11-12.14

   Berwala, Marwat Kundi Hills area, Northwest Frontier Province. Non-diagnostic. 1937.11-12.12, 13

   Dhur Nala, Marwat Kundi Hills area, Northwest Frontier Province. Non-diagnostic. 1935.10-13.7, 10-11

   Kargocha Nala, Marwat Kundi Hills area, Northwest Frontier Province. Non-diagnostic. 1935.10-13.5, 9

   Malagan, Marwat Kundi Hills area, Northwest Frontier province. Non-diagnostic. 1935.10-13.6

   Pezu Wagai, Marwat Kundi Hills area, Northwest Frontier Province. Non-diagnostic. 1935.10-13.2, 4

   Seikh Nala, Marwat Kundi Hills area, Northwest Frontier Province. Non-diagnostic. 1935.10-13.1

   Sheri Gasha, Marwat Kundi Hills area, Northwest Frontier Province. Undiagnostic. 1935.10-13.3

   (For further reference to collecting area, see Morris, 1938.)

Seton Karr, H.W.
   Indus Valley. No further provenance. Neolithic.

Single, J.
　Rohri Hills, Sukkur District, Sind Province. Neolithic/Chalcolithic. 1890.12-17.1-58

Todd, K.R.U.
　Karachi Site (River Lyari), Karachi District, Sind Province. Mesolithic. 1950.7-1.121-139

University College London, Institute of Archaeology.
　Beckli, Quetta-Pishin District, Northeast Baluchistan Province. Mesolithic/Neolithic.

　Jamal Garhi Cave, Mardan District, Northwest Frontier Province. Neolithic.

　Khairpur. Specific location unknown. This place-name is found in more than one area of Pakistan, as for example in Punjab Province and also in Sind Province, where it is a town and a district. Upper Palaeolithic/Neolithic.

　Mohenjodaro, Khairpur District, Sind Province. Neolithic/Chalcolithic.

　Ranaghundai, Zhob District, North Baluchistan Province. Mesolithic/Neolithic.

　River Sohan. No further provenance, Punjab Province. Lower/Middle Palaeolithic.

Unknown Collector(s)
　Punjab Province. No further provenance. Mesolithic/Neolithic.

SRI LANKA

Hartley, C.
　Bandarawella. Badulla District, Uva Province. Mesolithic/Neolithic. 1914.2-13.1-20

　Desert Tract 'A'. Specific location unknown. Possibly in North Central Province. Middle/Upper Palaeolithic. 1919.10-16.5, 14, 17, 24, 26

　The Kallumalai. Specific location unknown, North Central Province. Middle/Upper Palaeolithic. 1919.10-16.2, 4, 9, 12, 29, 30, 33

　Kangi Area. Specific location unknown, North Central Province. Non-diagnostic. 1919.10-16.19, 34

　Kudremalai. This may be Kudremalai Point, located in the Puttalam District of the North Western Province. Non-diagnostic. 1919.10-16.1, 10

　near Mana Villa (Game Sanctuary). Specific loction unknown, North Central Province. Non-diagnostic. 1919.10-16.27

　Minihagalkande. Specific location unknown, Southern Province. Non-diagnostic. 1919.10-16.3, 13, 20, 28, 32, 35.

　Moderagam Camp. Specific location unknown, North Central Province. Upper Palaeolithic/Mesolithic. 1919.10-16. 6, 15, 18, 23, 25, 31

Vannithi Villa. Specific location unknown, North Central province. Non-diagnostic. 1919.10-16.7, 8, 11, 36

Wellipatan Villa. Specific location unknown, possibly in North Central Province. Non-diagnostic. 1919.10-16.21, 22

Sri Lanka. No further provenance. Mesolithic/Neolithic. 1915.11-6.1-10

?Sri Lanka. No further provenance. Neolithic/Chalcolithic.

(For further reference to the site of Bandavawella in Uva Province, see Hartley, 1914.)

Noone, H.V.V.
Bandarawella. Badulla District, Uva province. Mesolithic/Neolithic. 1945.12-7.271

(For further reference to the collection area, see Noone and Noone, 1940.)

Wayland, E.J.
Bandarawella. Badulla District, Uva Province. Non-diagnostic. 1914.9-23.6

Rakwana, Ratnapura District, Sabaragamuwa Province. Non-diagnostic. 1914.9-23.3

Ratnapura, Ratnapura District, Sabaragamuwa Province. Non-diagnostic. 1914.9-23.1, 2, 4, 5

?Sri Lanka. No further provenance. Mesolithic/Neolithic.

BIBLIOGRAPHY

Agrawal, D P, Rekha Dodia & Mala Seth 1989. South Asian climate and environment at *c*.18,000 BP. In C Gamble & O Soffer (eds.) *The World at 18,000 BP*. Volume 2. *Low Latitudes*, 231-6. London: Unwin Hyman

Allaby, A & Allaby, M (eds.) 1990. *The Concise Oxford Dictionary of Earth Sciences*. Oxford: Oxford University Press

Allchin, B 1958. Moranha Pahar: a rediscovery. *Man* 58, 153-5

Allchin, B 1963. The Indian Stone Age sequence. *Journal of the Royal Anthropological Institute* 93, 210-34

Allchin, B 1966. *The Stone-tipped Arrow. Late Stone Age Hunters in the Tropical World*. London: Phoenix House

Allchin, B & Allchin, R 1968. *The Birth of Indian Civilisation: India and Pakistan before 500BC*. Harmondsworth: Penguin Books Ltd

Allchin, B & Allchin, F R 1982. *The Rise of Civilisation in India and Pakistan*. Cambridge: Cambridge University Press

Allchin, F R 1957. The Neolithic stone industry of the North Karnatak region. *Bulletin of the School of Oriental and African Studies (London)* 25, 306-30

Allchin, F R, Allchin, B, Durrani, F A & Khan M F (eds.) 1986. *Lewan and the Bannu Basin. Excavation and Survey of Sites and Environments in Northwest Pakistan*. Oxford: British Archaeological Reports, International Series 310

Anon. 1968. *India. A Physical Geography*. New Delhi: Government of India Press

Ball, V 1867. Stone implements found in Central India. *Proceedings of the Asiatic Society* 1867, 143-53

Bannerjee, K D 1965. Excavation at Attirambakkam, district Chingleput (Tamil Nadu). *Indian Archaeology - A Review, 1964-65*, 20. New Delhi: Department of Archaeology, Government of India

Black, G F 1892. Notice of stone implements etc. from Asia and Africa in the National Collection. *Proceedings of the Society of Antiquaries of Scotland* 26, 398-412

Blanford, W T 1867. Account of stone implements found in Central India. *Proceedings of the Asiatic Society of Bengal,* 1867, 136-47

Blanford, W T 1869. On the geology of the Taptee and Nerbudda Valleys, and some adjoining districts. *Memoirs of the Geological Survey of India* 6(3), 163-382

Bordes, F 1961. *Typologie du Paléolithique ancien et Moyen*. Bordeaux: Delmas

Bordes, F 1972. *A Tale of Two Caves*. New York: Harpers & Row

Cammiade, L A & Burkitt, M C 1930. Fresh light on the Stone Ages in Southeast India. *Antiquity* 4, 327-39

Carlleyle, A C L 1878. Report of tours in Eastern Rajputana in 1871-72 and 1872-73. *India Archaeological Survey Reports* 6. Calcutta: Government Printing

Carlleyle, A C L 1879. Report of tours in the Central Doab and Gorakhpur in 1874-75 and 1875-76. *India Archaeological Survey Reports* 12. Calcutta: Government Printing

Carlleyle, A C L 1883. Report of tours in the Gorakhpur District 1875-76 and 1876-77. *India Archaeological Survey Reports* 18. Calcutta: Government Printing

Carlleyle, A C L 1885. Report of tours in Gorakhpur, Saran and Ghazipur in 1877-79 and 1880. *India Archaeological Survey Reports* 22. Calcutta: Government Printing

Cockburn, J 1883. A short account of the petrographs in the caves or rockshelters of the Kaimur Range in the Mirzapur District. *Proceedings of the Asiatic Society of Bengal*, 1883, 125-6

Cockburn, J 1884. On the durability of haematite drawings on haematite rocks. *Proceedings of the Asiatic Society of Bengal*, 1884, 141-5

Cockburn, J 1899. Cave drawings in the Kaimur Range, North-west Province. *Journal of the Royal Asiatic Society*, 1899, 89-97

Corvinus, G 1968. An Acheulian occupation floor at Chirki on Parvara, India. *Current Anthropology* 9 (2-3), 216-18

Corvinus, G 1969. Stratigraphy and geological background of an Acheulian site at Chirki-on-Pravara, India. *Anthropos* (Freiburg, Switzerland) 63-64, 921-40

Corvinus, G. 1970. The Acheulian workshop at Chirki on the Pravara River, Maharashtra. *The Indian Antiquary* 4 (3rd series), 13-22

Corvinus, G 1981. *A Survey of the Pravar River System in Western Maharashtra, India*. 2 vols. Tübingen: Archaeologica Ventoria, Institüt für Urgeschichte

Cunningham, A 1873. Report for the year 1871-72. *India Archaeological Survey Reports* 3, IV-XIII

Daniel, G 1967. *The Origins and Growth of Archaeology*. Harmondsworth: Penguin Books Ltd.

Deshpande, M N 1975. *Indian Archaeology - A Review 1966-67*, 38-9. New Delhi: Department of Archaeology, Government of India

Drake-Brockman, D L 1909a. *Banda. A Gazetteer. District Gazetteers of the United Provinces of Agra and Oudh* 21. Allahabad: Government Press

Drake-Brockman, D L 1909b. *Hamirpur. A Gazetteer. District Gazetteers of the United Provinces of Agra and Oudh* 22. Allahabad: Government Press

Drake-Brockman, D L 1911. *Mirzapur, A Gazetteer. District Gazetteers of the United Provinces of Agra and Oudh* 27. Allahabad: Government Press

Dutta, P C 1971. Earliest Indian human remains found in a Late Stone Age site. *Nature* 233, 500-501

Evans, J 1860. On the occurrence of flint implements in undisturbed beds of gravel, sand and clay. *Archaeologia* 38, 280-307

Evans, J 1872. *The Ancient Stone Implements, Weapons and Ornaments of Great Britain*. 1st edition. London: Longmans, Green, Reader and Dyer

Fergusson, J 1884. *Archaeology in India, with especial reference to the works of Babu Rajendrala Mitra*. London: Trübner & Co.

Foote, R B 1866. On the occurrence of stone implements in laterite formations in various parts of the Madras and North Arcot districts. *Madras Journal of Literature and Science* 3 (2), 1-35

Foote, R B 1901. *Government Museum Madras. Catalogue of the Prehistoric Antiquities*. Madras: Government Press

Foote, R B 1916. *The Foote Collection of Prehistoric and Protohistoric Antiquities. Notes on their age and distribution*. Madras: Government Press

Ghosh, A K (ed.) 1956. *Indian Archaeology - A Review 1955-56*. New Delhi: Department of Archaeology, Government of India

Ghosh, A K (ed.) 1959. *Indian Archaeology - A Review 1958-59*, 27. New Delhi: Department of Archaeology, Government of India

Ghosh, A K (ed.) 1960. *Indian Archaeology - A Review 1959-60*, 22. New Delhi: Department of Archaeology, Government of India

Ghosh, A K (ed.) 1964. *Indian Archaeology - A Review 1961-62*, 57. New Delhi: Department of Archaeology, Government of India

Ghosh, A K (ed.) 1965. *Indian Archaeology - A Review 1962-63*, 37-8. New Delhi: Department of Archaeology, Government of India

Ghosh, A K 1970. The Palaeolithic cultures of Singhbhum. *Transactions of the American Philosophical Society* NS 60 (1), 1-68

Ghosh, A K 1973. Chrono-cultural perspective on the Palaeolithic industries of India. In D P Agrawal and A Ghosh (eds.) *Radiocarbon and Indian Archaeology*, 23-31. Bombay: Tata Institute of Fundamental Research

Ghosh, A K 1982. Pebble-core and flake elements: Process of transmutation and the factors thereof. In A Ronen (ed.) *The Transition from Lower to Middle Palaeolithic and the Origin of Modern Man*, 265-82. Oxford: British Archaeological Reports, International Series 151

Ghosh, A K (ed.) 1989. *An Encyclopaedia of Indian Archaeology*. 2 vols. New Delhi: Munshiram Manoharlal

Gordon, D H 1938. The microlithic industries of India. *Man* 38 (19), 21-4

Gordon, D H 1950. The stone industries of the Holocene in India and Pakistan. *Ancient India* 6, 64-90

Gordon, D H 1958. *The Prehistoric Background of Indian Culture*. Bombay: Madhuri Dhirajlal Desai & Bhulabai Memorial Institute

Hartley, C 1914. On the occurrence of Pigmy (*sic*) implements found in Ceylon. *Spolia Zeylanica* 10 (36), 54

Jacobson, J 1980. Investigations of Late Stone Age cultural adaptations in the Central Vindhyas. *Man and Environment* 4, 65-82

Jayaswal, V 1978. *Palaeohistory of India*. Delhi: Agam Kala Prakashan

Jayaswal, V 1989. Hunter-gatherers of the Terminal Pleistocene in Uttar Pradesh. In C Gamble and O Soffer (eds.) *The World at 18000 BP*. Volume 2. *Low Latitudes*, 237-54. London: Unwin Hyman

Joshi, R V 1968. Late Mesolithic Culture in Central India. In Bordes, F and Sonneville-Bordes, D de, *La Préhistoire. Problèmes et tendances*, 245-54. Paris: CNRS

Joshi, R V 1973. The significance of microlithic tools in post-Palaeolithic industries in India. In D P Agrawal & A K Ghosh, *Radiocarbon and Indian Archaeology*, 54-7. Bombay: Tata Institute of Fundamental Research

Joshi, R V 1978. *Stone Age Cultures of Central India*. Poona: Deccan College Postgraduate and Research Institute

Keeley, L 1980. *Experimental Determination of Stone Tool Uses: a Microwear Analysis*. Chicago: University of Chicago Press

Khatri, A P 1961. Stone Age and Pleistocene chronology of the Narmada Valley (Central India). *Anthropos* (Freiburg, Switzerland) 56, 519-30

Khatri, A P 1962. Origin and development of Series II culture of India. *Proceedings of the Prehistoric Society* 28, 191-208

Krishnaswami, V D 1947. Stone Age India. *Ancient India* 3, 11-57

Luard, C E 1907. *Rewah State. Central India Gazetteer series* 4. Lucknow: Newul Kishore

Medlicot, H B 1873. Notes on a celt found by Mr Hackett in the ossiferous deposits of the Narbada Valley (Pliocene of Falconer). *Records of the Geological Survey of India* 2 (3), 49-57

Menghin, O 1931. *Weltgeschichte der Steinzeit.* Vienna: Anton Schroll & Co.

Meyer, C I E & Cotton, J S (eds.) 1908. *The Imperial Gazetteer of India.* 26 volumes. Oxford: Clarendon Press.

Mishra, S 1992. The age of the Acheulian in India: new evidence. *Current Anthropology* 33 (3), 325-8

Misra, V D 1977. *Some aspects of Indian Archaeology.* Allahabad: Prabhat Prakashan

Misra, V N 1978. The Acheulian industry of rockshelter IIIF-23 at Bhimbetka, Central India: a preliminary study. *Puratattva* 8 (1975-76), 13-36

Misra, V N 1982. Evolution of the blade element in the stone industries of rockshelter IIIF-23 at Bhimbetka. In R K Sharma (ed.) *Indian Archaeology, New Perspectives,* 7-13. Delhi: Agam Kala Prakashan

Misra, V N 1989. Stone Age India: an ecological perspective. *Man and Environment* 14, 17-64

Misra, V N & Mathpal Y 1979. Rock art of Bhimbetka Region, Central India. *Man and Environment* 3, 27-33

Misra, V N, Rajaguru, S N & Raghavan, H 1988. Late Middle Pleistocene environments and Acheulian Culture around Didwana, Rajasthan. *Proceedings of the Indian National Science Academy* 54A (3), 425-38

Morris, T O 1938. The Bain boulder bed: a glacial episode in the Siwalik Series of the Marwat Kundi Range and Shekh Budin, North West Frontier Province, India. *Quarterly Journal of the Geological Society* 94, 385-421

Movius, H L 1949. The Lower Palaeolithic cultures of southern and eastern Asia. *Transactions of the American Philosophical Society* NS 38(4), 376-83.

Nelson, A E 1909. *Central Provinces District Gazetteers, Jubbulpore District.* Bombay: Times Press

Noone, N A & Noone, H V V 1940. The stone implements of Bandarawella (Ceylon). *The Ceylon Journal of Science, section G,* 3(1), 1-24

Oldham, T 1868. On the agate flake found by Mr Wynne in the pliocene (?) deposits of the Upper Godavari. *Records of the Geological Survey of India* 1, 65-9

Pant, P C 1982. *Prehistoric Uttar Pradesh (a study of Old Stone Age).* Delhi: Agam Kala Prakashan

Paterson, T T 1940. Geology and early Man I & II. *Nature* 146, 12-15, 49-52

Pellant, C 1990. *Rocks, Minerals & Fossils of the World.* London: Pan Books Ltd.

Ray, R 1982. Identification of transformation from Lower/Middle Palaeolithic with typo-technological marker (*sic*). In A. Ronen (ed.) *The Transition from Lower to Middle Palaeolithic and the Origin of Modern Man*, 283-94. Oxford: British Archaeological Reports, International Series 151

Rendell, H M, Dennell, R W & Halim, M A 1989. *Pleistocene and Palaeolithic Investigations in the Soan Valley, Northern Pakistan*. Oxford: British Archaeological Reports, International Series 544

Richards, F J, Cammiade, L A & Burkitt, M C 1932. Climatic changes in South East India during early Palaeolithic times. *Geological Magazine* 69, 193-205

Roy, S 1953. Indian Archaeology from Jones to Marshall (1784-1902). *Ancient India* 9, 4-28

Roy, S 1961. *The Story of Indian Archaeology, 1784-1947*. New Delhi: Archaeological Survey of India

Sahni, M R & Khan, E 1988. *Pleistocene Vertebrate Fossils and Prehistory of India*. New Delhi: Books and Books

Sali, S A 1985. The Upper Palaeolithic at Patne. District Jalagaon, Maharashtra. In V N Misra & P Bellwood (eds.) *Recent Advances in Indo-Pacific Prehistory*, 137-45. New Delhi: Oxford and IBH

Sankalia, H D 1956. Animal fossils and Palaeolithic industries from the Pravara Basin at Nevasa, District Ahmadnagar. *Ancient India* 12, 35-52

Sankalia, H D 1963. *The Prehistory and Protohistory of India and Pakistan*, 1st edition. Bombay: University of Bombay

Sankalia, H D 1964. *Stone Age Tools. Their techniques, names and possible functions*. Poona: Deccan College Postgraduate and Research Institute

Sankalia, H D 1974. *The Prehistory and Protohistory of India and Pakistan*, 2nd edition. Bombay: University of Bombay

Sankalia, H D & Banerjee, K D 1958. The Middle Palaeolithic Culture of the Deccan Karnatak and Central India. *Journal of the Palaeontological Society of India* 3, 158-69

Sankalia, H D, Deo, S B, Ansari, Z D & Ehrhardt, S 1960. *From History to Prehistory at Nevasa*. Poona: Deccan College Postgraduate and Research Institute

Seely, J B 1824. *The Wonders of Elora. The narrative of a journey to the temples and dwellings of Elora*. London: G & W B Whittaker

Sharma, G R 1973a. Stone Age in the Vindyhas and the Ganga Valley. In D P Agrawal & A. Ghosh (eds.) *Radiocarbon and Indian Archaeology*, 106-110. Bombay: Tata Institute of Fundamental Research

Sharma, G R 1973b. Mesolithic lake cultures in the Ganga Valley, India. *Proceedings of the Prehistoric Society* 39, 129-46

Sharma, G R, Misra, V D, Mandal, D, Misra, B B & Pal, J N 1980. *Beginnings of Agriculture*. Allahahabad: Abinash Prakashan

Sharmer, M J 1982. *The Upper Palaeolithic Culture in India*. Delhi: Agram Kala Prakashan.

Sieveking, G de G 1960. Moranha Pahar: or the mystery of A C Carlyle. *Man* 60, 98-100

Smith, R A 1937. *The Sturge Collection. An illustrated selection of foreign stone implements bequeathed in 1919 by William Allan Sturge*. London: British Museum

Smith, V A 1906. Pygmy flints. *The Indian Antiquary* 35, 185-95

Subbarao, B 1948. *The Stone Age Cultures of Bellary*. Poona: Deccan College Postgraduate and Research Institute

Subbarao, B 1955. The Chalcolithic blade industry at Maheshwar (Central India) and a note on the history of the technique. *Bulletin of the Deccan College Research Institute*, 17 (2), 126-49

Terra, H de & Paterson, T T 1939. *Studies on the Ice Age in India and associated Human Cultures*. Washington DC: Carnegie Institution

Thapar, B K (ed.) 1975. *Indian Archaeology - A Review 1974-1975*, 24-6. New Delhi: Department of Archaeology, Government of India

Thapar, B K 1980. *Indian Archaeology - A Review 1977-1978*, 51-2, 58-9. New Delhi: Department of Archaeology, Government of India

Thapar, B K 1985. *Recent Archaeological Discoveries in India*. Paris: UNESCO

Theobald, W 1860. On the Tertiary and Alluvial deposits of the Central portion of the Nerbudda Valley. *Memoirs of the Geological Survey of India* 2, 279-91

Tixier, J 1963. *Typologie de L'Epipaléolithique du Maghreb*. Paris: Arts et Métiers Graphiques

Tixier, J, Inizan, M L & Roche, H 1980. *Préhistoire de la pierre taillée. Terminologie et technologie*. Valborne: Cercle de recherches et d'études préhistoriques

Tixier, J (ed.) 1984. *Préhistoire de la pierre taillée 2. Economie du débitage laminaire: technologie et expérimentation*. Paris: Cercle de recherches et d'études préhistoriques

Todd, K R U 1939. Palaeolithic industries of Bombay. *Journal of the Royal Anthropological Institute* 69 (2), 257-72

Todd, K R U 1948. A microlithic industry in Eastern Mysore. *Man* 48, 28-30

Todd, K R U 1950. The microlithic industry of Bombay. *Ancient India* 6, 4-16

Tripathy, K C 1980. *Lithic industries in India. A study of south-western Orissa*. Delhi: Leeladevi Publications

Tuffreau, A 1984. Le paléolithique dans le Nord de la France et la Picardie. *Cahiers de Geographie Physique* 5, 5-29

Varma, R K 1965. Morhana Pahar and Baghai Khor shelter 1. In V N Misra and M S Mate (eds.) *Indian Prehistory - 1964*, 73-6. Poona, Deccan College

Wakankar, V S & Brooks, R R 1976. Stone Age Painting in India. Bombay: D B Taraporevala Sons & Co.

Wickramapathirana, E 1984. *The Stone Age of South India and Sri Lanka. A critical review*. Oxford: British Archaeological Reports, International Series 228

Zeuner, F E 1952. The microlithic industries of Langhuaj, Gujarat. *Man* 52, 129-31

INDEX TO GLOSSARY

Adze 33, 36, 39
Adze flake 33, 36
Agate 42, 43
Anvil 41
Arrowhead
    transverse 38
Awl 33
Axe 39-42
Basalt 35, 42, 43
Biface 31, 34
Blade
    backed 37
    crested 36
    obliquely truncated 37
    plunging 36
    tanged 38
    unmodified 35
Bladelet 35, 37, 38
    backed 37, 38
Borer 33, 37
Burin 37
Celt 39, 40
Chalcedony 42, 43
Chert 34, 35, 42, 43
Chisel 40
Chopper 30, 31
Chopping tool 30, 31
Cleaver 30, 31
Core
    blade 35-37
    complex 31
    discoidal 31
    Levallois 31, 32
    unprepared 30
Core trimming flake 33, 36
Denticulate 34
Drill 38, 40
End scraper 35, 37
Fabricator 41
Flake
    debitage 32, 33
    Levallois 32
    prepared 31-33
Flake tool 30, 32
Flint 34, 36, 43
Gneiss 43
Granite 43

Grooved grinding surface 41
Haematite 42, 44
Hammerstone 41, 42
Handaxe 31
Jasper 43
Lunate 38
Marble 43
Microlith 30, 35, 37-39
Muller 40
Palette 42
Pick 31, 40
piercer 38
Point
    backed 37, 38
    beaked 34
    bifacial 34
    obliquely blunted 37
    pressure flaked 34
    retouched 33, 34
    tanged 34
    unmodified 33
Polisher 42
Quartz 42-44
Quartzite 36, 43, 44
Raw material 30, 34, 35, 39, 42
Retouch 32-35, 37-40
Rhomboid 39
Ringstone 40, 41
Saddle quern 40
Sandstone 44
Saw 34, 37, 38
Scraper 34, 35, 37, 40
Silica 34, 36, 42
Steatite 43
Stone ball 40, 42
Stone disc 42
Trapeze 39
Trapezoid 35, 38, 39
Triangle 38, 39
Utilised piece 30, 40
Wedge 40
Weight 40

INDEX TO CATALOGUE

1. Amila Moruha 46
2. Amila Nala 46
3. Ashtbhuja 47
4. Babura 47
5. Baghai Khor 47
6. Baghmara Pahar 49
7. Banda 51
8. Barkor 55
9. Bhagatpura 55
10. Bhainsawar Nalla 56
11. Bhaisand 56
12. Bharkacha 57
13. Bharkura 59
14. Bundelkhand 59
15. Chilâhwa Nâla 64
16. Chitrakot 64
17. Dhir 64
18. Gâdur Hâta 64
19. Gaur River 65
20. Gharwa Pahâri 68
21. Jabalpur 69
22. Jathi 70
23. Jogran Dari 71
24. Jonoa Pahar 71
25. Kabrai 71
26. Kalinjar 71
27. Ken River 73
28. Kodaili Pahar 74
29. Liknaya Pahar 74
30. Lurhwûru Pahar 75
31. Magardar 75
32. Maharajapur 76
33. Mahrela Chacki 76
34. Mangawan 77
35. Manohar Tali Pahar 77
36. Marfa 78
37. Mirir Gaon 81
38. Moretha Pahar 89
39. Morhana Pahar 81
40. Nagir Ka Pahar 90
41. Nao Gaon 90
42. Naon Ka Pahar 90
43. Narmada Valley 91
44. Naro 92
45. Parari, Pathar-Kachhar 93
46. Partap Ganj 94
47. Rajapur/Rajpura Rewa 94
48. Sarsi 94
49. Vindhya Hills 95
50. Unprovenanced 96

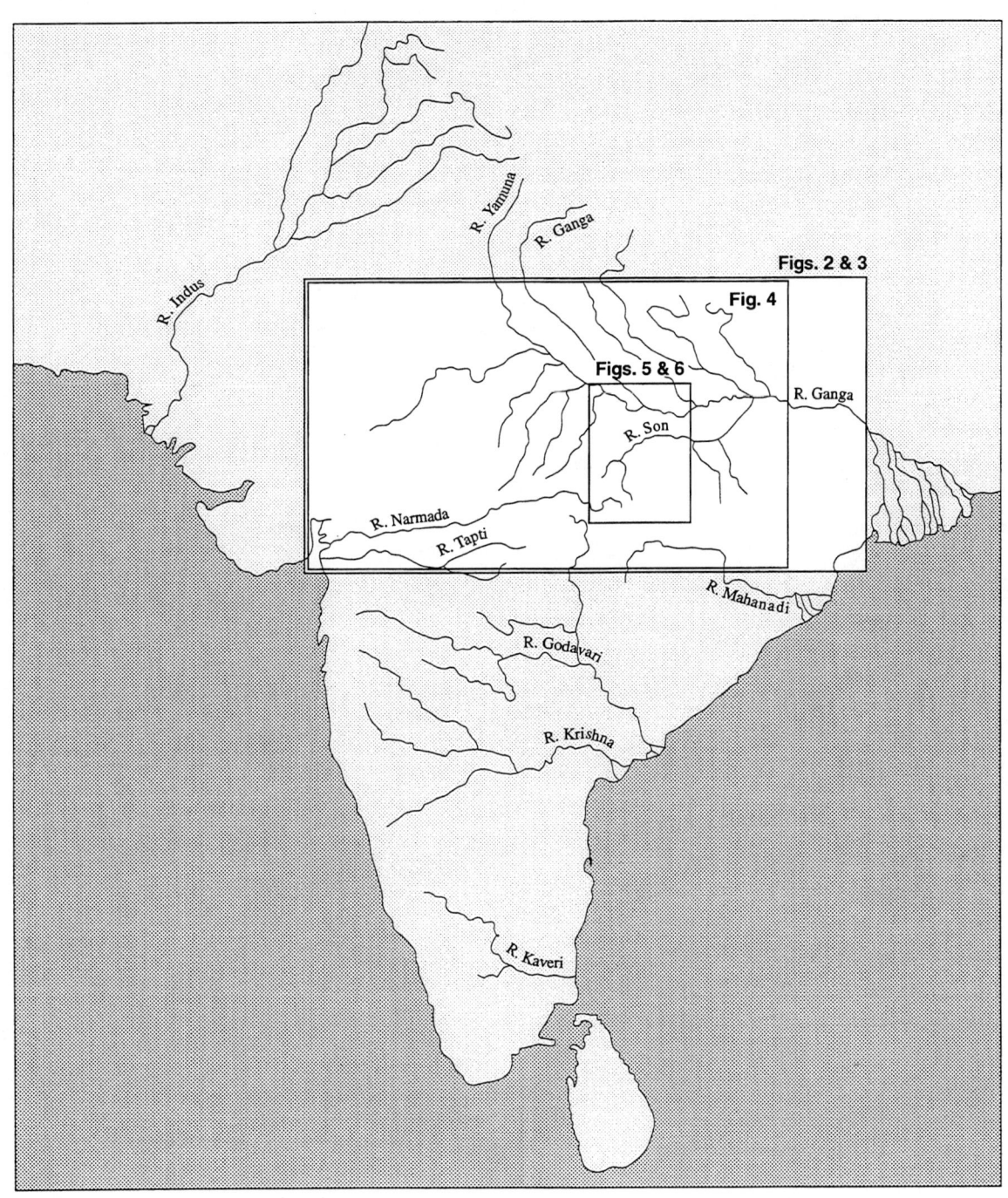

Fig. 1   The Indian sub-continent showing areas enlarged in figures 2-6

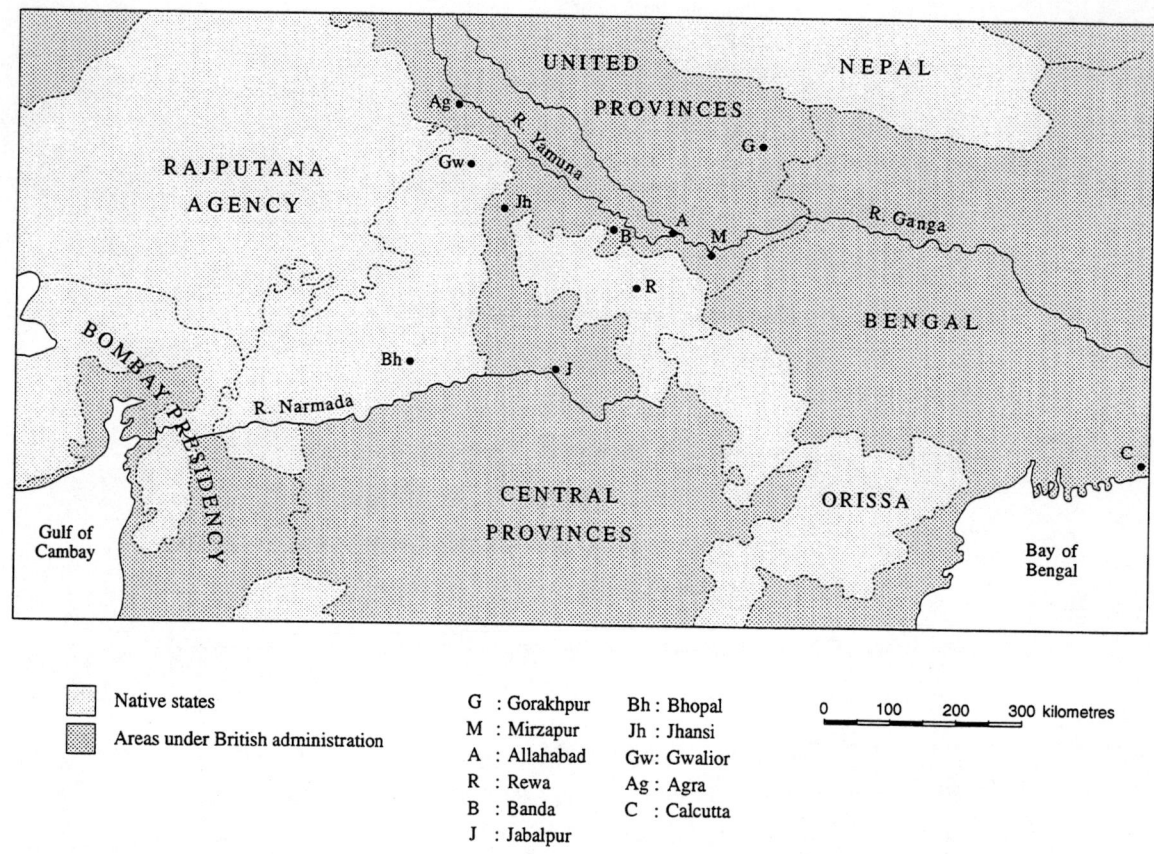

Fig. 2   Central India in the late nineteenth century

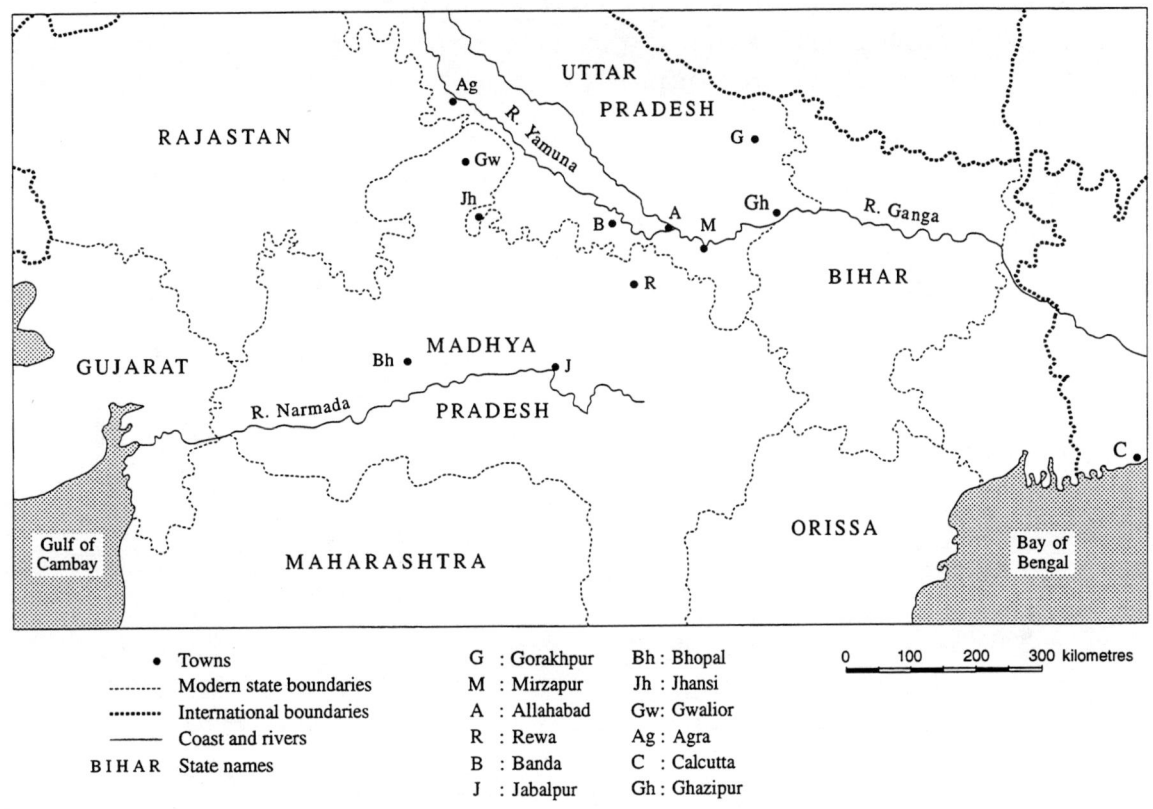

Fig. 3   Modern states of Central India

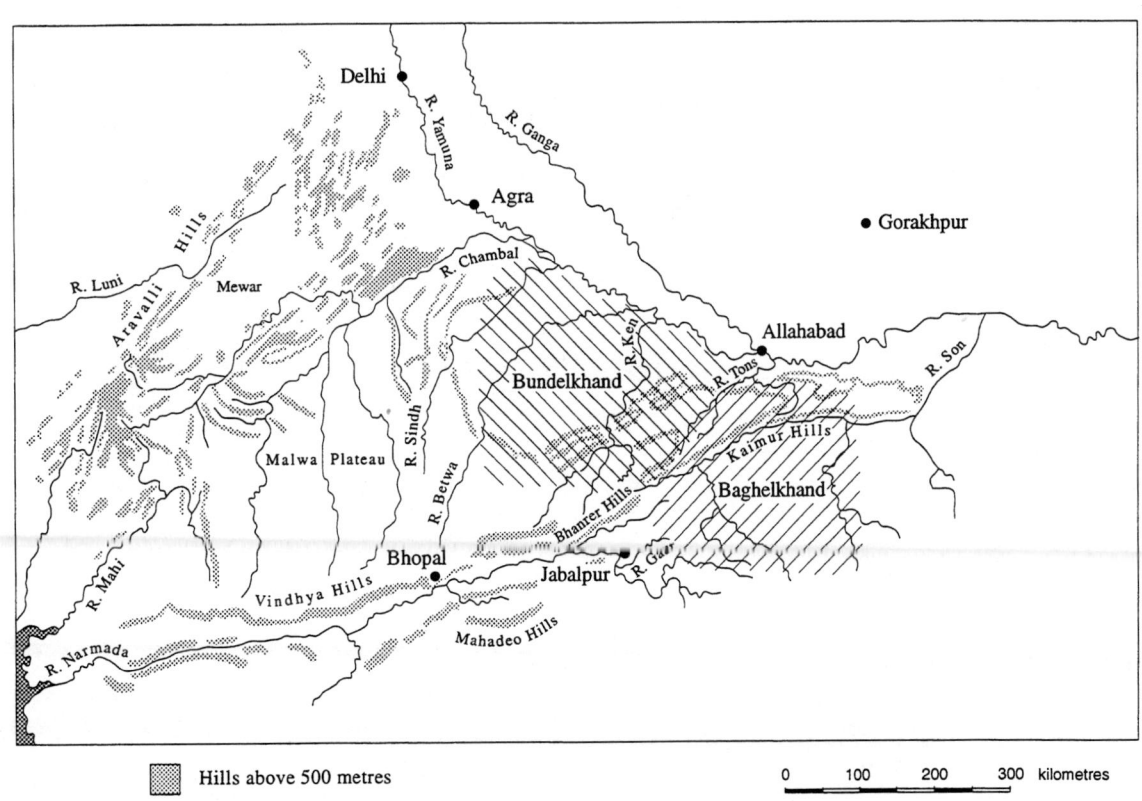

Fig. 4   Physical geography of Central India

Fig. 5 Districts and main towns visited by Carlyle

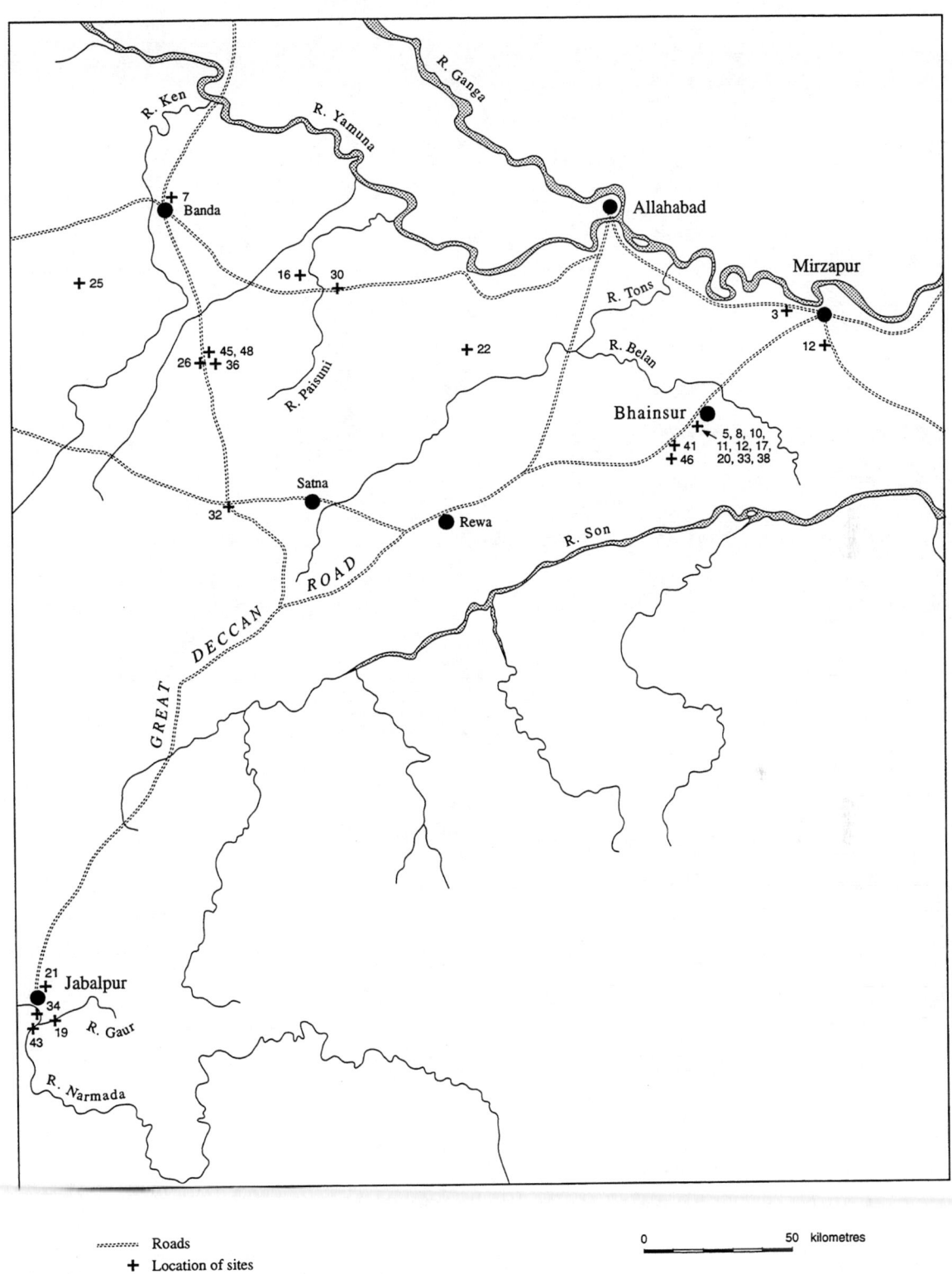

Fig. 6   Location of Carlyle's sites identified by their catalogue numbers

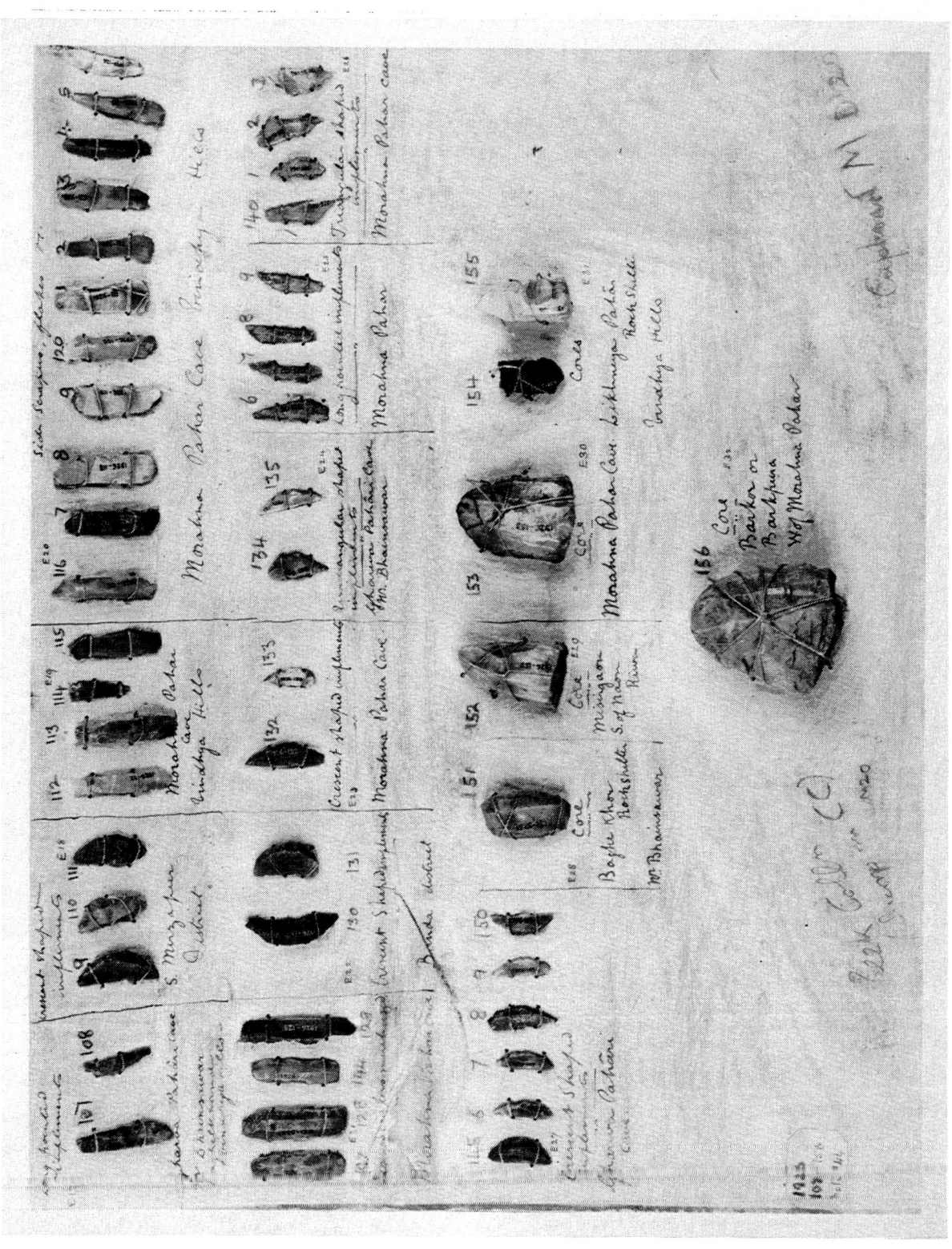

Fig. 7 Artefacts collected by Carlyle and sold by Charles Seidler to Sir Wilfred Peek before acquisition by the British Museum for the Christy Collection. The writing is that of Seidler.

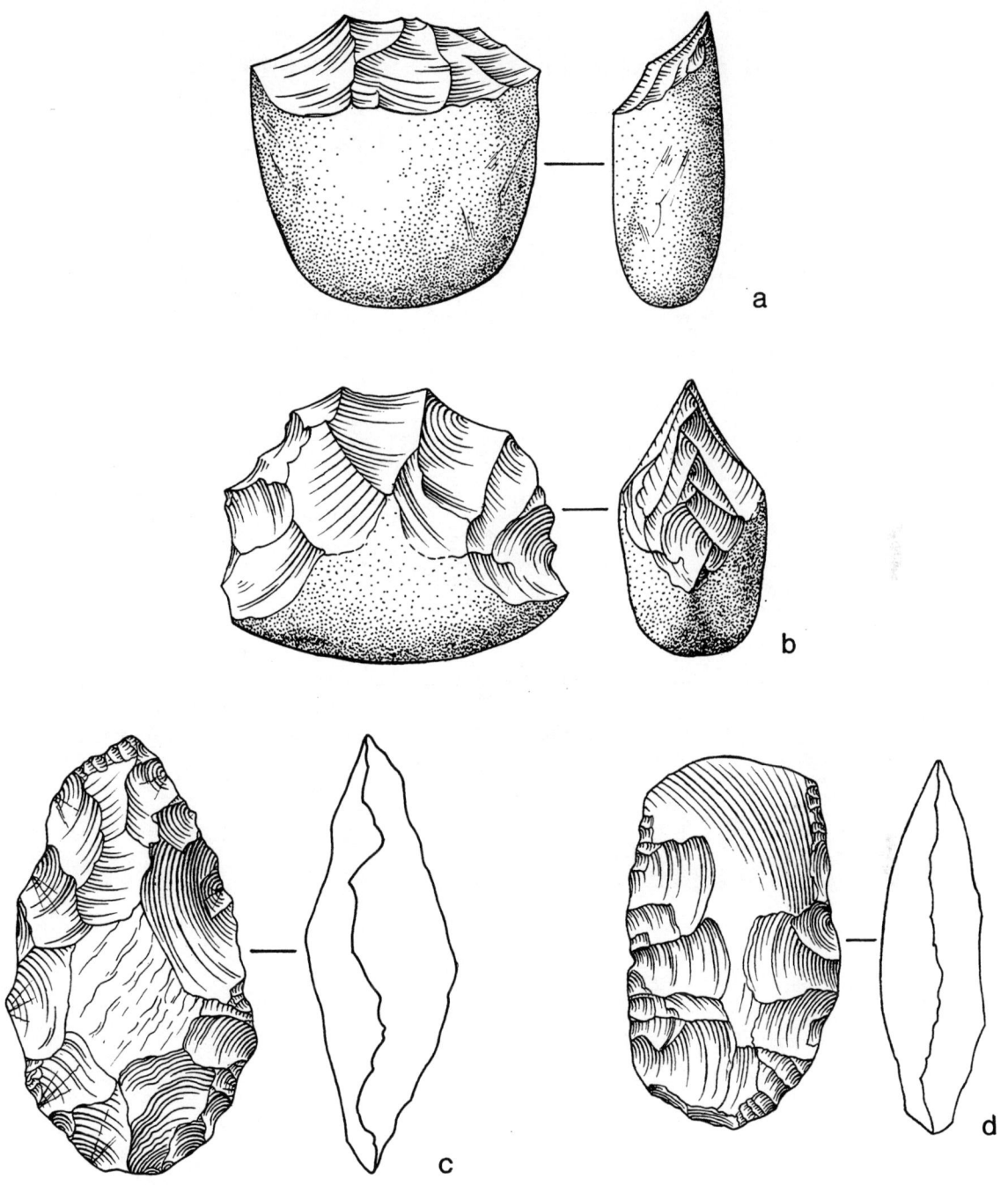

Fig. 8   Flaked artefacts: chopper (a), chopping tool (b), biface (c), cleaver (d)

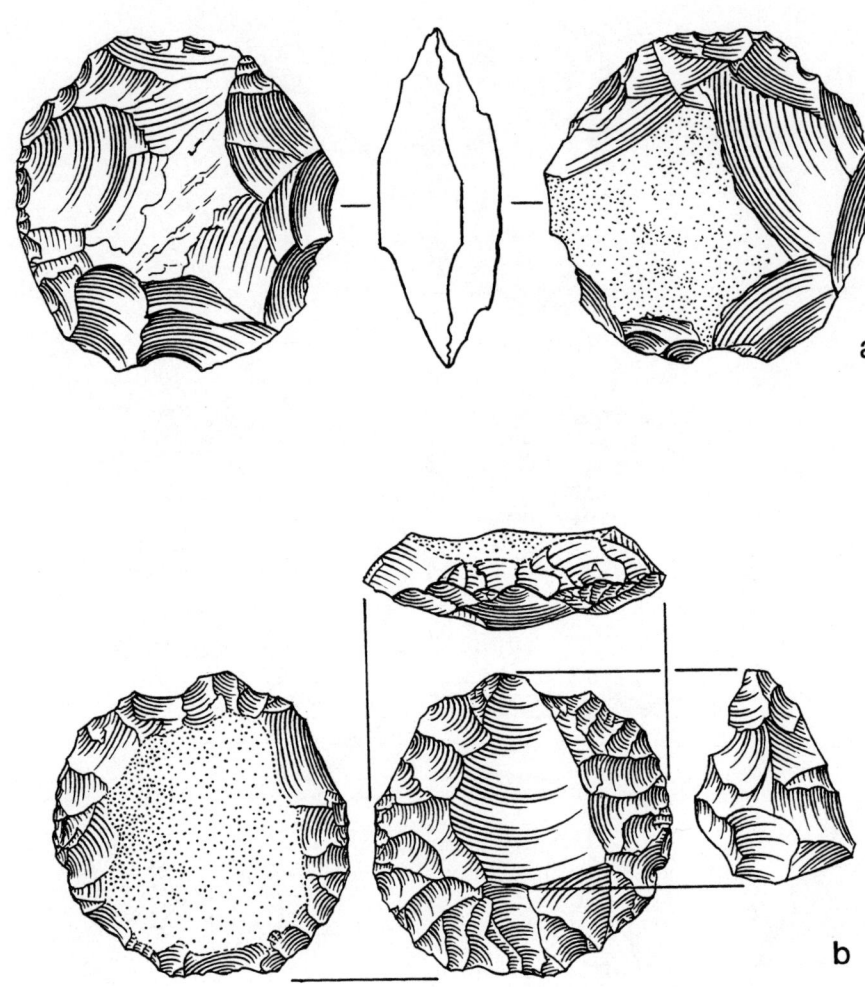

Fig. 9 Complex cores: discoidal (a), Levallois core and flake (b)

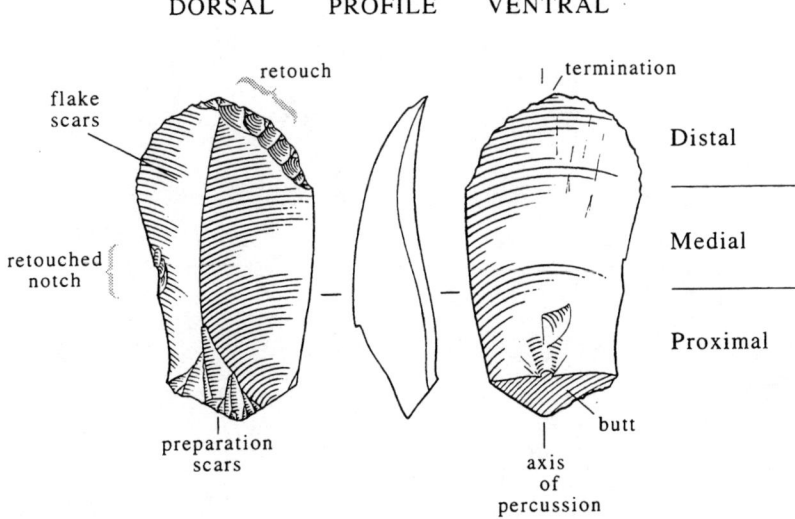

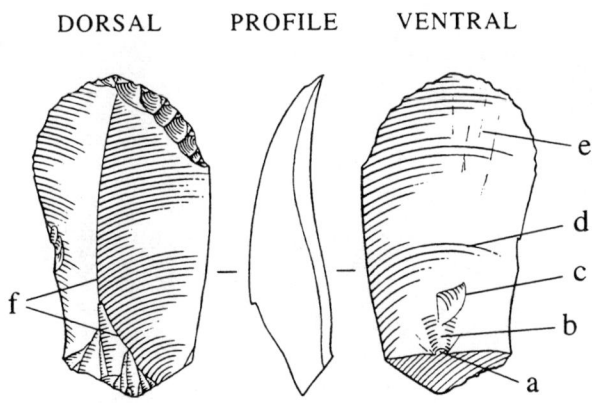

a: cone of percussion. b: bulb of percussion.
c: bulbar flake scars [éraillure]. d: ripple marks.
e: fissures. f: arêtes.

Fig. 10   Nomenclature used to describe features of struck flakes and blades

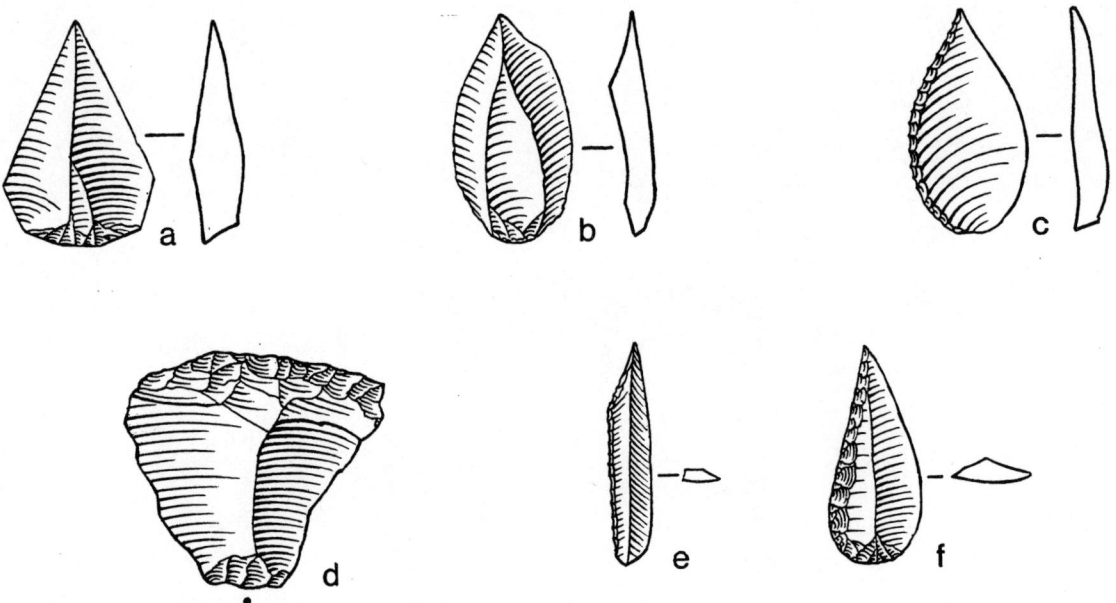

Fig. 11   Flake and blade tool types: unmodified triangular (a) and leaf (b) points; single edge point (c) with inverse retouch; transverse scraper (d); backed and obliquely truncated bladelet (e); flake with direct, semi-invasive retouch (f)

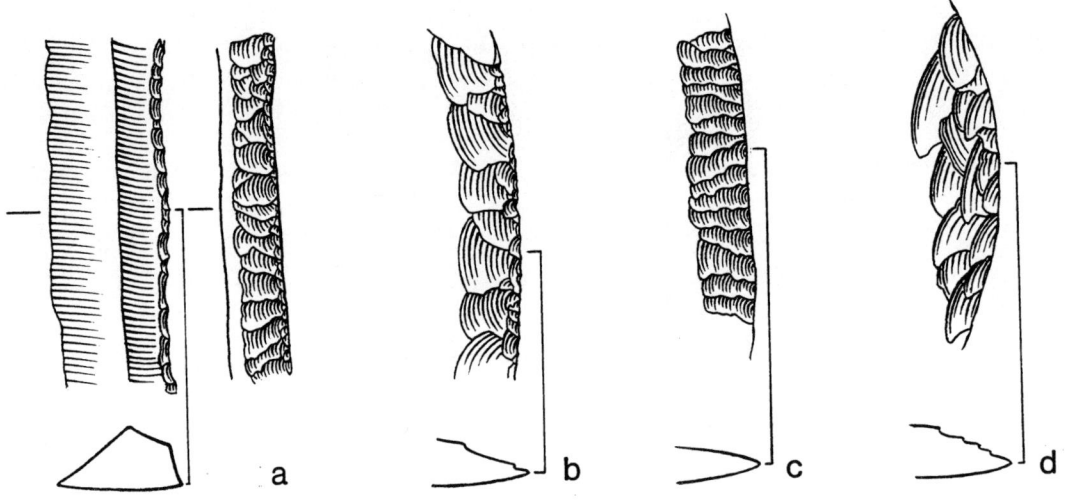

Fig. 12   Retouch types: abrupt or backing retouch (a); scalar retouch (b); sub-parallel retouch (c); stepped scalar retouch (d)

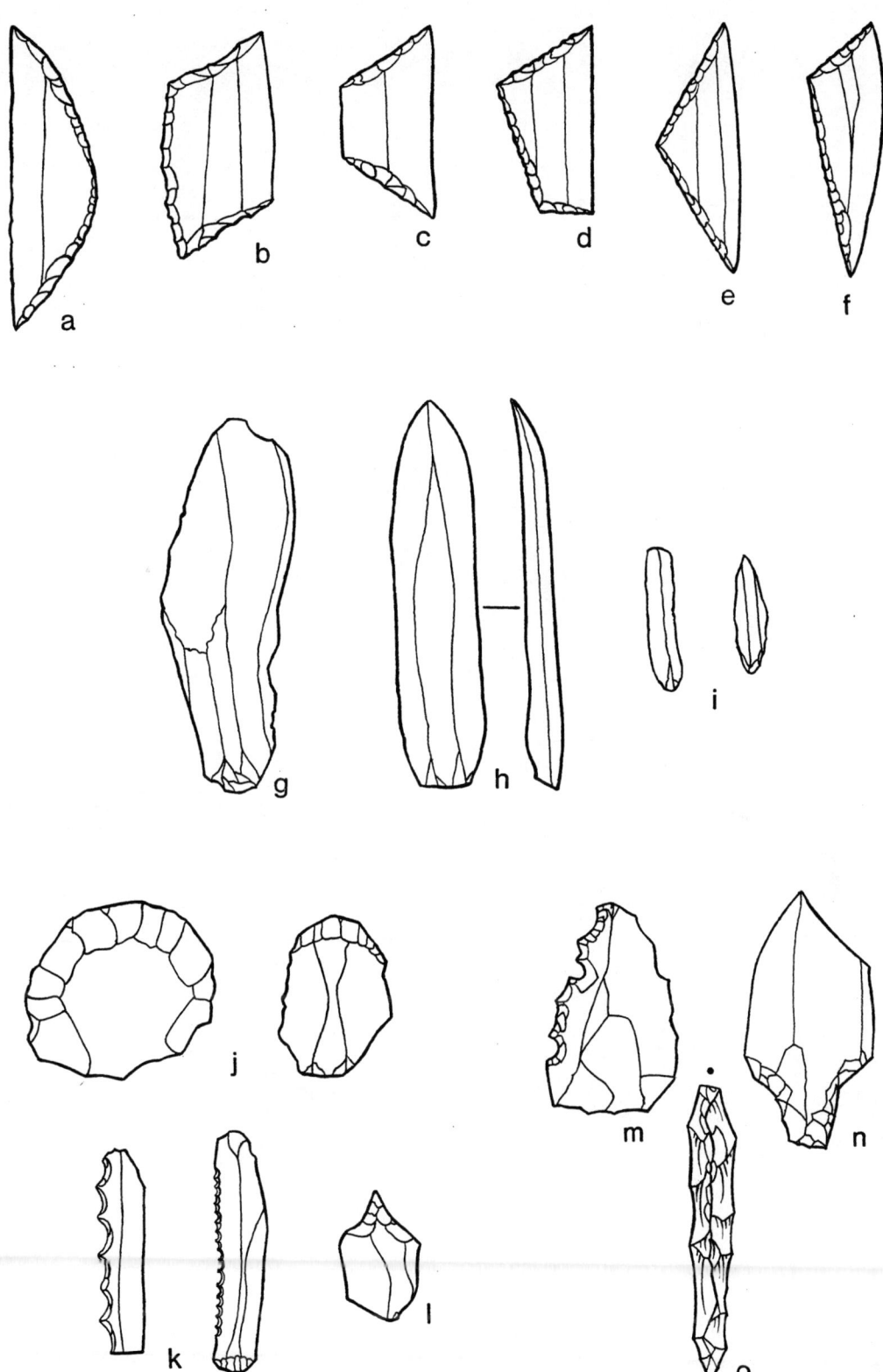

Fig. 13 Microlith forms (x2): lunate (a); rhomboid (b); trapeze (c); trapezoid (d); isosceles triangle (e); scalene triangle (f). Blade artefacts: unmodified (g); parallel-sided (h); bladelet (i); round and end scrapers (j); saws (k); borer (l); denticulate (m); tanged blade (n); crested blade (o)

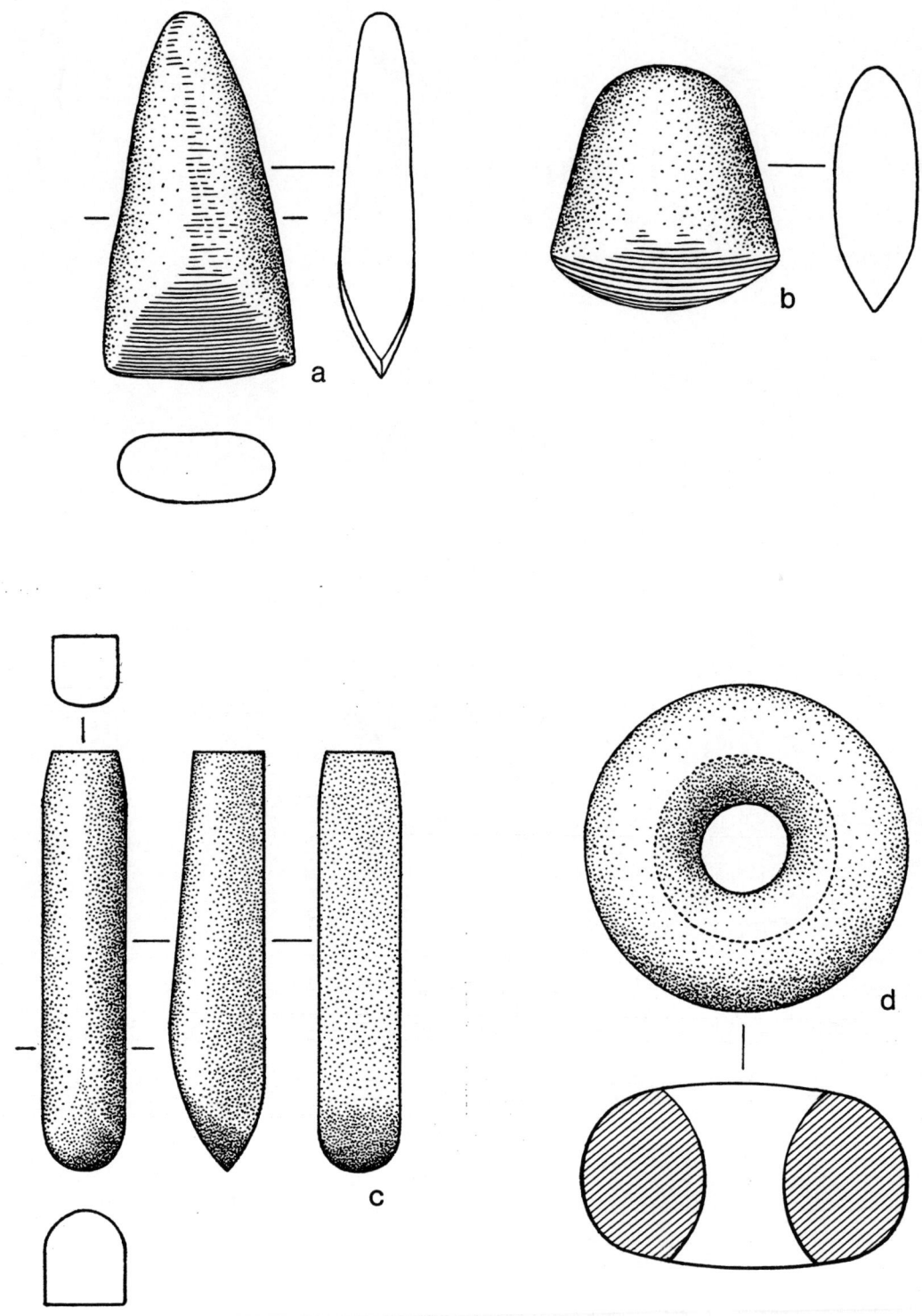

Fig. 14 Polished stone implements: polished axes (a and b); adze or 'shoe last celt' (c); ringstone (d)

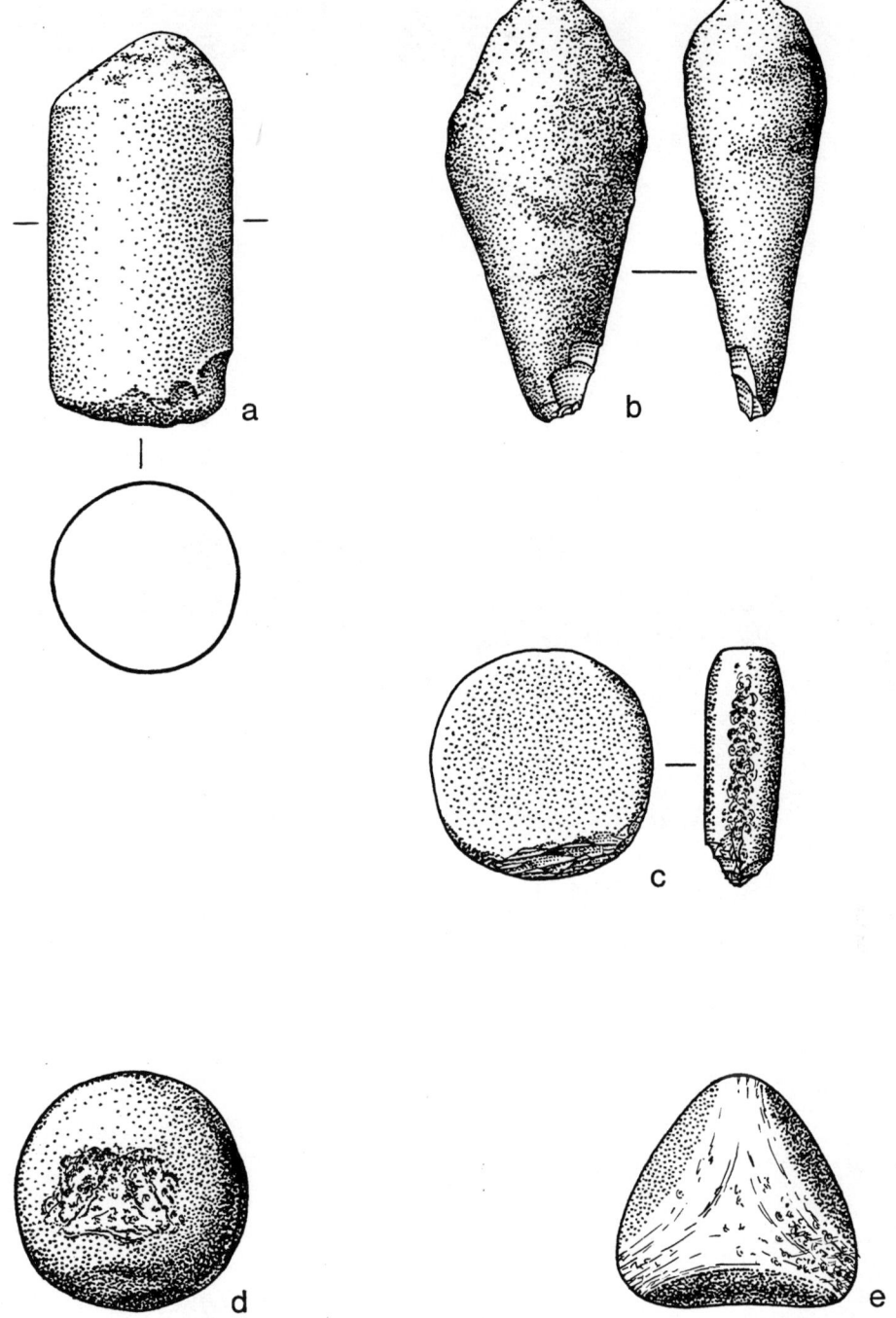

Fig. 15 Utilised stone artefacts: cylindrical (a), pointed (b) and discoidal (c) hammerstones; anvil stone (d); sling stone (e)

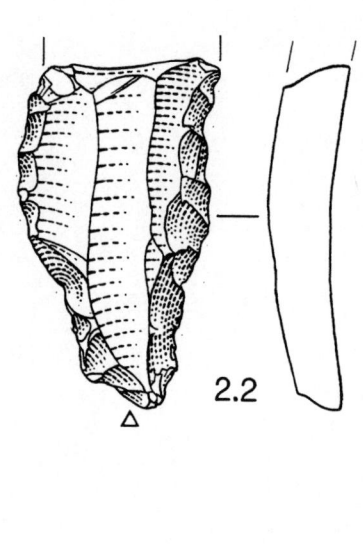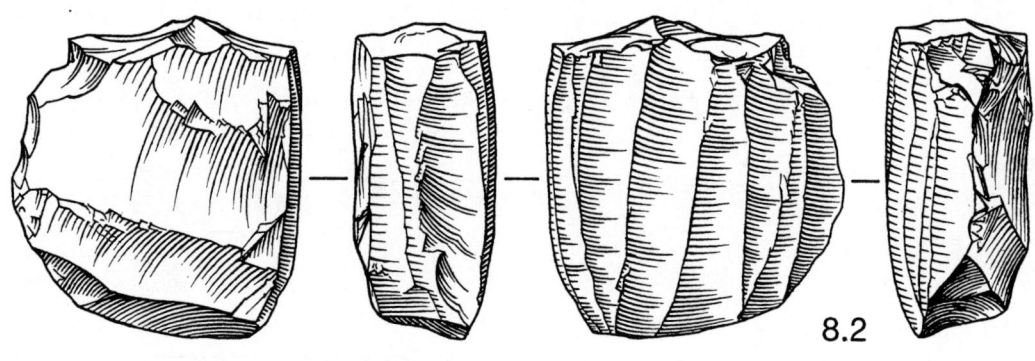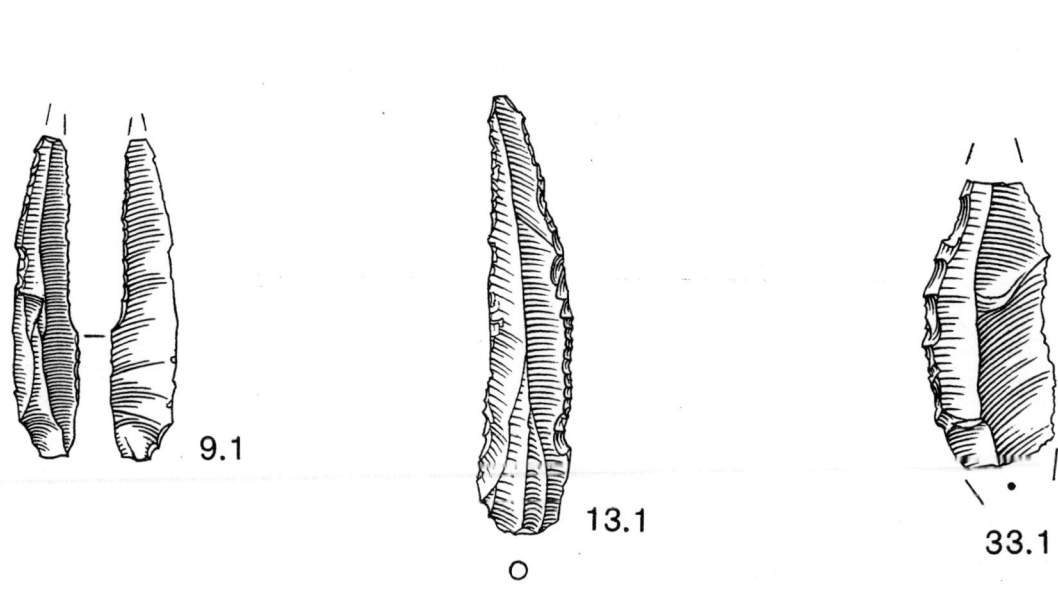

Fig. 16   Artefacts from Amila Nala, Barkor, Bhagatpura, Bharkura and Mahrela Chacki; (9.1, 13.1 and 33.1 at x2)

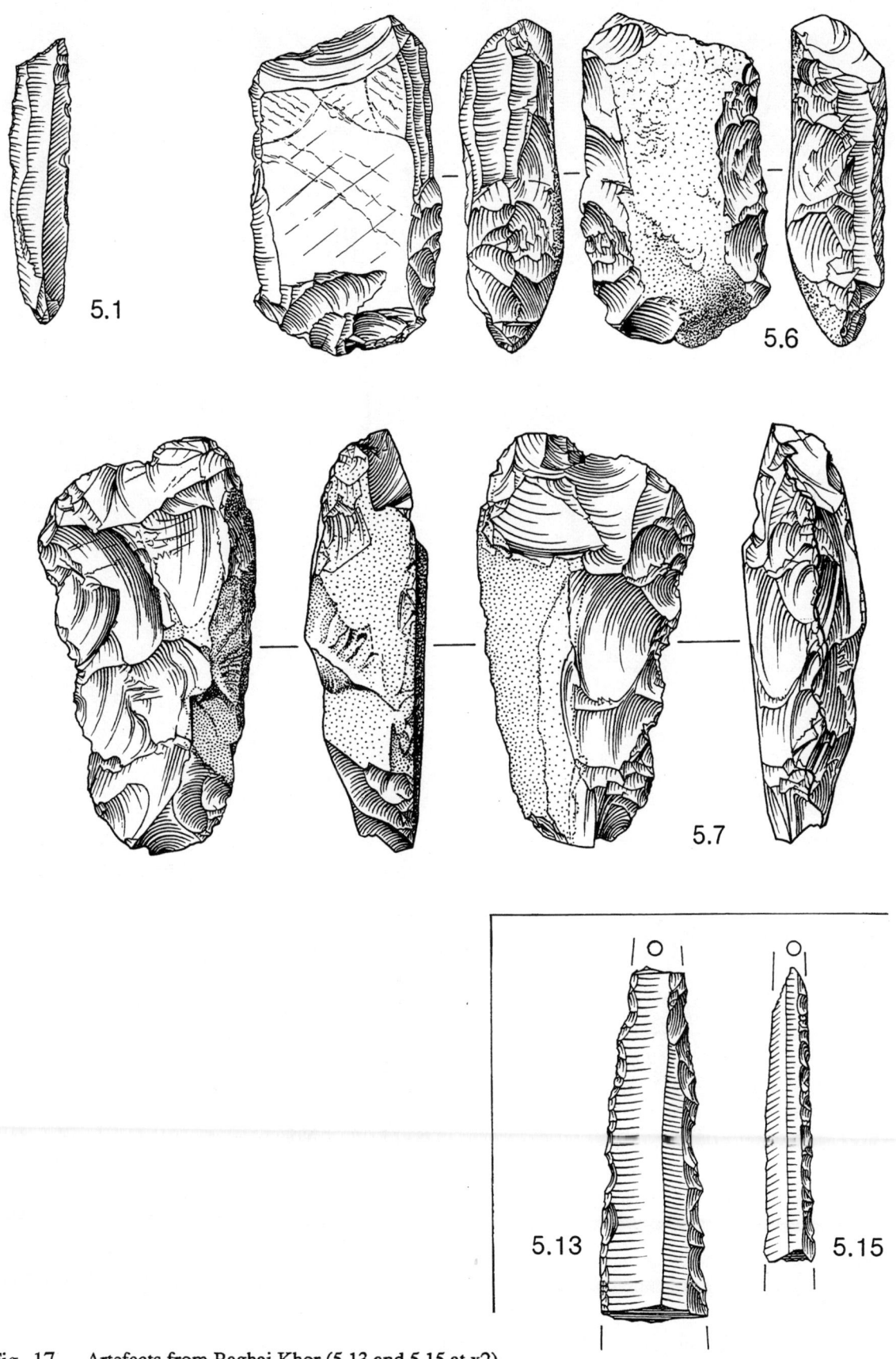

Fig. 17   Artefacts from Baghai Khor (5.13 and 5.15 at x2)

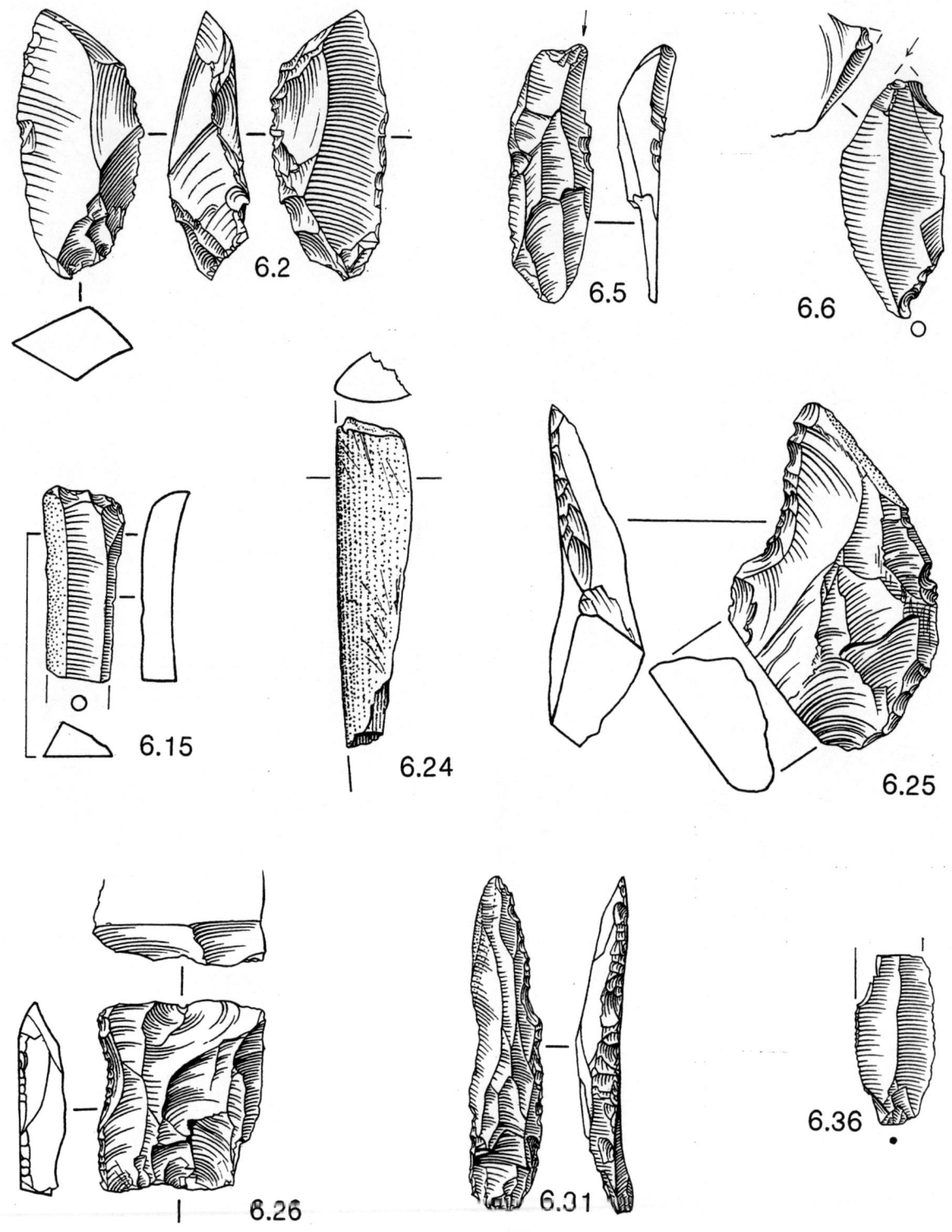

Fig. 18 Artefacts from Baghmara Pahar

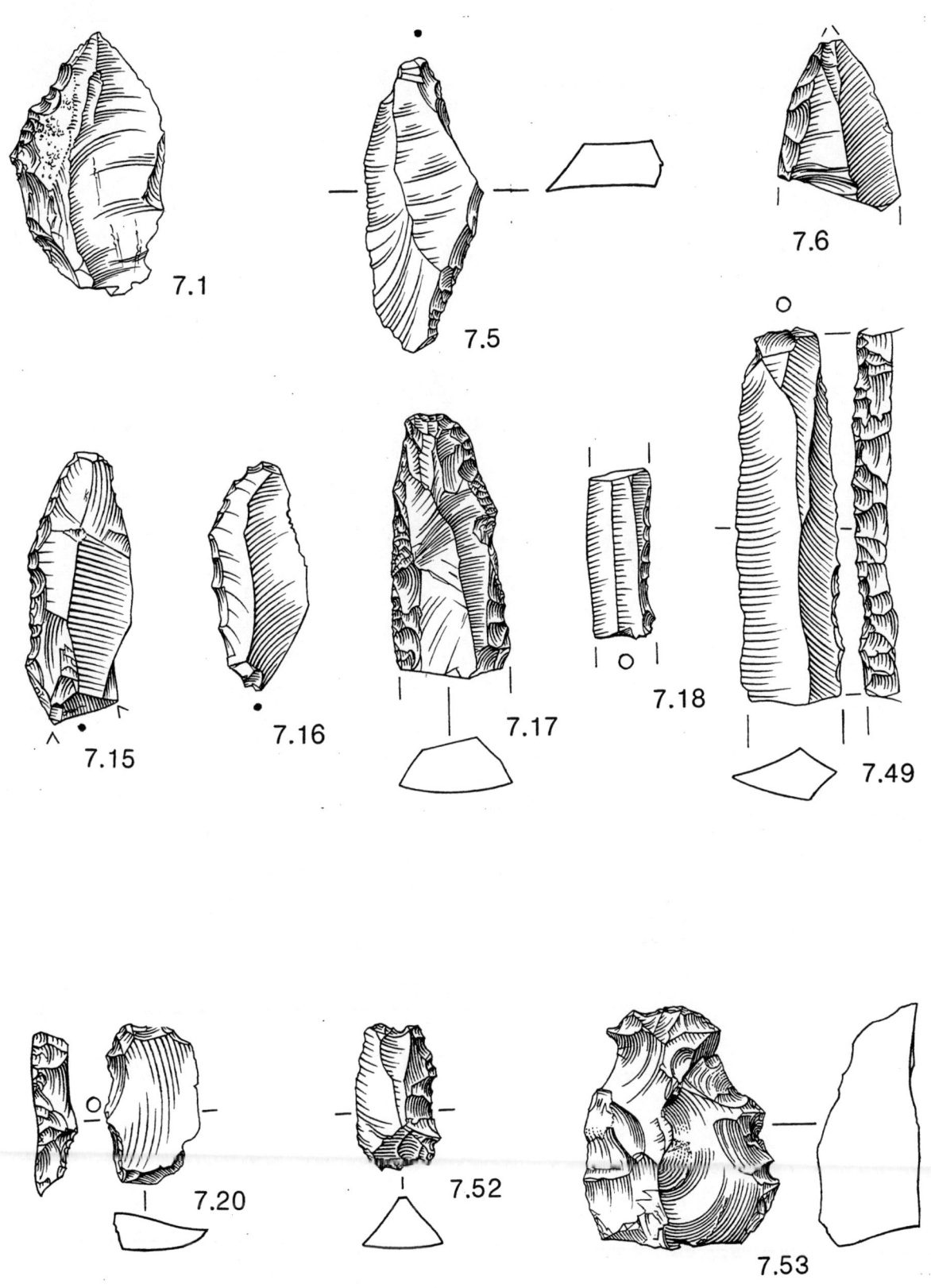

Fig. 19   Tools from Banda (7.1, 7.5, 7.6, 7.15-7.18 and 7.49 x2)

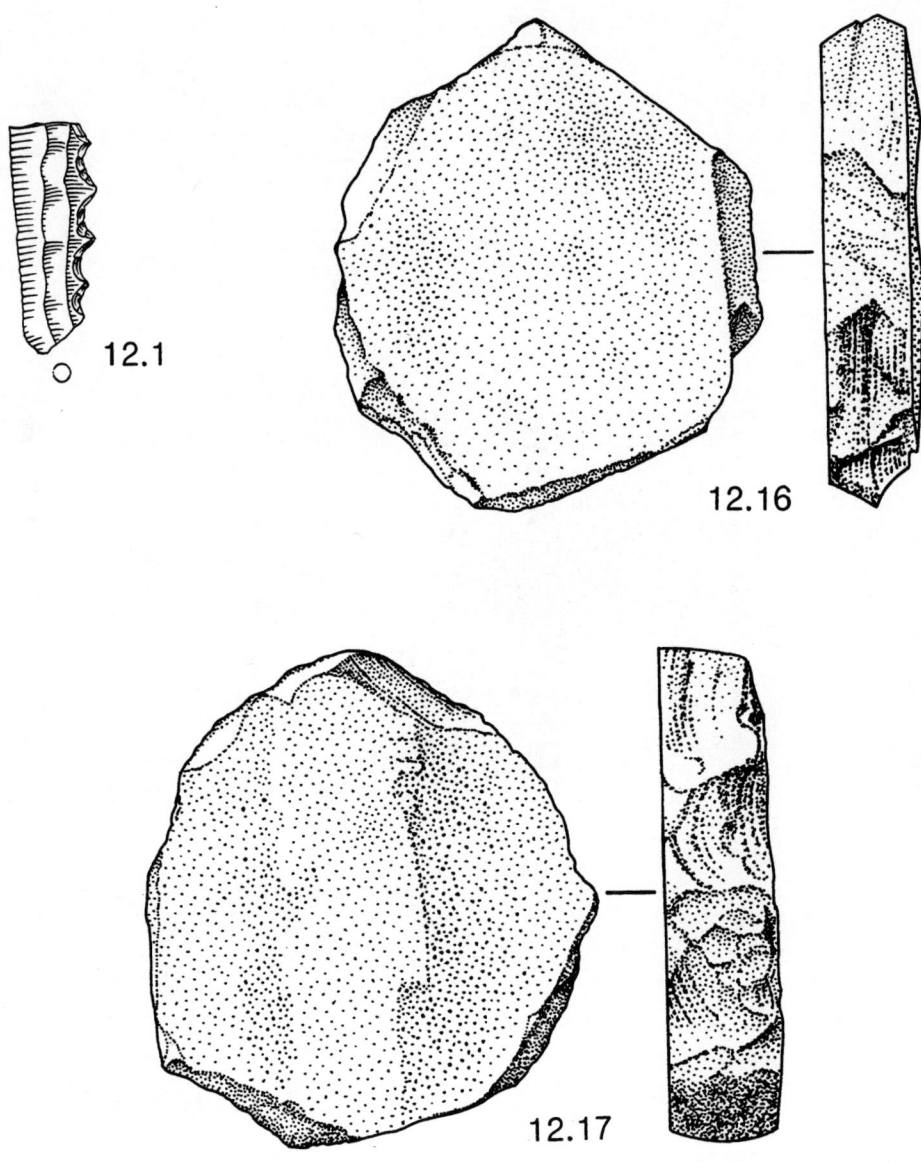

Fig. 20 Saw and palettes from Bharkacha

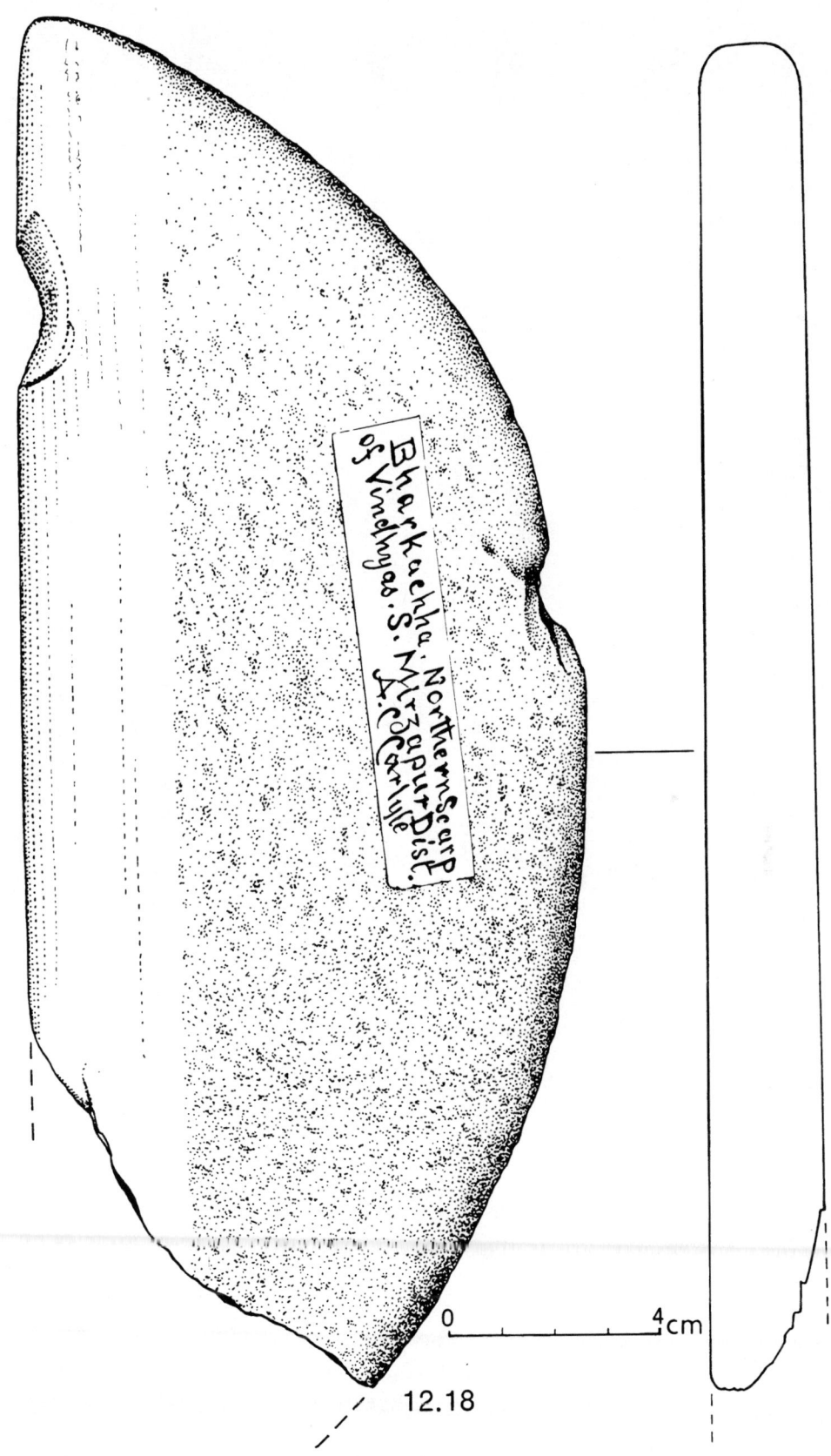

Fig. 21 Utilised sandstone slab from Bharkacha

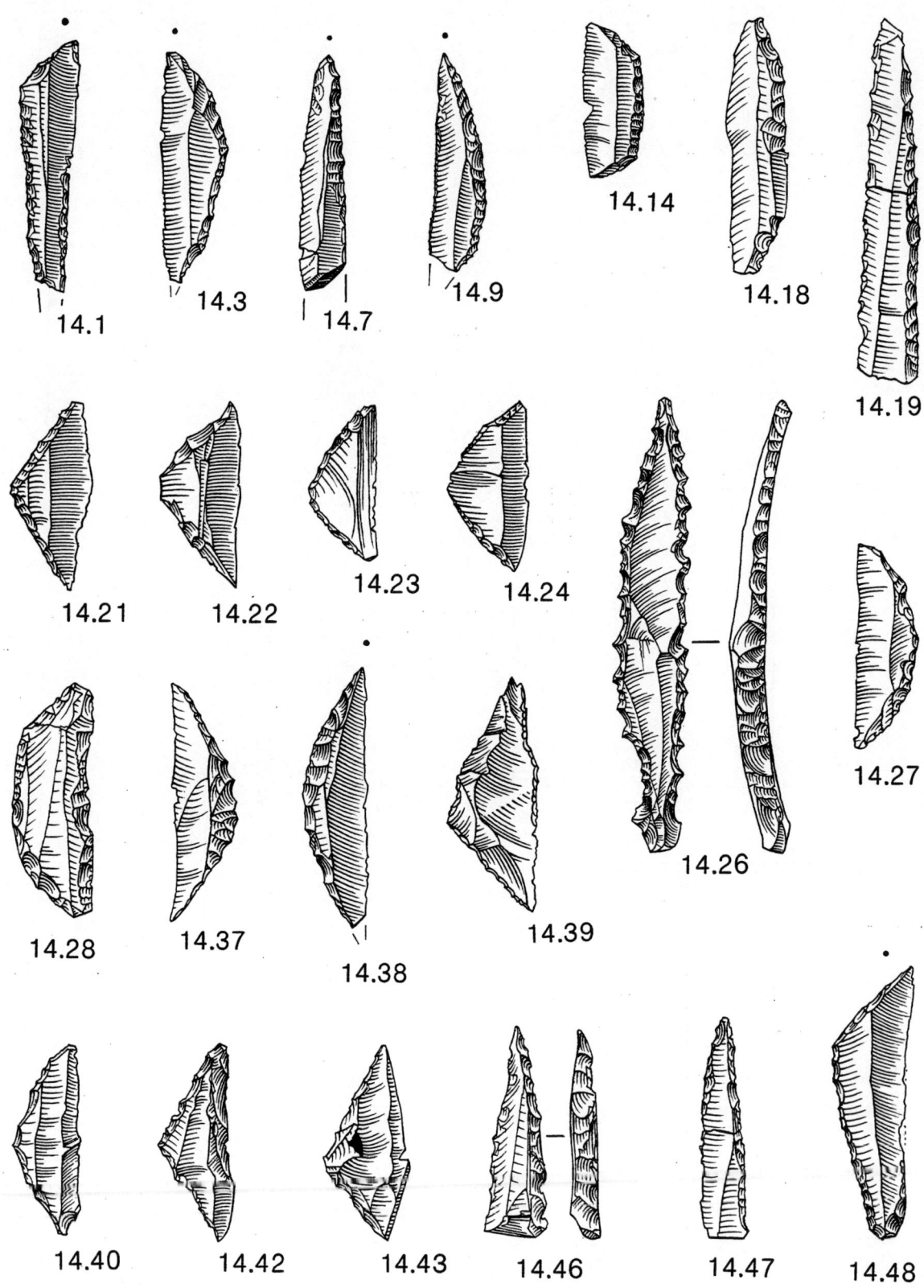

Fig. 22 Microliths from Bundelkhand (all at x2)

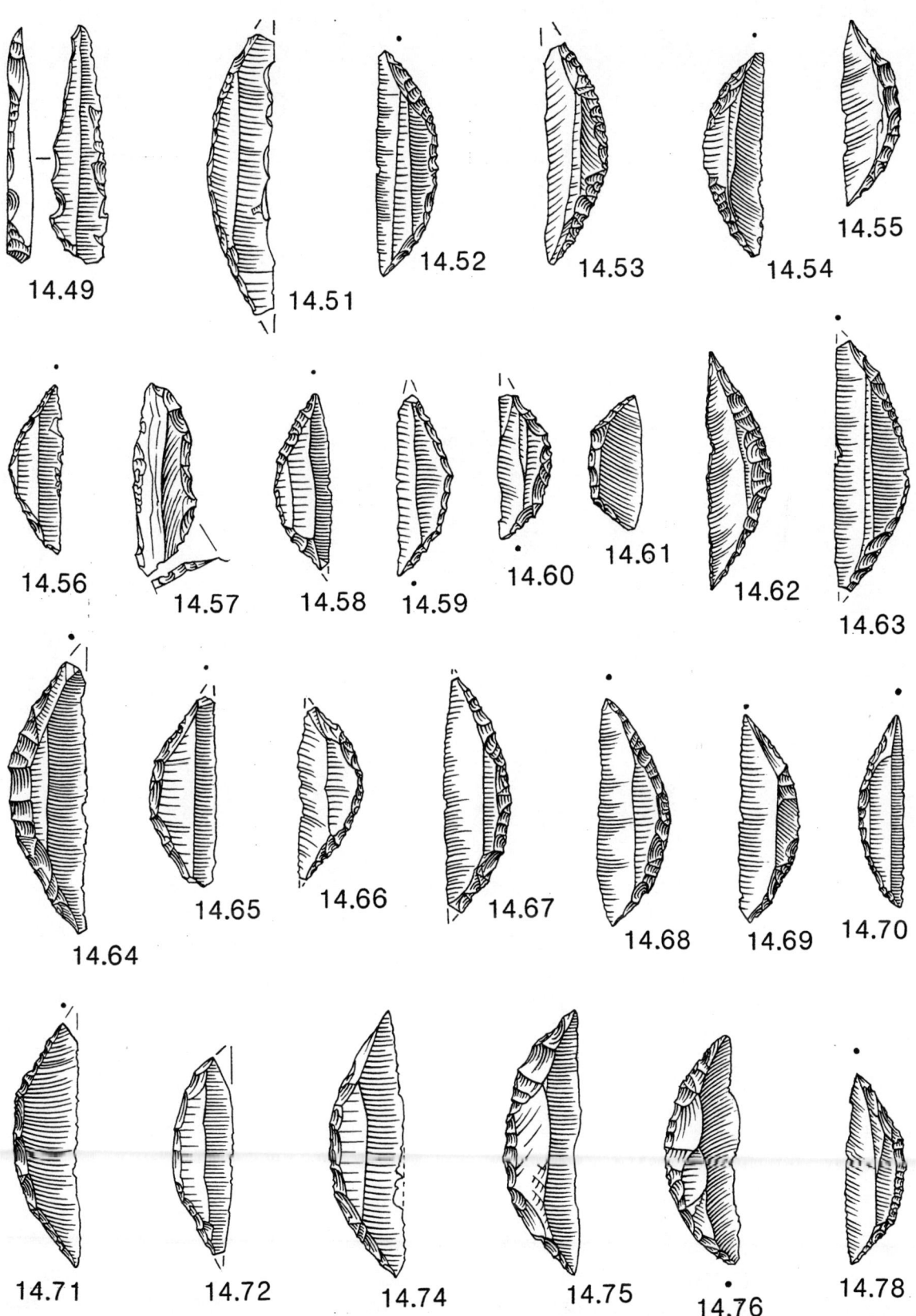

Fig. 23 Microliths from Bundelkhand (all at x2)

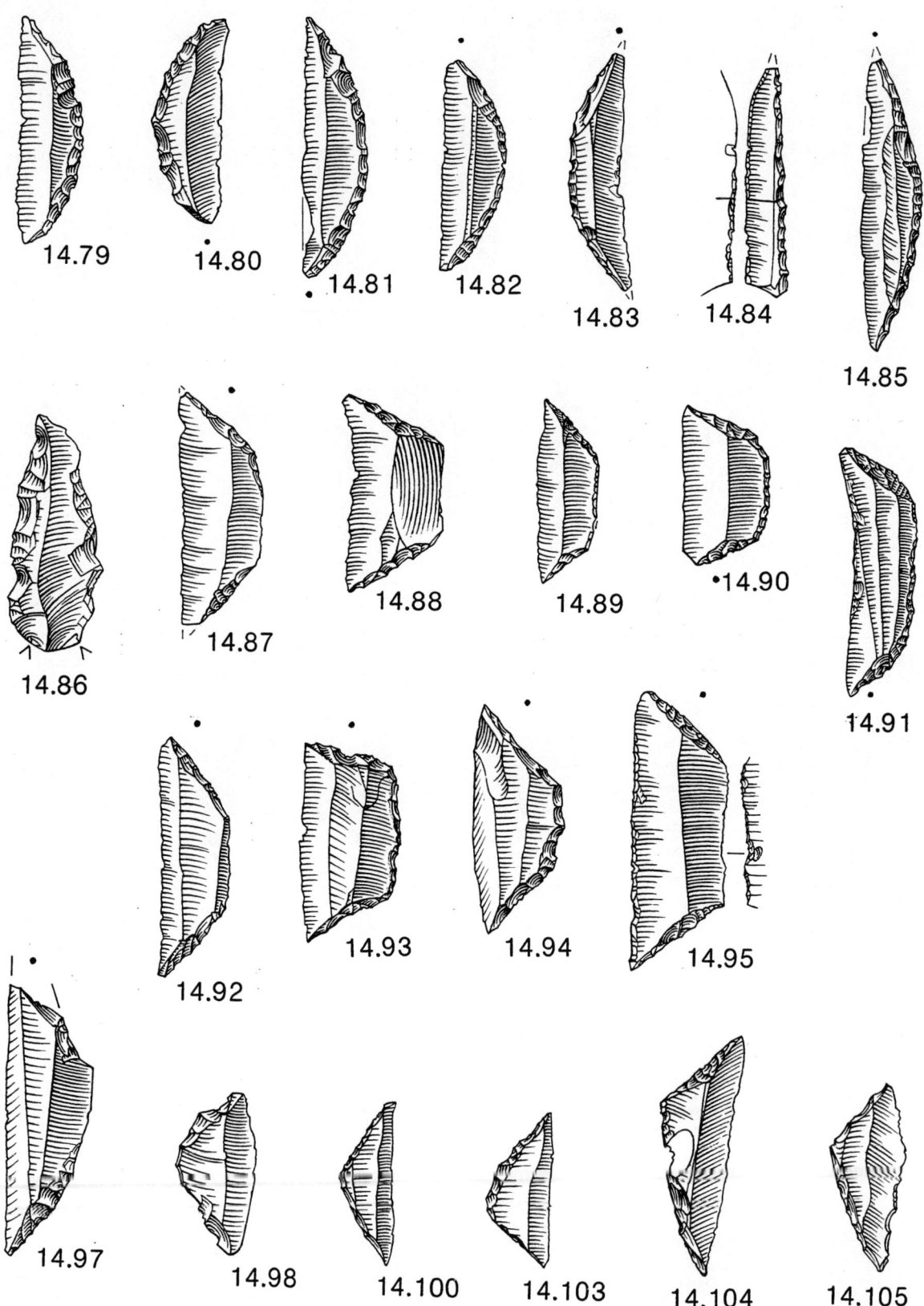

Fig. 24 Microliths from Bundelkhand (all at x2)

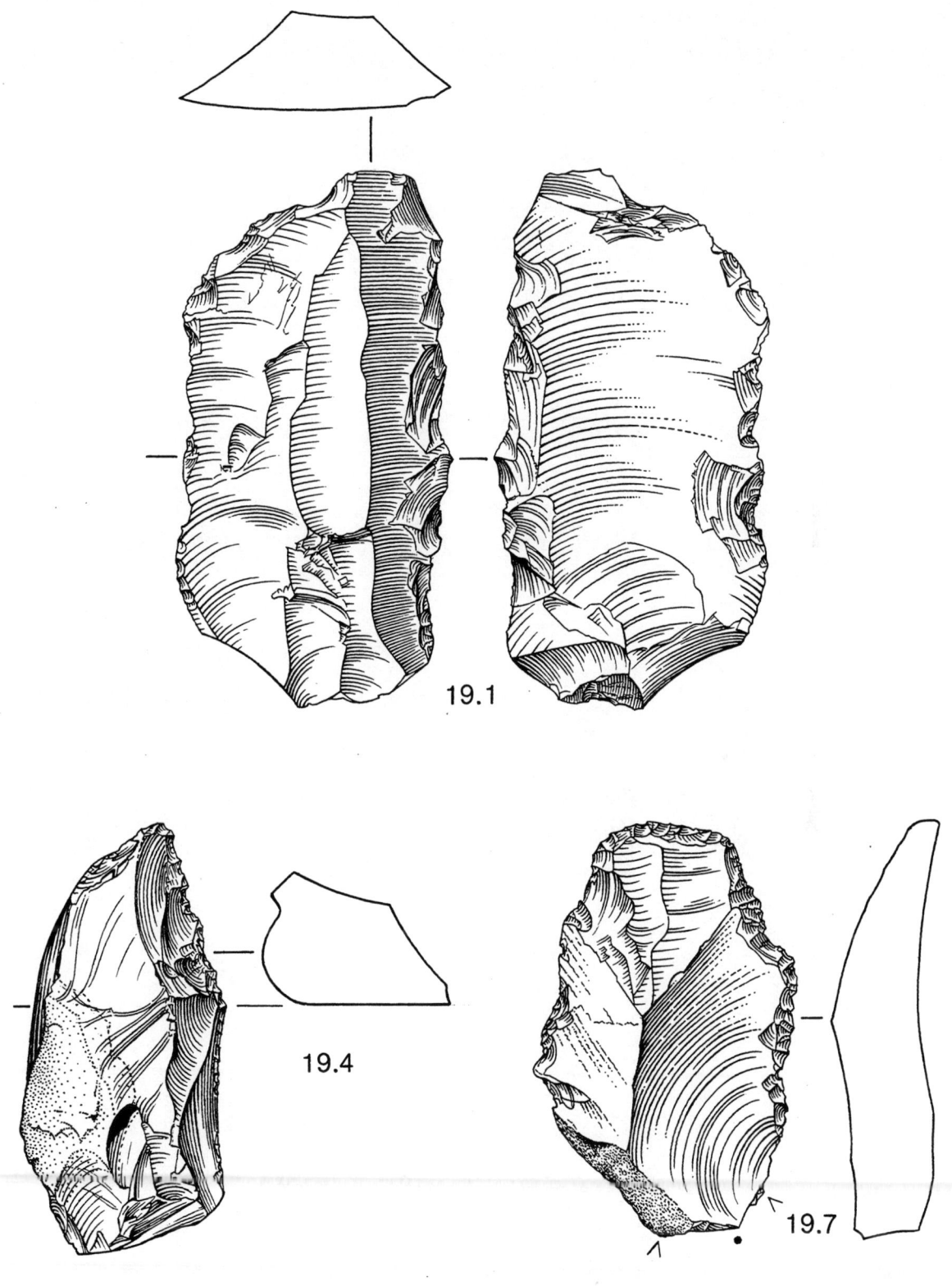

Fig. 25   Prepared and retouched flakes from Gaur River gravels

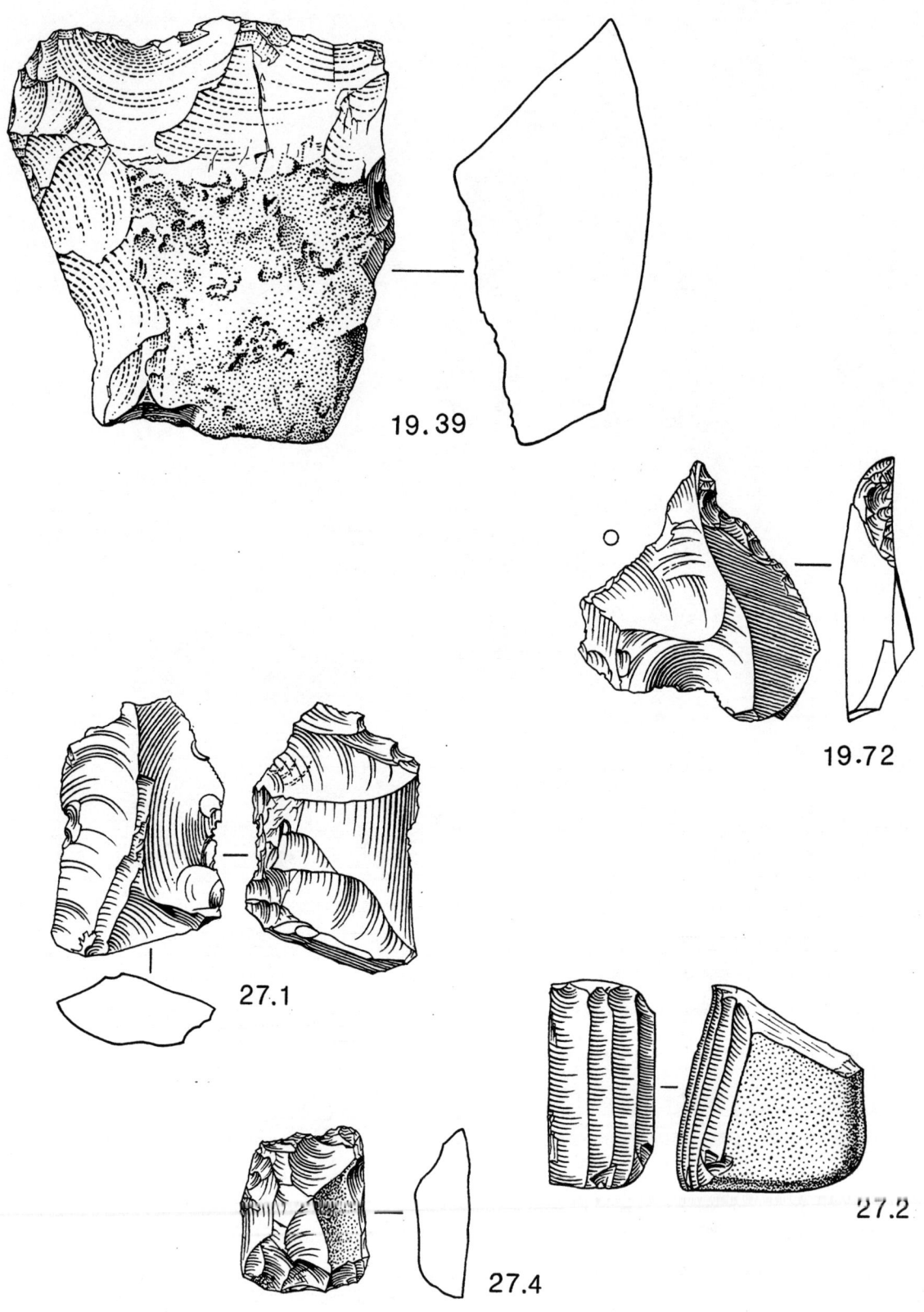

Fig. 26 Artefacts from the Gaur and Ken River valleys

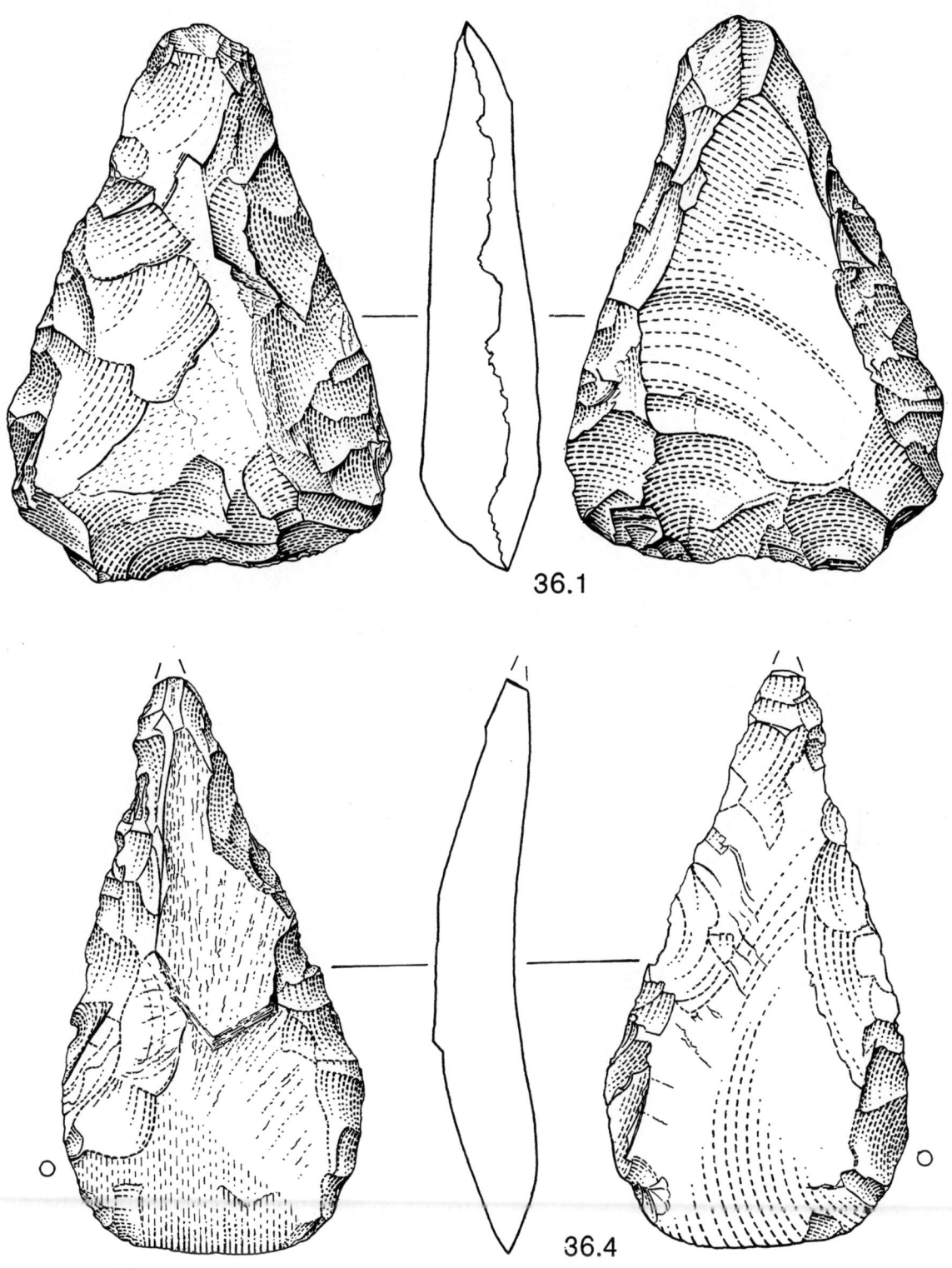

Fig. 27   Bifaces from Marfa

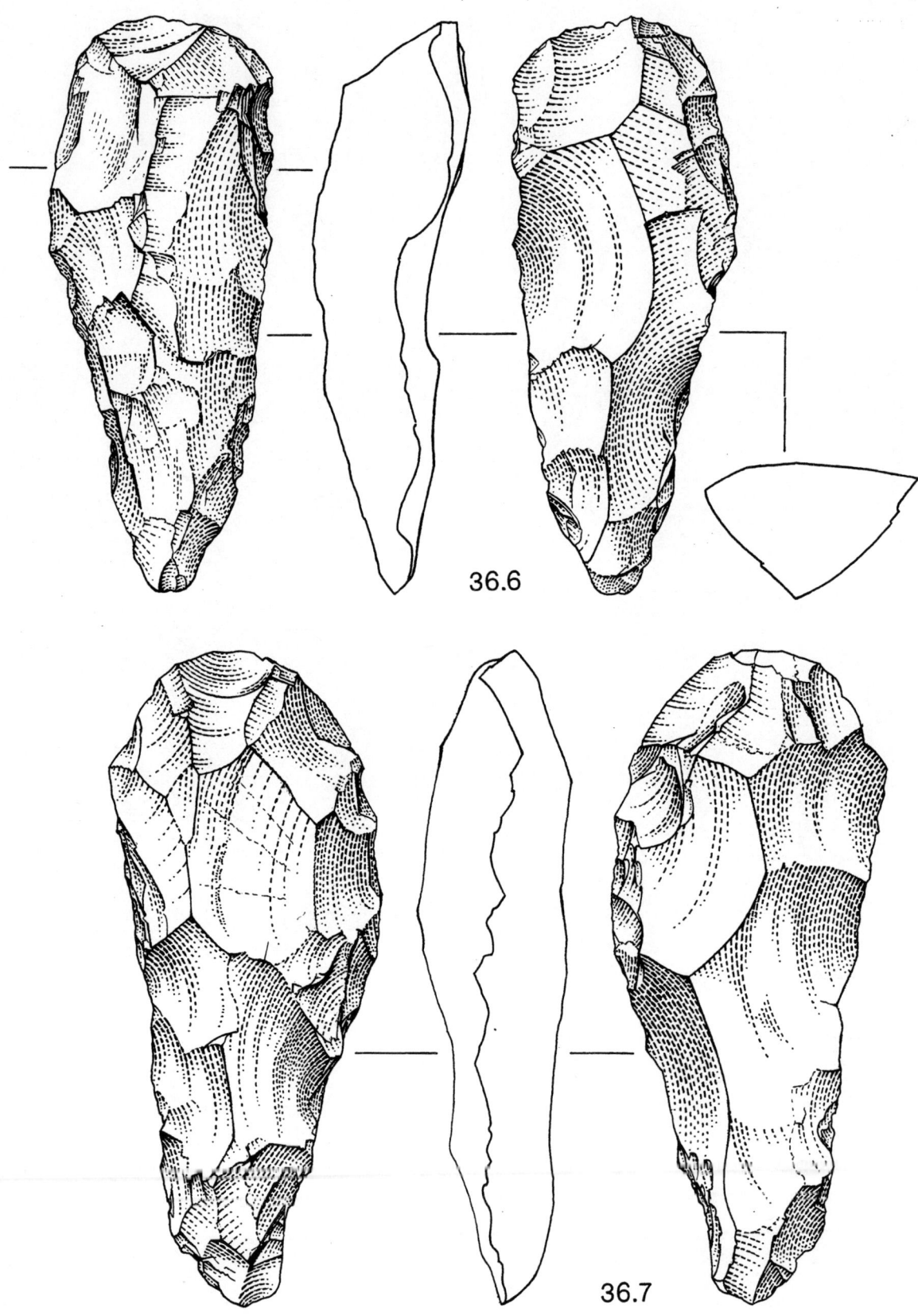

Fig. 28   Picks from Marfa

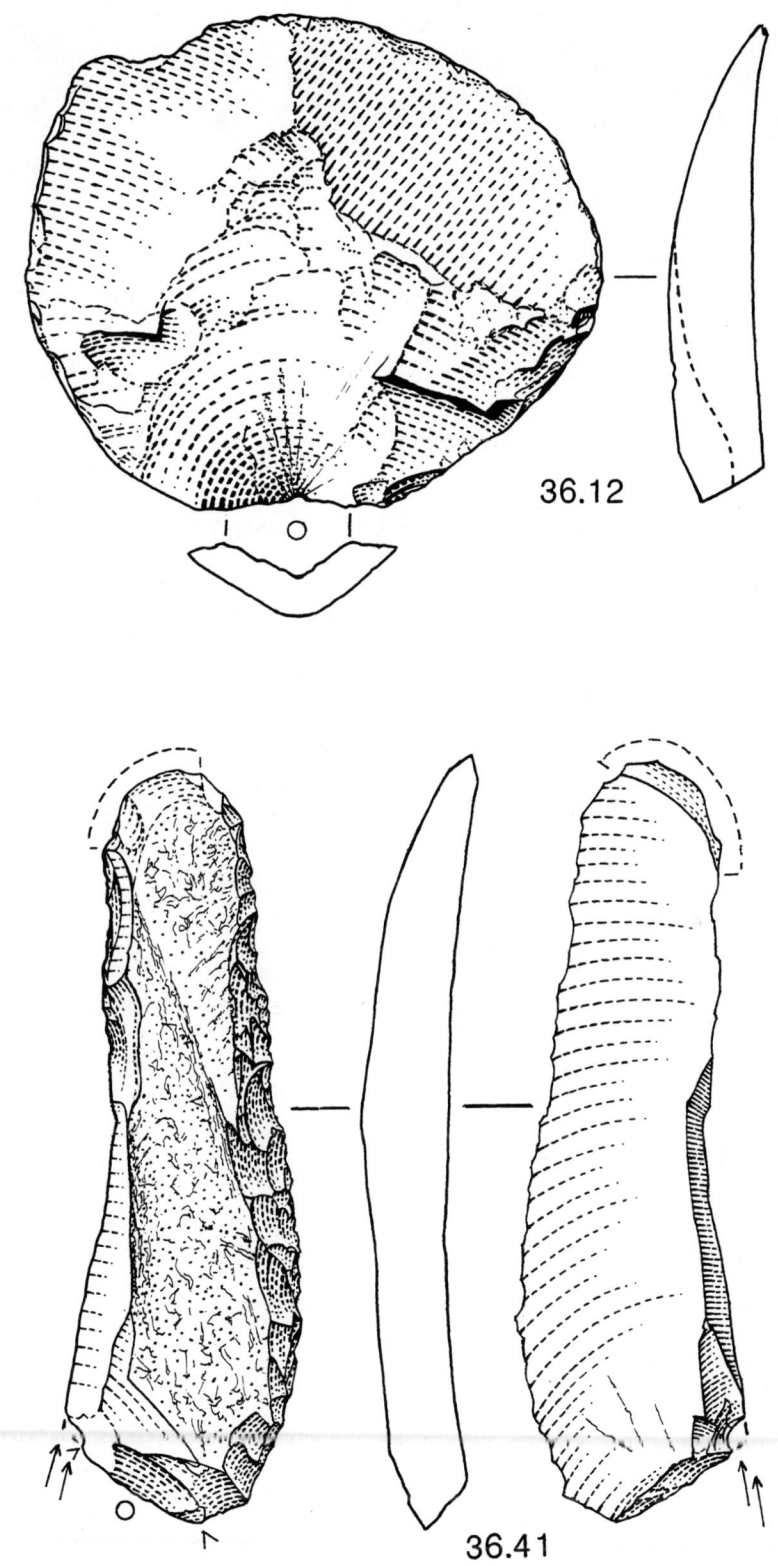

Fig. 29   Prepared flake and scraper from Marfa

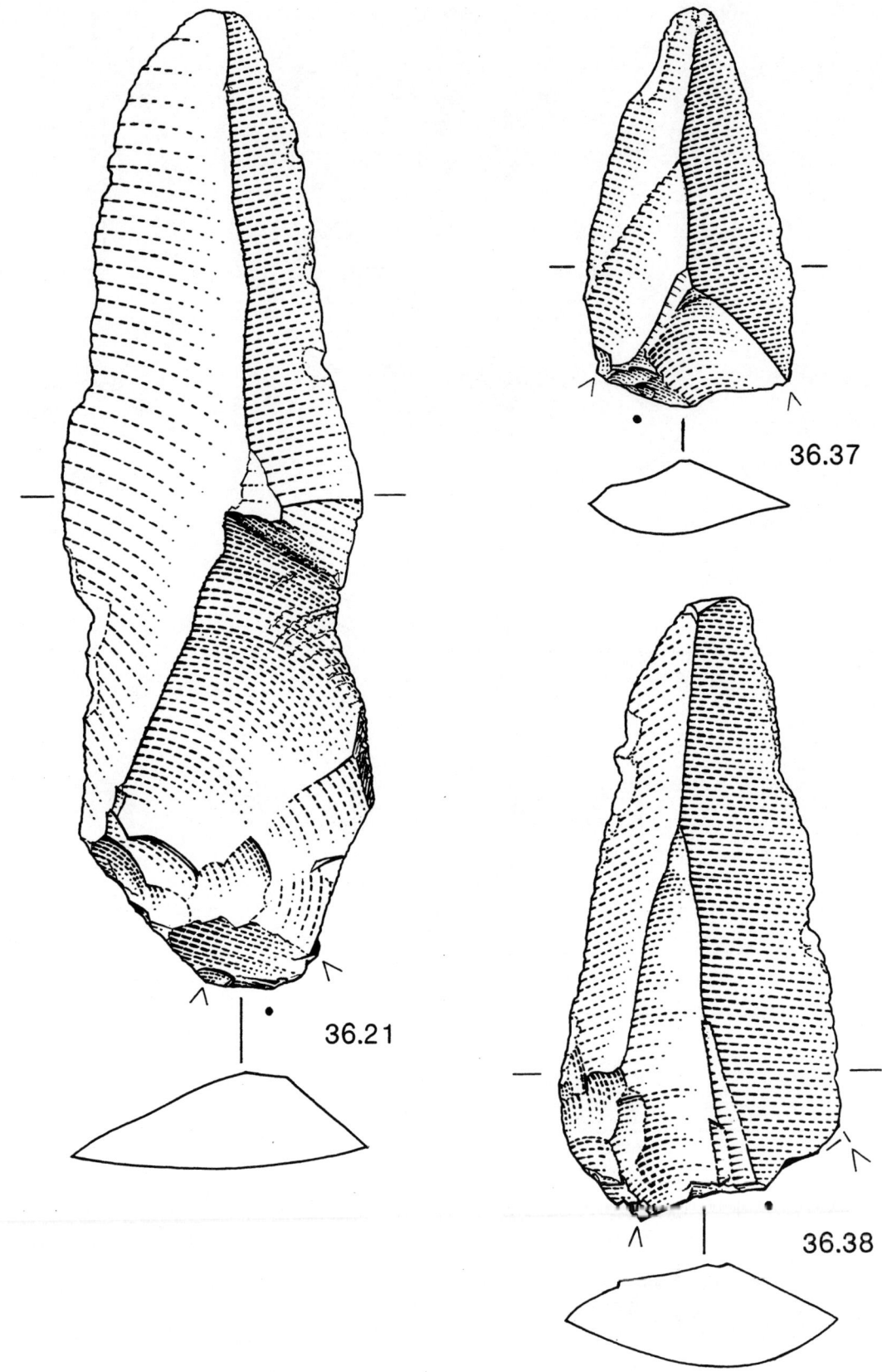

Fig. 30   Prepared flakes from Marfa

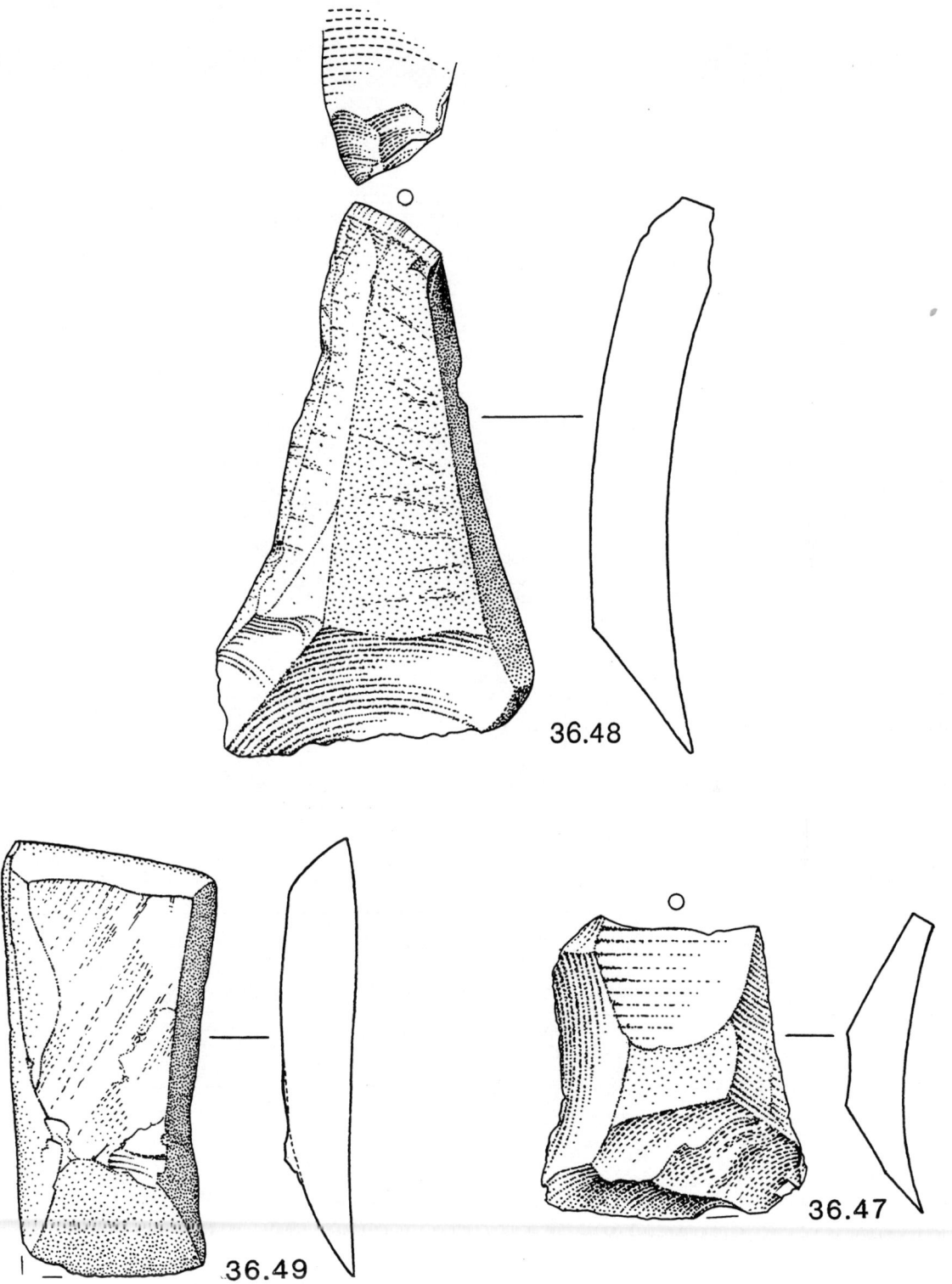

Fig. 31   Flakes from Marfa

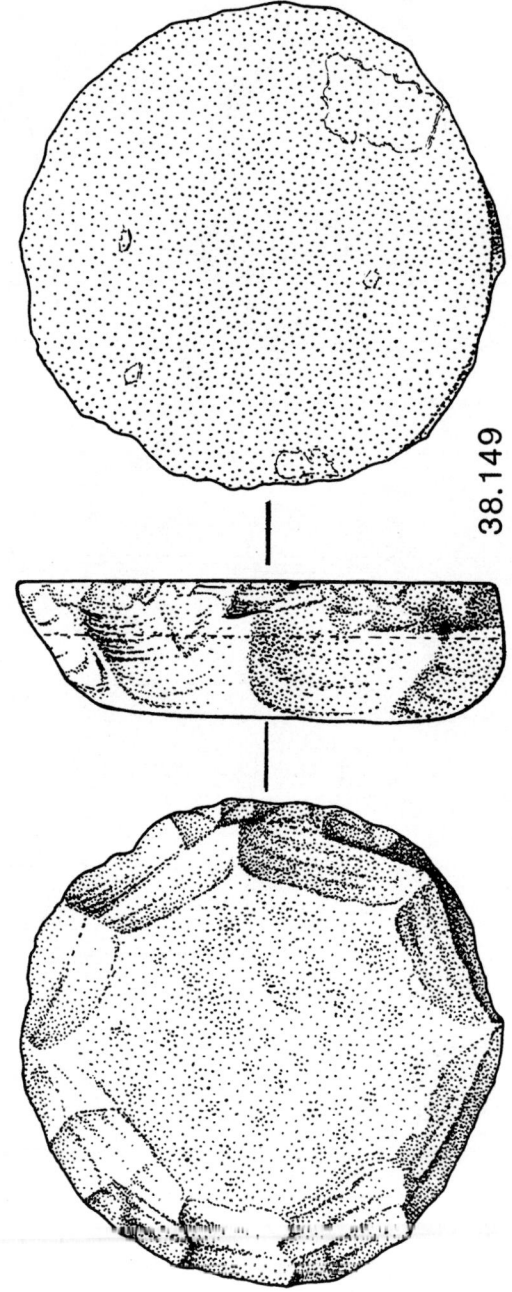

Fig. 32   Palette from Morhana Pahar

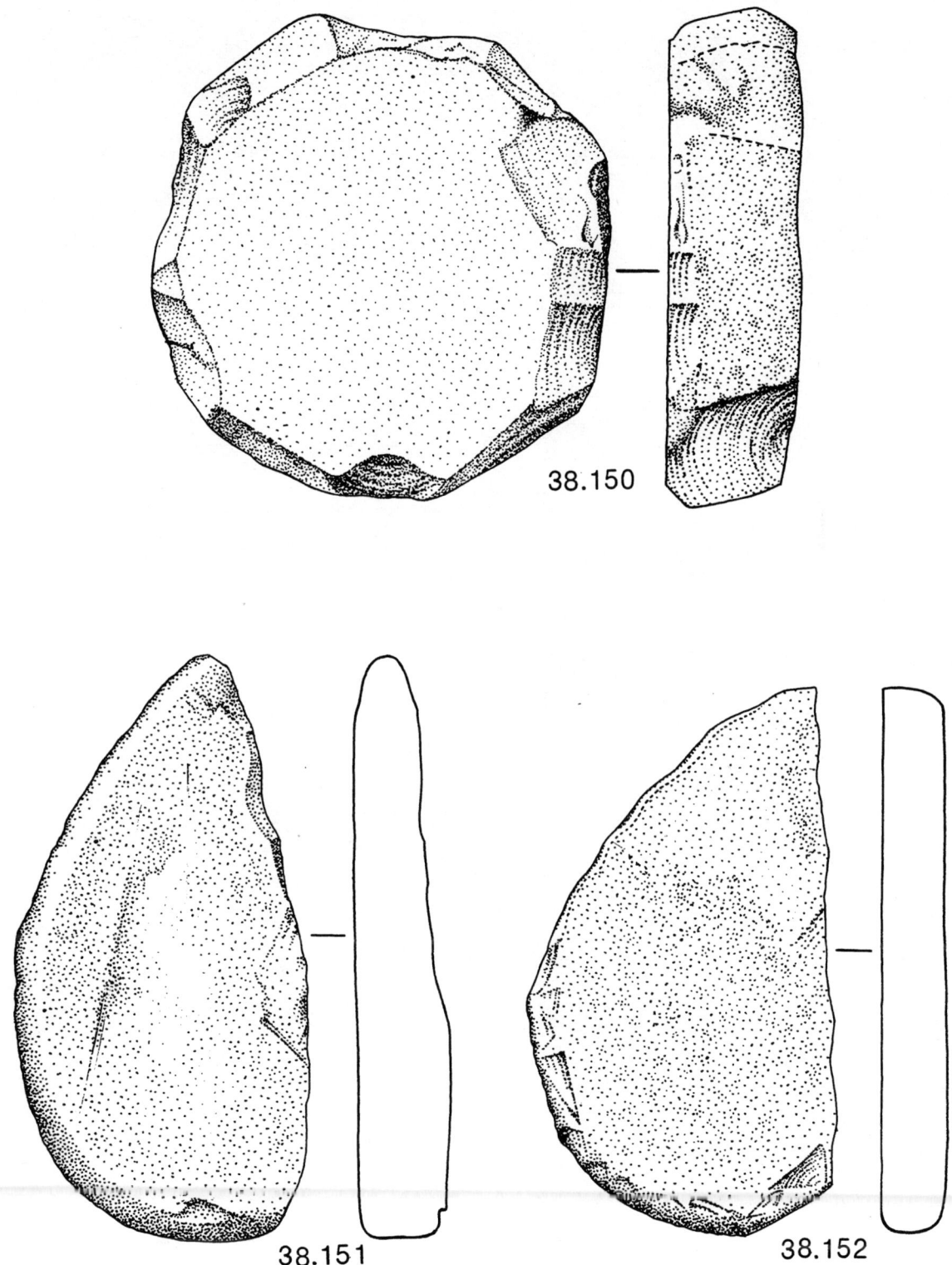

Fig. 33   Palettes from Morhana Pahar

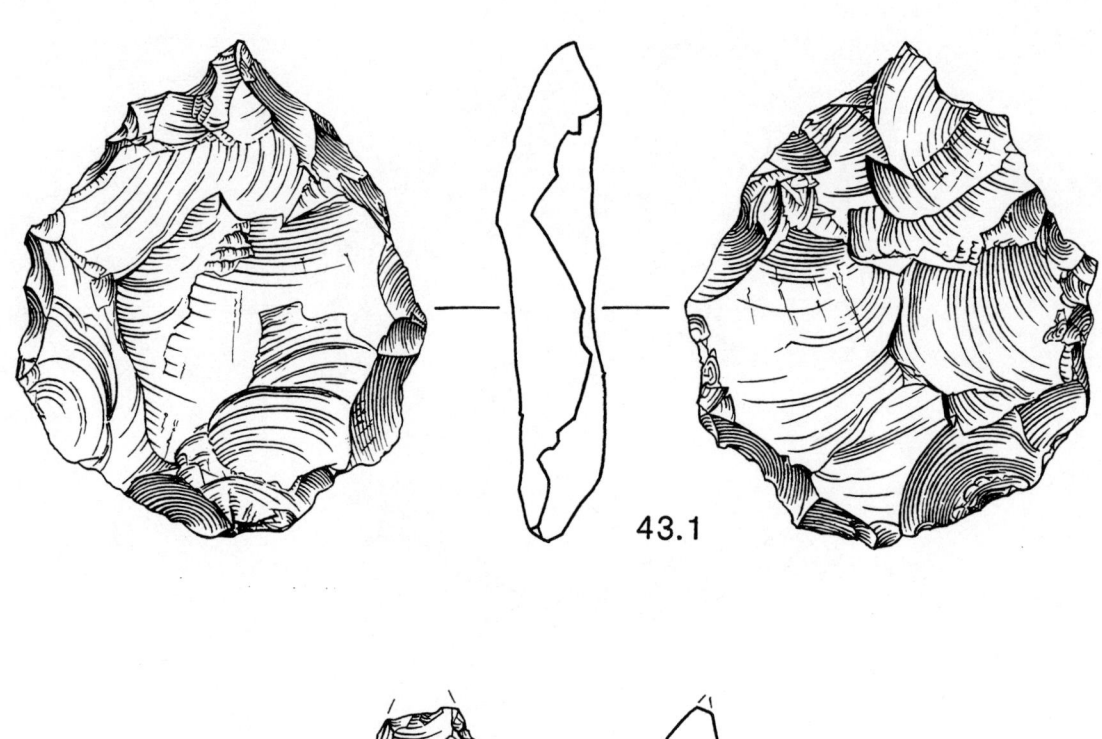
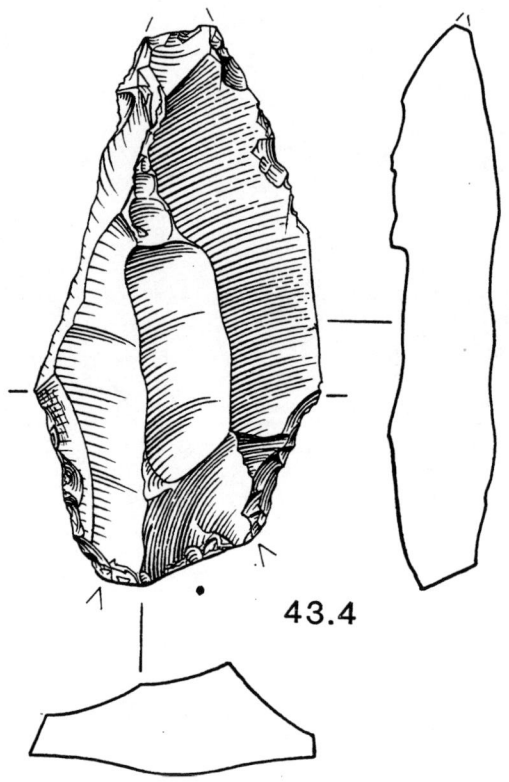

Fig. 34   Biface and prepared flake from the Narmada Valley

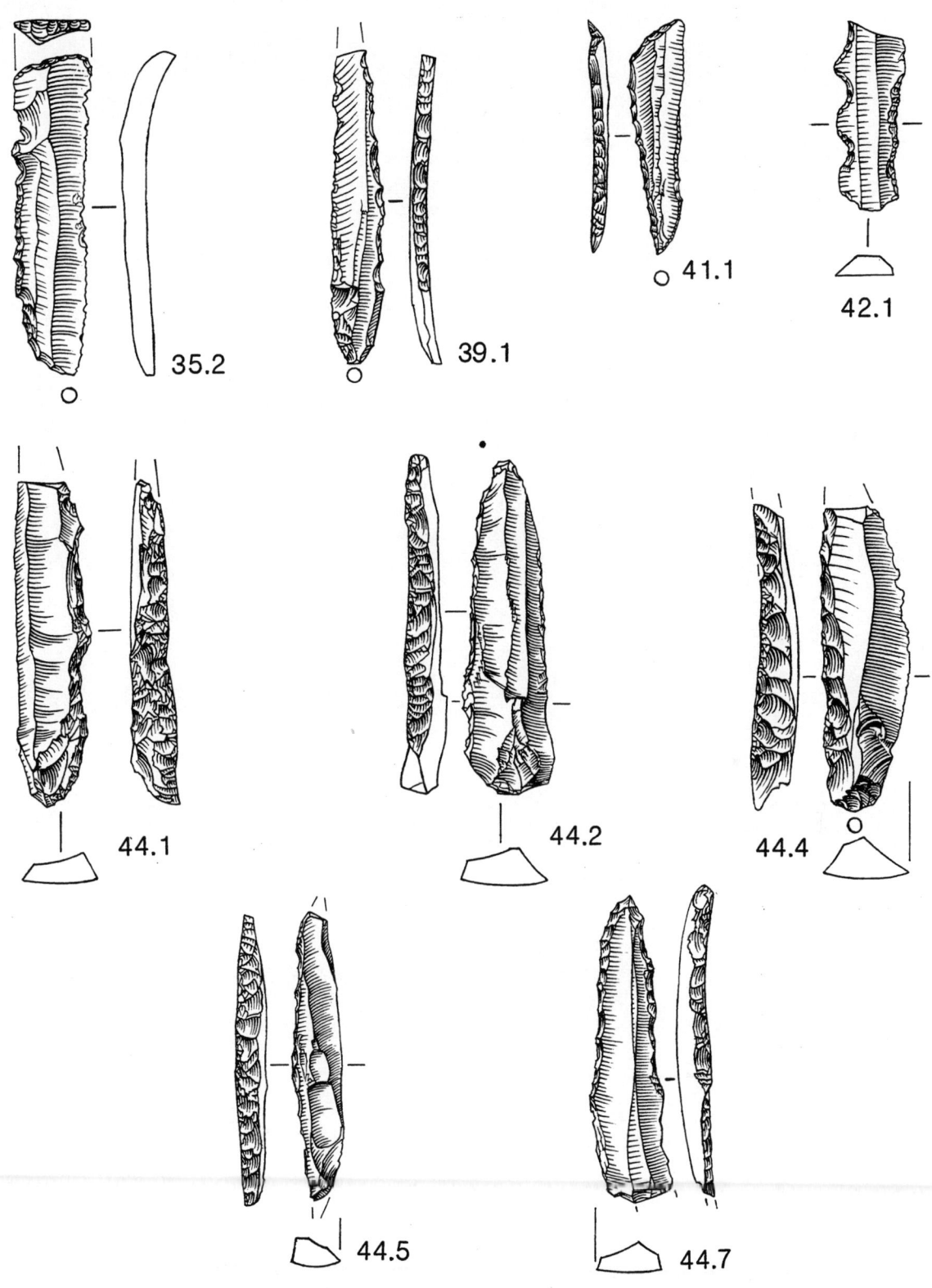

Fig. 35 Tools from Manohar Tali Pahar, Moretha Pahar, Nao Gaon, Naon Ka Pahar and Naro